Christian-
Jewish
Dialogue

Peter von der Osten-Sacken

Christian-Jewish Dialogue

Theological Foundations

Fortress Press   Philadelphia

Translated by Margaret Kohl

Translated from the German *Grundzüge einer Theologie im christlich-jüdischen Gespräch* copyright © 1982 Chr. Kaiser Verlag, Munich, West Germany.

Most of the biblical quotations are taken from the Revised Standard Version of the Bible, copyright 1946, 1952, © 1971, 1973 by the Division of Christian Education of the National Council of the Churches of Christ in the U.S.A. and are used by permission. But the wording has occasionally been modified where this was necessary for a correct rendering of the author's text.

Biblical quotations on pages 50, 120, 144, and 146 are taken from the King James Version of the Holy Bible.

Library of Congress Cataloging-in-Publication Data

Osten-Sacken, Peter von der, 1940–
    Christian-Jewish dialogue.

    Translation of: Grundzüge einer Theologie im christlich-jüdischen Gespräch.
    Bibliography: p.
    Includes index.
    1. Judaism (Christian theology) 2. Christianity and other religions—Judaism. 3. Judaism—Relations—Christianity. I. Title.
    BT93.08713   1986   230   85–45481
    ISBN 0–8006–0771–6

51,307

K897L85   Printed in the United States of America   1-771

For
A. Roy Eckardt, Pierre Lenhardt,
and Martin Stöhr

Contents

Preface

The scope and purpose of the present study are explained in detail in the opening chapter, so I may confine myself in this preface to a few words about the way in which the investigation came into being, and some of the circumstances that accompanied it.

Some of the central aspects discussed in the first five chapters were the subject first of all of a paper read in February 1978 in the Academy on Mount Leuenberg, near Basel, the subject I had been given being "A Christian Theology of Judaism." In a modified and expanded form and with what seemed to me a more appropriate title, this paper was read again in 1980 in the Protestant Academy in Bad Herrenalb, Baden, and in July of the same year in the Theological Academy in Celle. I have to thank Professor Rolf Rendtorff, Heidelberg, who conducted the conference in Bad Herrenalb, for encouraging me to develop the highly condensed paper read there into a more extended study. Dr. Friedrich Duensing, Bremen, was kind enough to read the paper with sympathetic and friendly understanding, and at a number of points to offer criticism that stimulated me to further thought. Similarly, Dr. Günther Morawe, East Berlin, subjected the two Old Testament excursuses to a critical examination.

Ricklef Münnich entered with sympathy and intuition into what was in part an almost illegible manuscript, transforming this first draft, step by step, into a legible typescript. His unabating interest in the progress of the work encouraged me to pursue it even when an increasing load of administrative work began to reduce the time at my disposal. An interruption to the final editing which then after all proved unavoidable gave me the opportunity to add a number of passages, especially discussions on literature that had meanwhile appeared. Lilo Grabau, and Karin Lange especially, undertook to put these additions into type. Manfred Weber of Chr. Kaiser Verlag, Munich, showed generous understanding when the book took on dimensions beyond those originally envisaged. Marion Gardei, with the help partly of Katharina Plehn, partly of Eva Brux, was indefatigable in her reading of typescript and proofs as well as in preparing the index.

To all these I should like to express my most sincere thanks. On the occasion of the English edition, it is also a pleasure for me to include in these thanks Margaret Kohl, who has translated the study chapter by chapter with great intuitive understanding and admirable comprehension.

I have taken the opportunity of the English edition to correct obvious slips and to draw attention in the notes to further important literature. I have also expanded the text at two or three points. These additions affect especially my remarks about the critical evaluation of Israel in Romans 9—11, at the end of the section "Reconciler of the Church with Israel," in chapter 3, and my indications of the links between Romans 11:26–27 and the Jewish Prayer Book, at the end of the section "The One Who Has Come and the One Who Will Come: Continuity and Discontinuity," in the same chapter. In chapter 8, I have considered a few of the important contributions to the subject that have appeared since 1981, trying to weigh up their arguments and to assess them in the light of the interpretation of the Christian-Jewish relationship I have put forward here.

I have employed the word "foundations" in my title, and my investigation as a whole was accordingly determined by the attempt to work out a few fundamental theological complexes. It was not my aim to pursue every factual link that might perhaps suggest itself or to strive for completeness as regards either the biblical testimonies or secondary literature. In particular, because of the wealth of the books and articles that have appeared on the subject, in recent years alone, it often seemed best to discuss one or several pieces of work as examples rather than to touch briefly on a multiplicity of contributions. Finally, in order to keep the book within readable bounds, I have frequently drawn attention to preliminary work of my own where the particular points under discussion are developed more fully.

This book is dedicated to three Christians who, in different places and in different spheres of life, have persistently demanded that a new relationship be built up between the Christian church and the Jewish people: Professor A. Roy Eckardt, of Lehigh University, in Bethlehem, Pennsylvania; Frère Pierre Lenhardt, NdS, at the Institut Ratisbonne, in Jerusalem; and the Rev. D. Martin Stöhr, Principal of the Protestant Academy at Arnoldshain. Right down to the present day, all three have played a very considerable part in developing a new relationship between Christians and Jews, each in his own way trying from the Christian side to overcome the paradox that has characterized the Christian-Jewish relationship from its very beginnings: whereas Jews have insisted that the church is *by no means as yet* the phenomenon it claims to be, the end-time community of Jews and Gentiles, Christians have countered by saying that the Jewish people is *no longer* that which it maintains it is, the people of God according to an unrevoked covenant. Both these noes have made history. And it was only at the beginning that the price of the mutual denial was paid by the Christian church. For far and away the greatest part of this history, the cost has been borne by the Jewish people. All three of the writers I have named have discerned, against the background of everything that has happened, that in the light of the gospel it is the Jewish and not the Christian no that can be legitimately grounded. And they have drawn the appropriate conclusions. This recognition unites all three scholars in spite of their different theological positions and work. The present investigation follows the path they have blazed through their own approach, and it is to them that it is therefore dedicated.

Since completion of the English translation in the autumn of 1984 I have had the opportunity of an extended stay in California. These weeks in January and February 1985 offered me an inestimable chance to gain some insight into Jewish life in the United States. As representing all those to whom I am indebted for much kindness during that time, my friends Professor Lewis M. Barth and Dr. Neil C. Sandberg, of Los Angeles, as well as Rabbi Joseph Asher, D.D., and Margaret and Leo Rosenthal, of San Francisco, are owed my sincere thanks. They conveyed to me a wealth of experience for which I am deeply grateful.

Berlin, October 1981/1986   PETER VON DER OSTEN-SACKEN

— 1

Introduction
Hermeneutical Points of Reference
for a Theology Developed in
Christian-Jewish Dialogue

THE PRESENT SITUATION: RECENT THEOLOGICAL
BOOKS ON THE SUBJECT

In recent years, two Catholic writers, Clemens Thoma and Franz Mussner, have published inquiries that are devoted to the task of developing
a "Christian theology of Judaism."[1] Mussner's title, *Tractate on the Jews*, is a
deliberate echo of a genre belonging to the early days of the church's
literature ("tractate *against* the Jews"). His play on this title is a way of dis-
sociating himself from it. Nonetheless, the first, main section of his work
begins with an "outline of a Christian theology of Judaism," and since
this section is fundamental to the whole, it may be said that the book falls
largely under this guiding conception. Both Mussner and Thoma have been
able to draw on a great number of earlier individual studies. The title they
have chosen (in Thoma's case for the whole book, in Mussner's for an
essential section) breaks new ground.[2] If we follow up the frequent use
of the phrase in lectures and discussion, we shall find that it has started
to become current coin in a relatively short period; as I indicated in the
preface, the present book also grew out of a study devoted to a "Christian
theology of Judaism." In spite of this, I have decided to dispense with the
term here, for a number of reasons, some of which have more weight
than others. I should like to explain these reasons in this introductory
section, developing the explanation further in subsequent chapters. I hope
that I shall thereby be able to bring out the structure of the "foundations"
I am trying to establish.

The first doubt is raised by the abstract nature of the term "Judaism."
As a comprehensive term, it is certainly helpful in particular contexts. But
it all too easily makes it possible for us to forget that it describes the
life and observances of men and women who are characterized by a unique
history and whose existence today cannot be isolated from the fact that
there is now a state bearing the name of Israel—a name that, throughout
time, has been the authentic term for the community of the Jewish people.

1

Accordingly, in his introduction to Thoma's study, David Flusser frequently talks about Israel instead of Judaism.[3] He makes it clear that this is not by chance when he postulates that in studying Judaism Christian theologians must accept that, according to the Jewish view, "it was not a religion that was chosen but a group of human beings, not the Jewish religion but Israel."[4] But, he also points out, "The country is part of the people of Israel."[5] Flusser is therefore convinced that "a Christian theology of Judaism that does not affirm the divinely willed tie between Israel and the Land [is] impracticable in our day."[6]

It seems questionable whether Thoma's study can stand up to the criterion apparently quite deliberately developed by Flusser in his introduction. In the final paragraphs, speaking quite expressly as a "Christian theologian of Judaism," he comes to talk about the existence of the state of Israel. This passage is characterized first of all by a series of statements that define all the things the state of Israel is *not*. A positive statement then follows: Israel as state "should be accepted out of feeling of fellowship, in the interest of Jews and non-Jews who have their home there."[7] But this proposition avoids making a theological statement. Here Mussner goes much further in his approach, even though with the appropriate caution. Not only does he treat the subject of Israel and its land much more broadly; he also interprets the existence of the state of Israel theologically, as a sign that "God has not excluded the Jews from his guidance." In this sense the state is "a sign of hope as much for Israel as for the church."[8]

But there are two obvious objections to the choice of the term "Israel" rather than "Judaism." On the one hand, does not the Jewish people include more than the state of Israel? Yet today it is the state that is associated first of all with the name Israel. And on the other hand, one may well doubt whether Christian theology does well to take its bearings from such an equivocal phenomenon. To some extent the answer to the first objection includes the answer to the second. The state of Israel does not see itself as separate from the Jewish Diaspora, since every Jew in the world is a potential citizen of that state and has the right to emigrate there. Nor, with a few exceptions, do Jews in the Diaspora see themselves as without any relation to the land of the patriarchs and the state that has been newly founded there. The case is somewhat different: the political existence of Jews in the world is two-dimensional. Jews are citizens of their own particular countries and at the same time have a special relationship to the state of Israel.[9] This is the structure in which Jews now live. A Christian theology that ignored it—for example, by using the term "Judaism" in an insufficiently precise way—would again, as in the past, be in danger of forgetting history and reality; although in fact one of the services the Jewish people should perform for the Christian church is to force it into reality.[10] Just as we have both to hold together *and* to distinguish between the state of Israel and the Diaspora in its relation to Israel, so too the definition of the word "Israel" must include a pointer to the multifarious movements or groupings within the Jewish people—which can be indicated, for example, through such adjectives as "orthodox," "conservative," "liberal," and "secularized."[11]

All this is Israel, as distinct from the Gentiles—this may be said to be the Jewish position.

All this is Israel, as the community that does not share the bond with Jesus Christ—this sums up the Christian viewpoint.

By defining the word "Israel," we make it possible to perceive two further dimensions of the term that must be kept in mind and that to some extent mean a departure from the Jewish interpretation. Jewish Christians also belong to Israel as Jewish people, according to their own view. In addition, Christian tradition maintains that the church as a whole is "Israel according to the Spirit." These two modes of interpretation belong closely together, although this fact is generally ignored. The Christian church was able to term itself Israel according to the Spirit only because of its Jewish roots (even if this fact was all too soon forgotten); and these roots are represented by no one better than the Jews who have come to believe in Jesus. Ecclesiologically, these Jewish Christians form the bridge between Israel and the gentile nations, the Jewish people and the Christian church. And this is so right down to the present day. If we may take it to be a general principle that a church (and a theology) can be tested by its attitude towards the Jews, then it is equally true, if not more so, that a church (or a theology) can be tested by its attitude towards its Jewish Christians; though of course these two tests are not alternatives. These reminders are intended to provide a clue, which we shall pick up again later; for Hebrews or Israelites in the church are bound to play an important part in the framework of a theology that is trying to work out its relationship to Israel in a new way. To have left this aspect unconsidered—that is, to have left present-day Jewish Christians in the shade—is a deficiency in the theology presented by Thoma and Mussner; and it could well be due in part to their choice of Judaism as overriding concept. It must be added in all fairness that Jewish Christians are in any case only given particular attention by groups that still cling to the idea of the "mission to the Jews"—even if it is very often no more than an ideology—and this is a fundamentally dubious matter, both in the abstract and practically.[12]

Another deficiency too is at least as important as the limitations of the idea of a Christian theology of Judaism that we have already touched on. The title shows the weakness that, as we know, belongs to all "theologies of . . .": they pick a particular complex or collection of facts out of the realm of theology as a whole and make these the subject of a special theology. The complexes Thoma and Mussner develop under their chosen term would therefore be much more appropriately described under a heading such as "Judaism from the viewpoint of Christian theology."[13] Seen in this light, what the authors have achieved in their work emerges much more sharply. This achievement lies above all in their struggle to give concrete form to the task arising from Vatican II's declaration *Nostra Aetate:* the task of interpreting Judaism or the Jewish people theologically as a positive entity. In fulfilling this charge, Thoma and Mussner succeed in making an essential correction to the dismal and negative picture of the Jewish people (particularly in its early days) that is current coin in Christian theology. And that is no small achievement.[14]

Apart from the points we have touched on, the theological limitations of the two studies are obvious. Both of them are more or less colored by the view that is is possible to redefine Israel's position in the framework of Christian theology without subjecting that theology itself to any essential change, redefinition, or restructuring. This makes itself felt in the relatively strong apologetic tendencies that determine both monographs at some of their key points. One example is the treatment of "anti-Judaism," especially in the New Testament.

Thoma plays down the problem of what he calls "possible anti-Judaism in the New Testament" wherever he can,[15] and brings his remarks to a head in an irritable and over-hasty statement that is important in its implications. "If one wishes by any means to subsume the New Testament under anti-Jewish literature," he says, "then the Hebrew Scriptures should be called even more antisemitic."[16] If this statement were to apply to Jesus of Nazareth instead of to the testimonies of the New Testament, it would be correct in its intention, even though it would still be incorrect in its wording,[17] but as it stands it is confuted by one simple and historically indisputable fact: none of the Old Testament writings presupposes a religious community of Jews *and* Gentiles; but it is just this which is the presupposition of *all* the New Testament testimonies under discussion. This fundamental difference apart from any other reasons shows that a straight comparison between the polemic of the Old and the New Testaments is illegitimate. The apologetic trend continues to some extent in Thoma's "Remarks on Christian Anti-Judaism" during the history of the church; but we need do no more than touch on that here.[18]

In Mussner the apologetic tendencies show themselves rather in the contradictoriness of what he says. On the one hand, he can talk about "anti-Judaism" "in the Gospels and in the entire New Testament," "distortions of Judaism" and "hostile images" even "in the time of the primitive Church,"[19] and he can concede that the Pauline doctrine of justification by faith in Jesus Christ meant that "naturally the life of the Jew according to the Law . . . was devalued, if not, indeed, often actually despised."[20] On the other hand, he asserts that in Paul the law was "a [phenomenon] pertaining to the whole world" and deduces from this that "it is nonsense to view the Pauline teaching of the Law and justification as an expression of the apostle's 'anti-Judaism.' It was actually only Christian theology after Paul that misused the apostle's doctrines in an anti-Jewish sense.[21] In the first statement I have quoted, Mussner rightly sees Paul's statements about the law as a factor in religious anti-Judaism.[22] But in the last extract I have quoted, the apostle is exonerated from the difficulty involved through the artificial construction of a "nonsense" that no one maintains—that Paul affirmed his doctrine of justification *because* he was anti-Jewish.[23]

The tendencies we are discussing come to the fore most strikingly, perhaps, when Thoma and Mussner give direct answers to the theological questions that sound out of the Holocaust. Thoma writes—and Mussner lends emphatic assent—"A believing Christian *should not find it so very difficult to interpret* the sacrifice of the Jews during the Nazi terror." One may well ask what can possibly follow a statement thrown out with such incredible ease. Thoma goes on (and is approvingly quoted by Mussner):

> His thoughts should be turned toward Christ to whom these Jewish masses became alike, in sorrow and death. Auschwitz is the most monumental sign of our time for the intimate bond and unity between the Jewish martyrs—who stand for all Jews—and the crucified Christ, even though the Jews in question could not be aware of it. Despite all separation, diverging routes, and misunderstanding, the Holocaust stands as a milestone for believing Christians of the inviolable oneness of Judaism and Christianity, based on the crucified Christ.[24]

Whereas Thoma goes on to say that "all witnesses to faith of all times," Christians and non-Christians, "belong to the people of Christ," Mussner proceeds,

> The Christian must, in face of the "total sacrifice" of the Jews in Auschwitz, openly confess his complicity in anti-semitism. However, he cannot grasp the meaning of this sacrifice without the crucified Christ, who took up the sacrifice of Auschwitz into his glorified crucified body.[25]

This interpretation is preceded by comments on Israel as the Servant of God who suffers for the sins of the world—sufferings that are interpreted in the Christian sense (in line with Col. 1:24) as "filling up" or complementing the atoning sufferings of Jesus Christ. In these additional comments of Mussner's there are certainly signs of an interpretation that does not bring the murder of the Jewish people within the hasty grasp of Christian theology. But unfortunately he does not develop the theological conclusions that follow from an acknowledgment that Jews died vicariously for the whole world, which means for Christians too: the soteriological and christological conclusions inherent in this interpretation remain undeveloped. Consequently, it is not clear what relation Mussner's interpretation bears to the emphatic statement in *Nostra Aetate* (which Mussner endorses) that Christ is the "source of *all* grace," and hence, as Mussner expounds, also died "for the sins of the Jews."[26] So we are left with the impression that the relevant statements are essentially intended to provide a hasty christological answer ("not . . . so very difficult") to the unanswerable questions of the Holocaust. The doubting question of the Jewish theologian Emil Fackenheim whether an answer will be given in the messianic era for the death of even one single child,[27] and his rejection of every attempt to find a religious meaning as blasphemous;[28] or even Amir's assertion that the question where God was in Auschwitz goes "beyond human capacity"[29]—all these statements show, by contrast, how impossible it is to cross the barrier that shuts us off from every attempt to *give* a meaning to these events. The only possibility seems to be to *wring* a meaning out of Auschwitz for the people living after it; and that means asking about the consequences, and especially the consequences for Christian theology. We have to ask these questions without apologetic bias as far as possible; and we have to try to win our way into the very center. So it seems questionable whether Thoma and Mussner sufficiently meet the criterion (formulated later by Johann Baptist Metz, but which they both anticipate) "no longer to pursue any theology that is so conceived that it remains untouched by Auschwitz or could remain untouched by it."[30]

Demands of this kind frequently give rise to protest in Germany. Elsewhere they have long since become accepted and have been taken up in a number of studies. Twenty years ago, in the United States, J. Coert Rylaarsdam already pointed out in an important little essay that the point of departure determining the Jewish-Christian encounter has changed in a quite essential way:

> The spiritual heartland of the Diaspora was once in Babylonia for fifteen hundred years; then it was in Spain for five hundred; and after that it was in central Europe for four hundred. Now it has crossed the ocean and is here in our midst. The tragedy of Spain and the tragedy of Germany measure the urgency of our [i.e., American] responsibility.[31]

By responsibility he means responsibility for an open-mindedness and mobility in dialogue such as was shown on the Jewish side by Franz Rosenzweig and Martin Buber before the years 1933–45.

It is in accordance with this fact that the demand for a decisive transformation of Christian theology in its relationship to the Jewish people should come from both the Christian and the Jewish side in the United States, perhaps not earlier than elsewhere but more emphatically and enduringly. The Jewish voices may be represented by Irving Greenberg. Faced with what Jews have suffered under Christians, he asks whether one must not decide that it would have been better if Jesus had not come.[32] Greenberg sees the future of the church as hanging in the balance, dependent on whether it can overcome the contempt for the Jews which it has inculcated in such multifarious ways. In the light of the Holocaust, he says, Christianity in its classic form "dies" in order to be born to new life, or it lives on unaffected, so as to die to both God and man.[33]

On the Christian side, pioneer work has been done by A. Roy Eckardt, especially in his study *Elder and Younger Brothers: The Encounter of Jews and Christians* (1967). Another important contribution was Franklin H. Littell's book *The Crucifixion of the Jews: The Failure of Christians to Understand the Jewish Experience* (1975). This initial thrust was followed up in subsequent years by these writers themselves in many different publications, and most recently, by the first two volumes of a theology by Paul M. van Buren, entitled *Discerning the Way: A Theology of the Jewish Christian Reality* (Vol. 1, 1980) and *A Christian Theology of the Jewish People* (Vol. 2, 1984). These books and similar American studies are important because of their approach. They do not merely meet the requirement of a different, more appropriate image of Judaism or the Jewish people. They do more: each of these writers, within his own individual theological contours, allows his theological work to be essentially determined by the criterion that Metz defines in the statement I have already cited.[34]

In Eckardt's early work the change that has come about is expressed most clearly, perhaps, in the following brief summing-up, which sounds like an early anticipation of the fundamental theological principles of the resolution of the German Protestant Church of the Rhineland "On the Renewal of the Relationship between Christians and Jews" (1980):

> A Christian theology of the Jewish-Christian relationship is called to proclaim from the Christian side what Franz Rosenzweig has expressed from the Jewish side: Judaism is the "star of redemption." Christianity the rays of that star. The church is "successor" of Israel *in only one respect and no other:* by virtue of the Christian gospel, the dividing wall between Jew and gentile is destroyed once and for all. The abiding covenant with Israel is decisively and definitively opened to the world in a way that Jewish faith does not provide.
>
> All Jews will not by any stretch of imagination ever assent to Rosenzweig's affirmation that the gentile world is able to come to God only through Jesus Christ. But the Christian church may testify that Rosenzweig is right, although of course it will do this only from the standpoint of its own christological persuasions. Here is the limited validity in the emphasis upon discontinuity. Yet it is the fact of continuity that demands preeminent stress. In carrying forward Israel's sacred role, the church does not annul the role of original Israel, nor can it ever, in human history, take the place of Israel. Original Israel continues as the people who "stay with God," whose enduring task is to sanctify the name of the Lord, to adore the God beyond all the hollow gods of men, to rejoice in and obey the precepts of Torah, to await the coming of God's messianic kingdom.[35]

In this century we are compelled to listen with the most intense concentration to the questions that the mass murder of the Jewish people force on us. This has led to further transformations in Eckardt's reflections on the relationship between God and man—reflections prompted by Jewish struggles to come to terms religiously with what has happened. In Zvi Kolitz's rebellious story "Jossel Rackower," Rackower, confronted by his murdered family and his own impending death, tells God that he has now ceased to stand in the relationship of a servant to his master; the relation is now that of a pupil to his teacher—more, it is like that of someone who not only owes a debt but is also owed one.[36] Irving Greenberg considers that at this point in history the only relation we can have to God is a relationship of anger and conflict.[37] Eliezer Berkovits sums up by saying that nothing can excuse God for the sufferings of innocent people in history, since God is responsible for having created a world in which human beings are free to make history.[38] Eckardt has taken up theologically what these other writers have said about the question of God, spelling out their views and taking them further both didactically and prayerfully:

> Can we believe in God, in this time after the Final Solution? No, it is out of the question. It is too late for such business. The camps of death have intervened. *Can* we believe in God in this time? Perhaps—in some unlikely place, down some out-of-the-way street. Life can come even out of death. Can we pray? No. There is no one left now to whom to pray. *Can* we pray? Perhaps—in some fleeting moment, maybe once or twice in a lifetime. God must be absent, that man may be; God must be present, that man may not perish.[39]

> LET US PRAY: Is anyone there, in the dark, the dark of the desolation? If you are still there, do not hide your Face another time. We could not bear that.
> We are here before you. Look at us! We are speaking to you. Listen to us! We who are your enemy. Are you our enemy? You are not our enemy. We need you. Do you need us? You do need us. We forgive you. Do you forgive us? You do forgive us. We love you. Do you love us? You do love us.
> Consume us, as you must. But then redeem us. Raise us, to live with you. And to live with each other. Without end. Through Jesus Christ, our Lord. Amen.[40]

Eckardt's work foreshadows a new understanding of revelation which includes contemporary history. The same may be said of the work of Littell and van Buren. Littell tries to find a meaning for Christian theology in the annihilation of the Jewish people in Europe and its rebirth in the form of the state of Israel. He sees the theological concepts of crucifixion and resurrection as the only categories that are appropriate for the theological dimensions of these events. Two points are particularly important here: First, he analyzes the Christian—and the church's—contribution toward making the annihilation a possibility and a reality. Second, he develops the need for a Christian counterculture that these facts lay upon us—a counterculture to totalitarian systems themselves and to the pseudo-value-free trends of modern societies and their institutions—for these only play into the hands of totalitarianism. This counterculture, Littell believes, can only be learned through ties of commitment to the Jewish people:[41]

> If we are, as we profess, linked in "the communion of saints" across the generations with those who have died in the faith, we are also linked in a solidarity of guilt with those who taught falsely and with those who drew the logical consequences of false teaching. That false teaching has led in our own time to mass rebellion of the baptized against the God of Abraham, Isaac, and Jacob, and to wholesale apostasy.[42]

> The meaning of the Holocaust for Christians is at least this: when the baptized betray their baptism, when those who have been grafted into history flee back out of history, when the "new men" and "new women" in Christ cast off the new life and become part of the dying age again, the "old Israel" is left alone as the sign that the God who is God yet rules and that—in spite of all world conquerers and posturing false prophets—his Kingdom shall triumph in the end. *For Christians only:* We must begin our agonizing self-assessment and reappraisal with the fact that in a season of betrayal and faith-

lessness the vast majority of the martyrs for the Lord of history were Jews.
The Jewish people carried history while the Christians fled headlong from their
professed vocation.[43]

The restitution of Israel is the event which challenges Christians to take events,
history, and the world seriously again. The sterility of a "spirituality" in which
nothing important happens between the Ascension and the Second Coming has
been exposed to sight.[44]

The main characteristic and strength of van Buren's study *Discerning the
Way* is his choice of the biblical concept of the Way, and its dynamic
development, to describe the reality of the Christian-Jewish relationship.
According to van Buren, the Way is the swath cut through history for the
nations by the God of Abraham, Isaac, and Jacob through his Son Jesus
Christ, who in this event represents the specific revelation of the God
of Israel for the Gentiles. The event manifests a new step taken by God
along the way with his creation. But it does not therefore abrogate his way
with Israel, the people of God, for the revelation in Christ is an act that is
directed especially towards the Gentiles. In this framework van Buren is
able to give full significance to the church's traditional Christology, which
is shaped by the Trinitarian concept of God, in its very light being able
to find a theological approach to the people of God that does not infringe
the authenticity of Israel's relationship to that God. God and Jesus Christ
are not one and the same; but the Son reveals how God acts, and what he
wants for us:

God steps back to leave us free to work His will, if we will, and suffers with
us in all our failures. Therein lies the power and majesty of His infinite freedom, that He is free in the fullest power of personal love to hold back, to
sit still and to suffer in agony as His children move so slowly to exercise
in a personal and loving way the freedom which he has willed for them to
have and exercise.[45]

This perspective is, I believe, the same as that to which Dietrich Bonhoeffer
had come at the end of his life: It is God's will that we live *before Him* as
though He were not. To live in full responsibility in the world is precisely
to live as God wills us to live whether at the moment He be present or
absent.[46]

We know no God but the one whom we have seen in the face of that suffering man. It is therefore not out of order, if extremely hard to say, that God
must have been present in the ovens of the deathcamps and in the mass graves
of Eastern Europe. Where else could He have been than there precisely where
His beloved sons and daughters were being tortured and slaughtered? The God
of the philosophers may have withdrawn. The God of Golgotha—who is no
other than the God of Abraham, Isaac and Jacob—would have had to be there.
Some may have been aware of Him there. Most, perhaps, were not. So it has
always been. But to say He was not there because He did not act—independently, as it were, apart from human action, removing from us the responsibility for righting the wrong we had brought about—assumes that God should
have done what He could not have done without ceasing to be the God of
love and freedom who has in His love conferred responsibility and free cre-
ative power on His creatures.[47]

We may leave on one side here the question of whether the Holocaust, because it is unique,[48] must be interpreted theologically as a "source of revelation" comparable to the biblical testimonies. More important and more appropriate than to reduce the inferno of that event to a theological concept is to hear the call that goes out from it to theology and the churches, or to theologians and Christians in general; and as we discern this call, to approach the life of the church and its biblical and postbiblical traditions with new eyes and ears. This call is taken up in a similar way in the work of Eckardt, Littell, and van Buren. We can perhaps describe it best in the message unremittingly preached—and rightly so—by Abraham Heschel: that it is not only human beings who need God; God also needs human beings, on the way which he is taking with his creation.[49] This insight may be possible even without the event of the Holocaust. But the endless suffering inflicted on the Jewish people in our century makes it seem *inescapable*.

The fact that Thoma and Mussner deal either too cursorily or not at all with work belonging to "theology after the Holocaust"[50] shows perhaps more clearly than anything else the limitations of their investigations. Significantly enough, most of the American work I have cited has avoided the somewhat detached title "Christian theology of Judaism." On the contrary, these writers all more or less, in the very way they formulate their subject, show how necessary it is to find a different form for Christian theology in its relationship to the Jewish people—a form *based on* that specific relationship. Only van Buren has given his second volume a title that comes close to "Christian theology of Judaism": *A Christian Theology of the Jewish People*. But though some of the questions mentioned above concern the title of this volume as well, the volume as a whole counteracts these misgivings. To make the point quite clear, let me say again that Thoma and Mussner are deserving of real gratitude. But—without depreciating their achievement—the present study aims at a deeper transformation of Christian theology and is therefore much more closely related to the American work I have referred to, with its rejection of any kind of christologically based absolutism, either in title or content.

The present book differs, however, from the American studies already discussed in two ways. First, since it is written by someone concerned with biblical exegesis, the book attempts to enter into a broader dialogue with the New Testament traditions, searching for ways—or even hints of ways—in the New Testament that might provide us with a theological approach to a sounder relationship between Christians and Jews, an approach free of destructive Christian absolutism. The context described in this introduction, then, is presupposed throughout, and can hardly be overestimated in its importance as hermeneutical aid. Eckardt, for example, is right when he doubts whether Romans 11 helps us to find a different relationship with the Jewish people if we read the chapter in the traditional or fundamentalist way.[51] But matters look different if we penetrate more deeply into the text in our reading and if—realizing the difference of the times—we become aware of what is hidden beneath the surface of the text. It is with this in mind that I am attempting in the present book to indicate in broad outline how the suggested necessary transformation of Christian theology in its relation to the Jewish people can be based more firmly on New Testament contexts.

The present study differs from the books already considered in another respect as well—and to a considerable degree this is certainly due solely to its New Testament orientation: I have tried here, as I have already suggested, to do more justice theologically to the group of Jewish Christians than the American studies we have looked at. It is true that it is difficult to find an appropriate place for them in the Jewish-Christian encounter in view of the great strain the actual existence of Jewish Christians has caused in the history of the church[52] and still causes today (in some cases; for example, through the movement Jews for Jesus, in the United States). But it hardly seems justifiable simply for that reason—or indeed for any reason at all—to leave Jewish Christians on the fringe of theological reflection from the outset, whether we are considering the past or the present.[53]

We have already gone a little way toward showing the connection between the Holocaust event and its challenge to Christian theology today. In order to clarify this further, we have now to look more carefully into the historical position of theology and church in their encounter with the Jewish people.

THE HISTORICAL SITUATION

Under National Socialist rule a crime against the Jewish people was committed in Germany and in German-occupied territory by Germans belonging to the churches. This crime can only be fragmentarily imagined, for it was of inconceivable frightfulness. During the time when the Jews were being persecuted and robbed of their rights, they were helped by individual Christians and Christian groups. But the churches themselves were silent. They permitted state violence to have its way and applauded the campaign against "the Jews." These twelve years of terror and horror from 1933 to 1945 have put their impress on life in the state of Israel and on Jewish life generally. But they have also stamped the life of the church, above all in its relation to the Jewish people. The people who today live in, for, and from theology and the church are the surviving contemporaries of both the evildoers and the victims who survived. Or, if born later, they are called not to judge but not to palliate either. When we ask what made the unfathomable depths of the years 1933–45 possible, we are at the same time asking about the church's share in the accumulated load of guilt that began with the partly voluntary, partly enforced betrayal of Jews who were citizens of the same country. What was wrong, what was irresponsible about theological doctrine, the church's proclamation, its instruction, and much else too? What went wrong in those years? What went wrong before? And what conclusions do we have to draw from all this? Theology and the church can only evade these questions if they pay the price of surrendering their own identity. And even when the generation of survivors no longer exists, Christians will not be able to escape this history, especially in Germany, except at the cost of themselves.

In considering the bond with the Bible, which is constitutive for theology and the church, it is certainly highly questionable to suggest that a path leads directly from the New Testament to the Holocaust. Nor can we maintain that Christians before Hitler desired what the Nazis brought about in so diabolical a way. But at the same time it cannot be disputed that, throughout the centuries, churches and theologies have again and again, to a depressing degree, aroused and encouraged attitudes that were hostile to and contemptuous of the Jews, appealing to the Bible to support them; and the consequences have often been deadly. Even when the churches did not directly violate Jewish life in the physical sense, they contributed, to a degree that can hardly be overestimated, to the fact that, when attacks were made on Jewish existence, the power of resistance and readiness for protest was either not allowed to spring up at all or was undermined. The readiness for partly active, partly passive betrayal of the Jews before and after 1933 grew up on fertile ground—ground prepared theologically and by the church over a period of centuries.[54] And it was this inward readiness that had such fateful consequences for everything that followed. But the main source of the anti-Jewish attitudes engendered by churches and theologies is their more or less strongly marked anti-Judaism *in principle*, and this by no means ended with the end of Nazi rule. We find its essential characteristic in a number of different variations, but its avowed grounds are christological. It consists of the theological denial of Israel's—or the Jewish people's—right to exist as the people of God that pursues its path of life with the Torah.

Almost twenty years ago, as thoughtful a scholar as Heiko Miskotte already put his finger on the essential connection I have suggested: the church, he wrote, proclaimed that it had now *taken the place* of God's people. It taught the nations an almost unbounded contempt of the Jews and not infrequently spurred them on to organized massacre. From Spain in the extreme west to Poland in the extreme east, the *corpus christianum* was the scene of a single great hunt. Rhine and Rhone became the training ground for the crusades, as the ghettos went up in flames and men and women were slaughtered in Christ's name.

Do not let us forget, he writes—seeing this as the vital point—that *one of the essential factors that made this possible was preaching.*[55]

In saying this, Miskotte does not make it clear whether the history he is thinking about is any later than the Jewish pograms of seventeenth-century Poland. But the link between anti-Judaism in principle and the deadly threat to the Jews in cold fact applies equally to the end of the nineteenth century and the beginning of the twentieth. The Jewish historian Uriel Tal has shown that this is true, and in what sense. He sums the matter up as follows:

> It would seem that racial anti-Semitism and traditional Christianity, although starting from opposite poles and with no discernible principle of reconciliation, were moved by a common impulse directed either to the conversion or to the extermination of the Jews. . . .
>
> When we recall the traditional Christian bias against the Jews—the collective guilt of deicide and the external curse of the world that rests upon them because of their unpardonable defection (Matt. 27:22, 25; 1 Thess. 2:15), the official policy of the church as formulated in such councils as the Synod of Elvira in 306, Clermont in 535, Toledo in 681, or the Third Lateran in 1179 and the Fourth Lateran in 1215, the preachments of Martin Luther against the Jews and his incitement to violence, especially after 1543 when he was disillusioned in his efforts to convert them, the blood libels and accusations in which the persecuted wandering Jew became the symbol of sin and abomination—when we recall all this, we see how Christianity created the patterns of prejudice, hatred, and calumny that could readily provide a rationale to justify organized violence. The anti-Christian elements of racial anti-Semitism were interpreted in such a way that the traditional theological concepts of Christianity were not completely rejected; only their meanings were changed by using a pseudoscientific jargon and applied to the historical realities of that day without the salutary correction of Christian discipline and belief.
>
> Racial anti-Semitism and the subsequent Nazi movement were not the result of mass hysteria or the work of single propagandists. The racial anti-Semites, despite their antagonism toward traditional Christianity, learned much from it, and succeeded in producing a well-prepared, systematic ideology with a logic of its own that reached its culmination in the Third Reich.[56]

The policy decisions of the church to which Tal refers may, like Luther's verbal excesses, have been an old story at the turn of the nineteenth century. Prejudice, hate, and defamation were not. Nor were the accusation of murdering God and the false doctrine that the Jews were under the divine curse. And both these views were for their part merely the final extreme of a theological position that had existed for centuries. What this position was is accurately formulated by Tal himself: Judaism was an anachronism, for the new dispensation and the incarnation had made it superfluous and robbed it of its reason for existence.[57]

And yet this reason for existence is to be found quite simply in the Torah given on Sinai. A fifteenth-century Bible illustration may serve as an example of the views about the Jewish people that led to the denial of its life with the Torah *in principle* (not merely to possible criticism of particular aspects). The picture shows the funeral of the synagogue. The synagogue lies in a coffin, dead, the tables of the law in her hands. Ecclesia, crowned, stands at the head of the coffin; Jesus Christ, with raised finger (blessing? admonishing?), at its foot.[58] The picture is all the more significant because it shows the background of certain interpretations that are current coin even today. For here, in picture form, we have what is still unwearyingly reiterated in the slogan "Christ—the end of the law," though the slogan, being abstract, has less obvious consequences.[59] Then as today, anti-Jewish solutions were to hand even for the difficulties in which a now literally "law-less" church and its theology had become entangled. Thus in the Middle Ages it was maintained that it was not the Ten Commandments that were written on the tables of the law received by Moses. What was written on them was the "double commandment" to love God and one's neighbor that Jesus stressed (Mark 12:28–34).[60] Today no one would support this thesis in its overt form; but in intention it still continues to dominate Christian theology to a remarkable degree. For example, Ernst Käsemann endlessly reiterates that through Jesus Christ the Torah "as such was abolished," or that Jesus restored the true sense of the Mosaic Torah, which had been perverted by the Jews; and these assertions really come down to the same relationship to the Torah.[61] In the framework of interpretations like this, there is no longer any trace of Paul's at least indirect admonition to "become a Jew to the Jews" (1 Cor. 9:20)—though writers readily appeal to this passage.[62]

We might therefore vary the definition of anti-Judaism put forward in connection with the medieval picture of the dead synagogue: we might say that a theology or proclamation is anti-Jewish or hostile to the Jews if it sees the life of the Jewish people in its present relationship to God solely under the sign of judgment or death (or both), interpreting the promise as having lost its present-day efficacy. It is hardly necessary to produce more evidence than what has already been adduced to show how far theological thinking of this kind has run right through the history of the church and its theology.[63] The germ of this thinking and its consequences (whether they are theoretical or, in certain circumstances, practical) have put their stamp on many Christian traditions. And these traditions, with their impress, exercise their own compulsion. This is probably one of the main problems—if not *the* main problem—that faces a theology developed in Christian-Jewish dialogue.[64] If this theology is not simply to fan the flames, theologians on the Christian side must be aware of the destructive character of theological or religious anti-Judaism, and the theology they develop can itself only be conceived as a contribution to the overcoming of anti-Judaism in theology and the church. This means that not only must information about the Jewish people be provided that is more precise, more comprehensive, and more appropriate. It means too that we must seek and struggle for more fundamental, necessary transformations in Christian theology itself, particularly in its appeal to the New Testament. In this sense, to keep the historical position in mind helps to define one function—perhaps the central one—of a theology whose upholders, remembering everything that has happened, try to take up the call to "repentance and renewal"[65] in a theological sense.

The historical situation described in outline here again finds specific expression in a social context, and this context is one of special importance for all our considerations of the subject.

THE *SITZ IM LEBEN* AND THE TASK

All the writers who in recent years—or even in recent decades—have helped through their work to give a new definition to the relationship between the church and Israel had, or have, their place in the framework of the Christian-Jewish dialogue. We may think—to name only a few— of Alice and Roy Eckardt, Hans-Joachim Kraus, Helmut Gollwitzer, and Günther Harder; then of Franklin Littell, Friedrich-Wilhelm Marquardt, Martin Stöhr, and Hans Hermann Henrix; and most recently of Franz Mussner, Clemens Thoma, Rosemary R. Ruether, Paul van Buren, Johann Baptist Metz, and the instigators of the Declaration of the Rhenish Synod. The Jewish-Christian dialogue can hardly be thought of apart from their thinking, and it was these writers who gave that thinking its impress. This means that, though the encounter between Jews and Christians is certainly only in its first beginnings, this encounter can easily be discovered to be the *Sitz im Leben*—the situation in life—for recent theological approaches to the Jewish people from the Christian side. This fact is, on the one hand, the main reason for the title chosen here: the theological foundations of Christian-Jewish dialogue. It also brings out another characteristic to which that theology has to be true if it remembers the *Sitz im Leben* from which it springs. Being itself rooted in *conversation*—to whatever degree this conversation may have emerged and may be possible[66]—its outline has to be developed as far as possible out of listening and questioning.

This means that we cannot start from the apparently safe refuge of dogmatic tradition, defining from there what Israel and the Jewish people are or have to be—or what the gospel and the church are or have to be. On the contrary, remembering the ever-present tendency towards anti-Judaism in this tradition, we have to take up and incorporate into our understanding and development of Christian theology essential aspects of the self-understanding of the Jewish people themselves, and we have to do this from the very beginning and in as comprehensive a sense as possible. Theological reflection about the Jewish people and the church in their ties with Torah and gospel respectively, and in their relationship to each other, therefore implies for Christians a double learning process from the very outset. On the one hand, it means acquiring and accepting new perceptions about the people of Israel; and on the other, it means acquiring and accepting new perceptions about the life of the Christian church before God, especially in its relationship to God's people of Sinai.

The title of the present book could give rise to a misunderstanding that we have to avoid at this point. It is true that Christian theology, when it enters into a new relationship with the Jewish people, has its specific *Sitz im Leben* in the Christian-Jewish encounter. But this certainly does not mean that this is a theology designed purely for the Christian-Jewish relationship (although special emphases are of course required). Both the biblical testimony itself and its reception today make any such isolation fundamentally impossible. The New Testament testimonies have certain things in common. One of these shared characteristics is that they are throughout, or almost throughout, written or edited by Jews—Jews who believed in Jesus—and, as a whole, reflect the varying stages of the process whereby the Christian congregations broke away from the Jewish people. The dispute, first of all with other groups within the Jewish nation, afterwards with "the Jews," is therefore the structure—sometimes implicit, sometimes explicit—that has essentially molded the writings gathered together in the New Testament. Whoever is concerned with the New Testament has to take account of this structure, as well as the everywhere-inherent relationship between the second part of the canon and the first. This is so even if what is being considered is in no way a subject specially relevant to the relationship between Christians and Jews, or if the relationship between the "New" and "Old" Testaments is not under discussion at all. Perhaps the most enduring component of the disastrous hostility of Christians toward Judaism was the uncritical reiteration in paraphrased form at a later date and under completely different conditions of those early Christian disputes with their largely anti attitude toward the Jewish people.

This hostility cannot be overcome by ignoring, denying, or trivializing it. We can only see to it that, through our study and application of Scripture, the encounter between the church and Israel for which the way has now been paved is lent hermeneutical weight. But if this takes the place of the anti structure that permeates the text, often into its finest ramifications, it then inevitably includes just as many theological areas as the biblical testimonies themselves. In this sense Christian theology can fundamentally *only* be theology in Christian-Jewish dialogue, however limited the possibilities open to such a conversation may be at the moment, especially in Germany. The Jewish-Christian encounter (as the *Sitz im Leben* under discussion), whether it takes place directly or indirectly, will therefore continue for a long time to have a primarily heuristic function, the function of helping Christians to undergo the undoubtedly wearisome and lengthy transformation of theology, proclamation, and instruction in its present largely anti-Jewish form.[67] The action taken by the synod of the Protestant church of the Rhineland in January of 1980,[68] and its resolution, as well as the subsequent work of the regional synods in Baden and Berlin,[69] has surely endorsed this emphatically on the level of the churches; and these things have an exemplary value that goes beyond the actual work performed.

In the foreground of the investigation is the question about the form a theology should take if it departs from the traditional, well-worn, and often highly subtle anti-Jewish attitudes and if it takes the factors we have indicated into account. And because of the central importance of Christology, the main emphasis must inevitably be on the task of working out an understanding of Jesus Christ that is not in its very nature anti-Jewish in structure but whose presupposition is rather the theologically grounded affirmation of Israel as people of God. But before this task can be undertaken, and after a first, transitional elucidation of the reference to Scripture, the first thing that must be done is to try to define Israel's identity as God's people. In line with what has already been said, we must attempt this first of all as part of Christian theology. Corresponding importance must be given to the question about the definition of the church and its relation to the Jewish people. This will follow the section on Christology, for it is in that context that these questions must be seen. But the question about the attitude of the Christian church already crops up continually in the christological section. This is due to the structure of New Testament Christology itself, with its indissoluble correspondence between the acts of Jesus Christ and the acts of the church.

THE RELATION TO SCRIPTURE

For Christian theology, the relation to Scripture is constitutive, Scripture meaning the Christian Bible, that is, the Old and New Testament, on whose combined testimony the Christian church is founded. What has just been said outlines the presuppositions that arise from the *Sitz im Leben*— that is, the dialogue—for our reference to the Scriptures. We have also been reminded that the paths of Jews and Christians (as the converts were called after a time) deviated very quickly after only a few decades. For this reason especially, it would seem obvious to go back to the earliest possible testimonies of the New Testament. These plainly have to be our discussion partner if we wish to acquire the cardinal data for a theology that will affirm Israel as God's people. Chapters 9 to 11 of the Epistle to the Romans are therefore of fundamental importance. Karl Ludwig Schmidt[70] and Karl Barth,[71] for example, already recognized this, and Franz Mussner[72] has recently stressed the same thing in his consideration of Romans 11. However, as I have already indicated, it is not sufficient, for a number of reasons, simply to give an account of the content of these chapters or even to describe the conceptions that are either expounded or implied there.

1. Paul defined Israel's position before God christologically, which means dogmatically. In so doing he in part described Israel's understanding of itself quite accurately; in part he distorted it. What he distorted particularly was Israel's relationship to the Torah. But if we listen anew to what Israel says of itself and if this receptive attitude makes us capable of objective criticism, we cannot forget to listen just when it is biblical tradition that is under consideration.

2. The Jewish people survived Paul and after 70 A.D. entered a phase of their history of which the apostle knew nothing. The tacit assumption that Paul would have gone on clinging to his theology unchanged even if he had known this different era is a historically untenable supposition and theologically a highly problematical one. For in the course of this phase, which the church and the Jewish people shared, some essential presuppositions of Paul's theology changed—one of the many being its chronological premise. Underlying Pauline theology is the expectation of the imminent

Parousia. His theology was certainly open for a certain delay—but delay for a foreseeable period, not for two thousand years. This can already be seen in the later history of Pauline theology in the New Testament itself.[73]

3. One of the most important statements about Israel in Romans 9–11 is the promise that they receive mercy *now*, without the help of the church—that is to say, at the immediately impending consummation of the world. If, then, *euangelizesthai* in this sense is laid upon the church—that is, the testimony to God's immediate and unconditional mercy to his people (not conditioned, that is, by a particular relationship to the gospel)—theology and church have to ask how they can express this testimony without the daily expectation of the end that God is going to bring about; for this expectation is certainly no longer to be found. We must therefore look further, and this search leads us back again, first of all, to Israel's own testimony that God's loving commitment to his people is a present event. We are all the more earnestly enjoined to look in this direction since the most convincing words of forgiveness spoken after 1945 have come from Jewish lips.[74] And our search leads us, second, more deeply into Romans 9–11 itself.

Our concern therefore, as I hope to show in more detail, is not with all this to reject Jesus Christ but to end the rejection of Israel as God's people. We might also say that our concern is to bring more humanity into theology, a more intensive understanding, which will take in the religious traditions, the life, and the self-understanding of others. In the fifties and sixties a positively endless hermeneutical debate went on, accompanied by many high-flown contributions. Feelings then ran high. But if we look back on this debate, what is especially noticeable is an introvert confinement to one's own tradition; and this suggests a lack of biblical orientation. It is continually stressed that Christian existence in the light of the gospel is or should be determined by the command to love our neighbor or even our enemy. But if this is so, then this directive provides the yardstick for Christian hermeneutics as well.[75] Even if this doubtless runs up against certain limits, the Christian churches and their scholars must understand and interpret the traditions and testimonies of others—in this case the Jewish people—with the same love they bring to their own. And this understanding must still obtain, even when it is a matter of scriptural interpretation.

—— 2 ——————————————————

"They *Are* Israelites. . . ."
The Identity of the Jewish People

Who are the Jewish people? If we remember what was said in chapter 1, we see that the question requires an answer that, on the one hand, is based on the Christian tradition, and, on the other, gives the widest possible scope for the Jewish people's own interpretation of their identity. This implies that our answer must take the form of a dialogue. And we shall try to emphasize this conversational structure by occasionally comparing the Jewish and the Christian interpretations of particular facts and themes. The Jewish tradition is a rich one, and this means that all the different complexes can only receive a more or less fragmentary discussion. Certain points will have to be developed in later parts of our investigation; other subjects will have to be introduced there for the first time. What we have to say goes beyond pure information and is intended to be understood as part of a Christian theology. It therefore intends to show Christians who Israel is, from the Christian perspective, insofar as that people rejects the gospel, and it thereby also aims at the same time to show Jews who they are, as a part of the Jewish people, seen from the same perspective. Unless we are sufficiently clear about these things, we cannot enter into or pursue a dialogue at all, nor can the relation between the church and Israel be adequately and properly considered.

The Christian testimony to which we have to listen with particular attention in this context has already been touched on in the introduction. Here we cannot attempt a full exegesis of Romans 9—11, but it would seem indispensable to give at least an exegetical outline of a few essential aspects, for these chapters provide an initial approach to the rest of our discussion.

ROMANS 9:1–5 AS BIBLICAL GUIDELINE

As the apostle of Jesus Christ, Paul discovers that only a small section of Israel accepts the gospel. Most of the Jews (though Paul is biased here and gives the impression that it is only a few of them, Rom. 11:17) have closed

their hearts to the good news of Jesus Christ, although the promise applies
to Israel as a whole. Has God then rejected his people (Rom. 11:1–2)? Has
the word of God perhaps lost its validity (Rom. 9:6)? In these three long
chapters the apostle answers these questions with an unequivocal no. But
right at the beginning, in Rom. 9:1–5, he had already pegged out the
boundaries of what he was going to say, and he was no longer able to go
beyond this framework—he could only fill it in.

These few verses bring out three important aspects:

1. Trust for his people, love for his people, and hope for his people are
the constitutive characteristics of Paul's existence as apostle. In Israel's fate,
his own message as the servant of Jesus Christ is at stake (Rom. 9:1–3,
6ff.).

2. The people he is talking about—Jews who do not believe in Jesus
Christ—"are Israelites."[1] This decisive Pauline answer to the question of
who the Jewish people are cannot be remembered too insistently. They are
Israelites, not they were (as the picture of the synagogue's funeral suggests)
and not they will be, as the church in its bias has often interpreted the
matter. They are irrevocably: hoitines eisin Israēlitai. They are still unchanged from what they were before, bne Yisrael, the people of God. This is
the first thing Paul has to say about his people, in a whole catalogue of
concepts, and it would be natural to see the terms that follow as a closer
definition of what it (still) means to be Israelites and to bear that name.
Paul accordingly goes on as follows:

They are Israelites [and that means]:
To them belong the sonship [hē hyiothesia]
the glory of the divine presence [hē doxa]
the pledges and enactments of the covenant [hai diathēkai]
the law [hē nomothesia]
the cult [hē latreia]
the promises [hai epangeliai];
to them belong the patriarchs [hoi pateres];
and from them comes the Messiah [ho christos] according to his earthly origin.

All these things are not just additional attributes the Jews enjoy as Israelites. All this is their essential definition as God's people. This is what makes
them Israel. And we may well ask whether anything can well be said about
Israel that is more comprehensive, more tremendous, and more full of
promise than this.[2]

3. Paul does not end this sequence with the words "and from them
comes [or, to them belongs] God." Instead he completes the list with a
benediction, a berakhah: "The God who is over all be blessed for ever.
Amen." His reason for this utterance of praise is quite simply the gifts he
has just enumerated. Paul is able to conclude like this because he is certain
that everything God has given here will find its goal. At the end of chapter
11 he describes this certainty by saying that however, and for however
long, and even if, Israel denies herself to the gospel, the gospel itself by its

very nature means that "the gifts of grace and the call of God are irrevocable" (Rom. 11:29). It is because of this certainty that, at the end of the whole complex that makes up Romans 9—11, Paul is able to conclude—as he concludes the brief unit Rom. 9:1–5—with a rapturous utterance of praise. For his assurance includes the knowledge that "at the end all Israel will be saved"—that is to say, they will arrive at the divine shalom (Rom. 11:26). The present "disobedience" of most people in Israel is actually conduct that contributes to salvation, for through Israel's no, the gospel has come to the Gentiles (Rom. 11:11ff.).

In saying that all Israel will be saved, Paul is unveiling a mystery. On the basis of divine revelation, he is explaining to the community of Christ in Rome enough of Israel's way and destiny to make it possible for that congregation to avoid the failing of arrogance in its relation to Israel, but for it instead to live in the power of faith. The lengthy history of the church shows that the mystery Paul reveals was not able to prevent the attitude the apostle was already anxious to change, the no to Israel. It is therefore all the more necessary for Christians to listen to what Robert Raphael Geis calls "the unknown Judaism," to the mysteries of Israel's history, the history of the Jewish people—the history of God's people—and it is all the more important for Christians in their listening to be impelled by God's yes to his people, the yes the gospel itself underlines. I must again stress that what is in question here is not some arbitrary edict. But at this point perceptions about the present and an understanding of the changes the Pauline text requires (when it is read in a period different from its own) grow toward one another like the two ends of a bridge. For Paul does not expound the charismata he lists in Rom. 9:4–5 in his definition of Israel by explaining what they mean in positive terms (with the exception of the word "promise"). On the contrary, these gifts are simply presented as a pledge of the salvation to come. But in Paul this limitation has little or no importance, for at that time salvation was thought to be immediately impending—an expectation that sets the Pauline context apart from all succeeding periods down to the present day.

We must therefore now go on to consider more carefully the question, Who is Israel, who are the Jewish people? In attempting to find an answer, we shall draw on Paul's definition of Israel in Rom. 9:4–5, as well as on Jewish written and oral traditions and testimonies.

THE GOD OF ISRAEL

As our first approach to the text showed, Paul devoted extreme care to the composition of the last two verses of his introduction (Rom. 9:1–5). This is shown especially by the way the verses clearly build to a climax. The apostle lists a series of gifts of grace conferred on Israel, then, in a separate sentence, specially mentions the Messiah, and finally ends with an utterance about God. But although Paul can say that the gifts belong to the children of Israel and although he can acknowledge that the Messiah belongs to their lineage, a similar statement about God would turn things upside down. God, "who is over all," does not belong to Israel; Israel belongs to him. In Rom. 11:1 Paul defines this relationship by calling the children of Israel "his people." That is to say, the fundamental "mark" of Israel is that, from the very moment it appears in biblical history, it is gathered and bound into God's special relationship to it. This means that the theological question about Israel's identity is first of all the question about the One to whom Israel belongs. His characteristics, for their part, can be related to other realities—for example, creation as a whole. But they cannot be detached from that fundamental relation between God and his people. Israel's characteristic mark as God's people corresponds, on God's side, to his unswerving faithfulness, the faithfulness to which the testimonies of the *Tanach* (the Hebrew Bible) witness on almost every page, but to which Paul's own discourse in Romans 9—11 also testifies especially.

It is a reflection of this divine faithfulness in which Israel experienced and believed, when, after the flood, God promises the whole creation that "[w]hile the earth remains, seedtime and harvest, cold and heat, summer and winter, day and night, shall not cease" (Gen. 8:22). And it is the same faithfulness that stamps the narratives that follow—the stories about the God of the patriarchs and the way he takes with Abraham, Isaac, and Jacob. But the secret of the divine steadfastness is to be found in the name of God himself: "I will be there as the One I shall be there as" (Exod. 3:14).[3] The revelation of this name does not mean any diminution of the faithfulness itself—on the contrary, that faithfulness is revealed as a reality, as the "essence" of the divine name. The revelation simply stresses the free nature of God's faithfulness. It challenges Israel to a trusting confession of faith in her God—"Hear, O Israel, Yahweh our God, Yahweh is one and unparalleled"—and to trusting obedience with her whole heart, her whole mind, and whole capacity (Deut. 6:4–5). The responding faithfulness of Israel finds its unsurpassable expression in the *kiddush ha-shem*, the sanctification of the divine name in martyrdom. But the daily relationship of mutual faithfulness can seldom, surely, have been more aptly or beautifully described than by Joseph Roth in his description of east European Judaism:

> They are not God's rare guests. They are at home with him. They do not pay him an occasional state visit. They gather three times a day at his rich, poor, holy tables. In prayer they rebel against him, cry out to high heaven, complain about his strictness, and in God's presence plead their case against God, in order then to acknowledge that they have sinned, that all his punishments were just, and that they will do better. There is no other people whose relationship to God is like this. It is an ancient people, and it has known God for a long, long time. It has experienced his abundant goodness and his icy justice; it has sinned and bitterly repented. And it knows that, though it may be punished, it can never be forsaken.[4]

It in any case makes a fundamental difference whether an individual or a community *acknowledges for itself* that the sufferings endured are a punishment for sin, or whether this is the judgment of outsiders. But even if we bear that in mind, it is impossible to apply this kind of interpretation to the mass murder in the concentration camps, even from the Jewish side. Not a single victim among all the millions died because he or she had violated the covenant with God.[5] On the contrary, the murderous persecution of the Jews was pursued, unreasoningly and indiscriminately, simply because these people *were* Jews. In the same way, the rising in the Warsaw ghetto introduced a completely new dimension into Jewish understanding of the *kiddush ha-shem*.[6] But this does not put an end to the reality that is described under the key word of the relationship of mutual faithfulness between the God of Israel and his people. The words Emil Fackenheim attributes to the "commanding voice of Auschwitz"—words that parallel and supplement the Ten Commandments given on Sinai—are an expression of the struggle to understand this very reality after the Holocaust:

> Jews are forbidden to hand Hitler posthumous victories. They are commanded to survive as Jews, lest the Jewish people perish. They are commanded to remember the victims of Auschwitz lest their memory perish. They are forbidden to despair of man and his world, and to escape into either cynicism or other-wordliness, lest they cooperate in delivering the world over to the forces of Auschwitz. Finally, they are forbidden to despair of the God of Israel, lest Judaism perish. A secularist Jew cannot make himself believe by a mere act of will, nor can he be commanded to do so. . . . And a religious Jew who has stayed with his God may be forced into new, possibly revolutionary relationships with Him. One possibility, however, is wholly unthinkable. A Jew may not respond to Hitler's attempt to destroy Judaism by himself cooperating in its destruction. In ancient times, the unthinkable Jewish sin was idolatry. Today it is to respond to Hitler by doing his work.[7]

Christians have received from the Jewish people the Ten Words given on Sinai, and these additional words also contain a similar admonition, which they might always have already heard from their own gospel[8]—an admonition that has in fact occasionally been heeded.[9] As long as this world endures, the Jewish people, in Israel and in the Diaspora, are for Christians inviolable, in a sense that has to be continually rediscovered and reinterpreted.[10] It is this especially that is meant when in the context of the Christian church's relationship to the Jewish people we talk about reverencing the nature of the God of Israel and sanctifying his name.[11]

ISRAEL AS THE PEOPLE OF GOD

The Subject of the Promises

The sequence of terms in Rom. 9:4b is a separate, carefully constructed section of Paul's whole catalogue in v. 4b.[12] To them, Paul says, belong

hē hyiothesia kai hē doxa kai hai diathēkai
kai hē nomothesia kai hē latreia kai hai epangeliai.

The final stress lies on the last term, the promises. Two observations confirm our impression that for Paul this was the evident climax and goal of the sequence. First, the apostle picks up the concept again indirectly when he immediately continues, ". . . to them belong the patriarchs," for the patriarchs are the initial subjects of the promises. Second, in 9:6ff., the promise given to the patriarchs is immediately made the explicit theme, as the beginning of God's words and acts with Israel. Romans 4 and Galatians 3 are further witnesses to the preeminence of promise, rather than law, in Paul.

If we look at these indications of the trend of Paul's theology, it is already clear that the divine promise conferred upon the people of God, and given in their behalf, has to stand at the center of a Christian definition of Israel. Who is Israel? A community that lives from its reception of the divine word of promise and that has its foundation and continuing existence in that word. First come God's words and his acts. The acts of the people are a response to the word God addresses to them, a response given either in listening and obeying or in the refusal to obey.

This description certainly seems to conflict with a frequently cited Jewish tradition that doing comes before hearing—a tradition derived from the striking sequence in the promise given in Exod. 24:7: "We will do and we will hear"; first do, then hear (b. Shabbat 88a). There may even be traces of this sequence in the Sermon on the Mount, when Jesus puts doing before teaching (Matt. 5:19). But this tradition probably really has the function of a corrective, the justification of which is the same as that which later allows the Epistle of James to rebut a Pauline tradition that had been interpreted in a one-sided way: "Faith by itself, if it has no works, is dead" (2:17). Important traditions in Israel, at least, point in the direction of this interpretation. For in fact the very first word uttered to Israel, and the very first word Israel repeats in her fundamental confession of faith, in the Shema Israel, is "Hear!" And the sequence of the first and second sections of the whole Shema (Deut. 6:4–9; 11:13–21)[13] is traditionally explained as follows: "We should first of all take upon ourselves the yoke of the heavenly rule [that is, we should recognize God as Lord, and as One] and only then accept the yoke of the commandments" (Berakhot 2.2). The connection between the two things is given vivid pictorial form in the following parable, which is an exposition of the saying in Exod. 20:2 "I am the Lord your God" (Mekhilta on this passage):

Why are the Ten Words [that is, the Commandments] not uttered at the beginning of the Torah [that is, in Genesis 1]? A mashal was made. To what shall the matter be likened? It is like a man who went into a province. He said to the people: I will be king over you. They said to him: Have you done anything [good] to us, that you desire to reign over us? What did he do? He built a wall for them, made a channel to bring them water, and waged war on their behalf. Then he said to them: Now I will reign over you. They said to him: Yes indeed. So "the Place" [i.e., God] led the Israelites out of Egypt, divided the sea for them, sent the manna down to them, let the wells spring up for them, called up the quails for them, and on their behalf waged war with Amalek. Then he said to them: I will rule over you [that is, through the commandments or precepts]. Then they said to him: Yes indeed.[14]

But lest the attempt to think along the lines of Jewish tradition should seem too easy, we should consider another complex, which makes the matter more difficult. For the Jewish people, as for the Christian church, living from the promise means turning back to the patriarchs, especially Abraham. The way God took with Abraham begins with the saying "Go from your country and your kindred and your father's house to the land that I will show you. And I will make of you a great nation, and I will bless you, and make your name great, so that it will become a blessing" (Gen. 12:1–2). Abraham is caught between God's immediate address, which he has to obey, and a future for which there is no foreseeable foundation in the present, except for the pure, unalloyed promise of God himself: "Then I will make of you a great nation." This certainly means that he is also encompassed by the promise of divine action, which is what literally moves him. All the same, in the framework of that action, the first thing is, "Go, *lech*. . . ."

God's first word to Abraham is an order, a commandment. Jewish and Christian tradition seem to draw apart in their interpretation of this "go" (though it may sometimes also be different texts that are specifically under consideration). Christian tradition stresses that because Abraham "goes" in response to the promise, it is a matter of faith or trust. So faith or trust is the behavior that accords with the divine word. And because this trust is effected by that very promise itself, it has its foundation not in human beings but in God himself. Jewish tradition, on the other hand, stresses that the promise cannot be fulfilled unless Abraham *does* what he is commanded to do. Abraham is God's partner in the fulfillment of the divine promise. The background of these two interpretations is a different interpretation of human beings in their relationship to God. Jewish tradition finds perhaps its clearest expression in the declaration "Everything is in the hand of heaven, except the fear of heaven" (*b. Berakhot* 33b). In the Christian tradition, Paul sums up the different interpretation most succinctly in 1 Cor. 4:7: "What have you that you did not receive? If then you received it, why do you boast as if it were not a gift?" In the first case, a person's responsibility is always something he is faced with as the possibility open to him. In the second case, he always starts from a responsibility that has been misused, and can acquire responsibility only on the basis of God's merciful acts. On the one side, we find a limited degree of independence in relation to God; on the other, unbounded dependence.

This varying interpretation of the relation between human beings and God also comes out in the different understanding of redemption. According to the Jewish view, human beings are God's partners in the redemption of the world.[15] According to Christian ideas, redemption—which has already, in germ, begun—is the work of God alone. He merely makes use of human beings in the process.[16]

Particularly in complexes like this, we should surely give up the attempt to cut the various Gordian knots and instead ask how far Jews and Christians can help each other. Death constitutes a closed frontier beyond which Jewish cooperation in the redemption of the world cannot go. Yet in the form of obedience to the Torah, this cooperation is a living testimony that God will achieve sovereignty in this world through the hearing and doing of what he commands. The misery of this world constitutes a no less closed frontier for the Christian assurance of redemption. But as protest against the laws of this world, this certainty testifies that God is greater than what human beings desire and achieve. The strength of the Jewish people is its faithfulness to the Torah; but inherent in that very strength is a probably unavoidable weakness—a tendency to obey the commandment for the commandment's sake, irrespective of the question whether it is actually of positive value for life itself. The strength of the Christian church is its assurance of participation in the Spirit of the end time. But the weakness inherent in this strength is a no less dubious trend toward "enthusiasm." Both these tendencies in their different ways can stand in the way of God's rule. So whereas Christians can be encouraged by Jews and learn from them how to discover commandments that serve the kingdom of God, and hence also the gospel, Jews can perhaps learn from Christians that God's activity always goes beyond the commandment he has given.

I say perhaps: for in spite of the differences I have picked out, we are confronted with a question. In the context we have been discussing, are the Jewish and Christian traditions not after all closer to each other than would seem to be the case traditionally, according to what we have said? And do the standpoints perhaps not seem unduly hard and fast because of the way the questions themselves are traditionally framed? The Jewish interpretation that "everything is in the hand of heaven" teaches that the promise and the call to conversion are part of Israel's life as God's people, for that first challenge to Abraham already seems like what Jürgen Moltmann calls a "conversion to the future." Men and women can trust the divine promise, and the divine edicts that stand in the service of the promise; that is to say, they may, and can, turn again. This may be termed the fundamental assurance of the biblical and postbiblical Jewish tradition —an assurance that is continually stressed anew. This, so to speak, is the inviolable dignity conferred on human beings by God himself. In a New Testament context we may think here of the parable of the prodigal son (Luke 15:11–32).[17] The possibility of repentance and conversion (*teshuvah*) distinguishes human beings from the lost sheep, or the lost coin, which can *only be found*. If here the Jewish Bible and Jesus are in agreement, Paul's question about whether there is anything that human beings have *not* received affirms that repentance is not something that can be separated from God himself. Rather, it is a turning to his promise and to the will which that promise manifests. We can therefore only talk about repentance or conversion at all if the premise is God's own commitment toward human beings. But this understanding is in complete accordance with the intercession in the Eighteen Benedictions: "Do *thou* lead us back to thy instruction [*torah*]."

So it would seem that what was suggested as being a possible Jewish "help" for Christians, and a Christian "help" for Jews could in fact, in either case, quite well be learned from one's own history and tradition. But it can surely not be denied that the other tradition may make things easier because, where the relationship to God is concerned, the emphasis of the two traditions is different.[18]

Whether, then, we consider that the difference between the Jewish and Christian understandings of the relationship to God is considerable or very slight, what we have said provides the answer to our cardinal question, Who is Israel, who is the Jewish people? Israel is a community that lives from pledge and promise and is therefore continually pointed along the path of conversion (*teshuvah*).

The Firstborn Sons of God

The very first thing Paul says about Israel in the list that formed our starting point (Rom. 9:4–5) is that it has received the sonship as gift of grace. The concept of sonship takes us into the exodus tradition, which was already touched on in the rabbinic parable quoted above. For in the exodus from Egypt, with the liberation from the house of slavery, Israel became the son of God, the firstborn son (*bekhor/prōtotokos*; Exod. 4:22; Hos. 11:1) whom the Father loves especially.[19] For Paul, Israel is the firstborn son from beginning to end. That is why the gospel is proclaimed first (*prōton*) to the Jews (Rom. 1:16–17). And in the same way, the end of Israel means that it will enter into its full heritage, which is described in the assurance "All Israel will be saved" (Rom. 11:26). The term "sonship" carries the echo of Israel's election, which is a partial fulfillment of the promise given to Abraham. It is one of the primal facts about Israel, on God's way with his people. It is not abrogated just because the title of firstborn Son is applied to Jesus, since in the case of Jesus it is used in a strictly eschatological connotation. Jesus is the firstborn from the dead, by virtue of his resurrection, in which we believe (Rom. 8:29; Col. 1:18).

Israel's election in the exodus, which is comprehended in the term "sonship," is at once a reminder of salvation and the foundation for hope. According to rabbinic tradition (*Pesaḥim* 10.5), every Jew should look upon himself as having been himself led out of Egypt and therefore as someone who has been liberated. This remembrance is the unending source of hope for liberation out of new slavery, and hence hope for life in the land promised to the patriarchs.[20] The remembrance of salvation in the exodus has, not least, profound consequences for the behavior toward its neighbors which is enjoined on Israel. Recollection of their own existence as slaves in Egypt flows over to people in Israel's midst who are themselves slaves or without rights. Behavior toward these people is to be determined by the remembrance of Israel's own origin (Lev. 19:33–34). Here, by way of recollection, the way leads from exodus to Sinai, from the act of liberation to obedience to the commandment, which also covers the relationship to strangers.

The final aspect we must consider in this context touches directly on the understanding of God. The liberating God does not participate in the exodus simply as an observer. He is the One who is in the forefront. He goes with the people, suffers with them, shares their experiences. In this participation he shows himself to be the Father of Israel, his firstborn son. The people of the exodus correspond to the God of the exodus—the God who is present in that exodus, accompanying his people as, once before, as the God of the patriarchs, he accompanied Abraham, Isaac, and Jacob.

In the Splendor of the Divine Presence

These last observations already take us further into what is meant by another of the gifts Paul mentions: to them, he says, belongs the *doxa*, the divine presence in manifested form, the *shekhinah*.[21] The prophecy of Deutero-Isaiah is a single testimony to this assurance: God is present in the foreign land, after the exodus from the Israelites' own country, and he will be present when, for a second time (as the prophet expects), he leads his people into the land of the patriarchs. It is in accordance with this that, even before Deutero-Isaiah, Ezekiel had seen the *doxa*, the *kavod* of the Lord, leave the temple and move away in an easterly direction (Ezek. 12:22ff.). Later on, rabbinic tradition could describe the circumstances more precisely: the *kavod* did not leave the temple or Jerusalem at the same time as the priests or the other dignitaries. It was only when the children left that the divine presence went with them.[22]

This tradition and many others reflect the certainty that God's presence means his accompanying presence in Babylonian exile, just as during Israel's sojourn in the foreign land of Egypt. It is accompaniment in abasement and weakness, even in suffering and impurity.[23] Yet the conviction of God's presence in the foreign land is not restricted to biblical times. "God descends with Israel into *all* her exiles . . . he is with Israel in the suffering of exile today too."[24] The rabbis extend the conception of God's descent into the exiles of Egypt and Babylonia down to their own present time and "by taking God's suffering in exile quite seriously . . . logically see Israel's redemption from exile as the redemption of God himself too"[25] —the God who will reveal his presence in power in the coming liberation. This is the form in which, from this time on, Jews in the Diaspora were for centuries to live out the assurance Paul describes in the words "To them belongs the divine presence."

Partner in the Covenants

The idea of covenant echoes perhaps more strongly than anything else through all the other concepts listed in Rom. 9:4–5. "Covenant" is connected particularly closely with the gift of the promises mentioned at the beginning and with the gift of the law specified immediately afterwards in Rom. 9:4–5. The assurances given to the patriarchs are in each case the essential part of a *berit* that God makes with them out of his free goodness and through which he binds himself to fulfill particular promises.[26] Although Scripture mentions the patriarchs especially as the recipients of these divine self-imposed obligations, these commitments are not restricted to the early period. They are continually given anew in the history of God's people and include, for example, the continuance of the earth (Gen. 9:8–17) and the throne of David (2 Sam. 23:5) as well as the Levitical priestly office (Mal. 2:4–5, 8).[27] The essential mark of these personal divine self-imposed obligations is their unbreachable binding force.[28] In Romans 9–11 this comes out most clearly in the apostle's affirmation (which we have already touched on) that God's gift of grace and his call are irreversible (Rom. 11:29). This is the reason for the certainty that all Israel will be saved—simply that this is the fulfillment of the obligation God has imposed on himself in the covenant he has made (Rom. 11:26–27).

The sole guarantee, then, that the divine promise will be kept is the certainty that "God will keep his word";[29] but God can lay certain obligations on the people in the framework of the covenant he has established. The people have to keep these edicts, under threat of punishment if they disobey. But this does not mean that they can make their obedience a reason for claiming that the promises be kept.[30] In this sense *berit* (parallel to *torah,* "instruction," and *chok,* "statute") can mean "any deposition of the divine will as regards human beings."[31] The connection between the divine promise and human obligation is particularly emphasized in the interpretation of the *berit* on Sinai as "promise *and* command."[32] It is this link which demonstrates the closeness of *diathēkē* to *nomothesia,* the term that immediately follows.

As I have indicated, this biblical interpretation of the divine covenants as the expression of God's loving, steadfast commitment to his people is picked up by Paul in Romans 9–11. But it is also in Luke's mind when, in Zechariah's *benedictus,* he praises the beginning of Israel's redemption as the expression of God's recollection of his covenant (Luke 1:72–74). The conception of the divine covenant I have outlined persisted in postbiblical rabbinic Judaism as well. We can see this by a glance back at what was said about Israel as subject of the promises. In this later period, particular weight was laid on the interpretation that not only was God's own personal commitment the expression of his divine love but the same could also be said about the Torah—the obligation laid on the people. This interpretation emerges in exemplary fashion from the benediction that introduces the "Hear, O Israel":

With abounding love hast Thou loved us, O Lord our God, and great and overflowing tenderness hast thou shown us. O our Father, our King, for our fathers' sake, who trusted in thee, and to whom thou didst teach the statutes of life, be also gracious unto us and teach us. O our Father, merciful Father, ever compassionate, have mercy upon us; O put it into our hearts to understand and to discern, to mark, learn and teach, to do and to fulfill in love all the words of instruction in thy Torah. Enlighten our eyes in thy Torah, and let our hearts cleave to thy commandments, and unify our hearts to love and reverence thy Name, so that we may be never put to shame.[33]

We may trace the same line forward into the present and remember Martin Buber's well-known, moving scene in the Jewish cemetery in Worms, in which he describes his discovery of what it means to be a Jew. Here too what Buber is expressing is a primal biblical assurance, which is endorsed both by the New Testament and by the testimonies of rabbinic Judaism:

> I live not far away from the city of Worms, to which I am also attached through a tradition of my forefathers; and I visit it from time to time. Each time I am there, I go first of all to the cathedral. Here is a visible harmony of elements, a wholeness, a perfection whose equilibrium is undisturbed by any one individual feature. I wander round the cathedral, contemplating it with perfect joy. Then I go over to the Jewish cemetery. It is a graveyard full of crooked, split stones, without form or direction. I stand in the midst of it, looking up from its confusion to the glorious harmony beyond; and I feel as if I were looking up from Israel to the church. Down there there is not an iota of form. Nothing but stones and the ashes beneath the stones. One still has the ashes, however much they have become vaporized. One has the physical being of the men and women who have come to this. One has them. I have them. I do not have them as some physical being within the space of this planet. I have them as the physical form of my own remembrance, back down to the depths of history, back to Sinai.
>
> I have stood there, bonded to the ashes, and through the ashes to the patriarchs. And this is the remembrance of the event with God that is given to all Jews. The perfection of the Christian house of God cannot loosen my hold on this. Nothing can loosen my hold on Israel's time with God.
>
> I have stood there and have experienced it all, I myself. I have experienced all the death: all the ashes, all the disintegration, all the dumb lamentation is my own. But for me the covenant has never been revoked. I am prostrate, felled like these stones. But still it has never been revoked.
>
> The cathedral is what it is. The cemetery is what it is. But the covenant with us has never been revoked.[34]

We could hardly find anything that Romans 9–11 could endorse more emphatically. And it is not an infringement of the assurance to which Buber testifies when, in the face of a world threatened in our century as never before, Heschel, for example, asks "whether we should renew the covenant with God."[35] For this is a question that can only be put at all by someone for whom the covenant is, from God's side, a reality that may be open to attack but that is nonetheless a reality which endures.

Recipients of the Torah

The next gift mentioned by the apostle is the *nomothesia*, the law-giving, the Torah. We can do no more than touch on the wealth of references and relations surrounding this term. This is the instruction that enables the people to live in accordance with God's election and the covenant he has offered. It is therefore the proof of his love. Christians cannot talk about the presence of God without linking what they say with the gospel; Jews cannot speak of God's presence without the medium of the Torah. Given before the people entered the promised land, it enabled them to live even outside that land—to live, but above all to survive there. We find especially impressive interpretations of this link between exile and Torah in a testimony that was written even before the destruction of the second temple, in the Damascus Document, which belongs within the radius of the Dead Sea community. The document tells us that the community it is describing is itself living in exile or sees itself as an exiled community. In a free interpretation of Amos 5:26–27 and 9:11, the document defines the books of the Torah as a tabernacle, as the home of the congregation of Israel, as the room where Israel is preserved (CD VII, 15ff.).[36] In another midrash on Num. 21:18, the document again interprets "the law" as a spring of water, as the elixir of life that guarantees the community's existence in the foreign land (CD VII, 2–3). Whereas the first interpretation is peculiar to the Damascus Document, the second (which is similar in substance) is shared by rabbinic tradition.[37] When Paul says that the Torah is given "for life" and "for good" (Rom. 7:10, 12), his statements are probably elucidated best from a Jewish standpoint by interpretations such as the two we have cited: through the gift of the Torah God preserves Israel as his people. But according to the Jewish view, the Torah shows the power of this preservation in its twofold—written and oral—form; for both are the "Torah of Sinai" given to Moses (*Avot* 1.1) and both of them contain haggadah and halakhah, haggadah being the broad sector of exhortation in narrative form, and halakhah containing binding instruction for everyday conduct.[38]

The Torah is designed for life and for good because it is through the Torah that God preserves his people. This is obvious in one sense, and yet it takes a paradoxical form, so to speak. Preservation through the Torah can be positively deduced from the very fact of the Jewish people's continued existence for thousands of years, so we may speak of the trend "for life"; and yet this trend has almost always borne the signature of suffering. The "mystery of Jewish suffering" is "indistinguishable from the experience of the Torah, the experience of election, and—as the reverse side of that, so to speak—the experience of grace."[39] In 2 Cor. 4:7–8, Paul sums up *his* experience of preservation and suffering: "But we have this treasure in earthen vessels, to show that the transcendent power belongs to God and not to us. We are afflicted in every way, but not crushed; perplexed, but not driven to despair; persecuted, but not forsaken." If we do not apply these sentences to Jesus Christ or the *pneuma*, like the apostle, but relate them in the heuristic sense to the Torah, as the treasure in earthen vessels, then they are a very precise summing up of what I have suggested the law means for Israel as God's people.

In the Nazi murder camps many Jews lost this treasure of the Torah. Others lived it in a way that we could describe in Paul's very words.[40] In view of life lived like this in the power of the Torah as God's gift, what sense does it make to go on talking about Jesus Christ as the end of the law, and referring such statements to Jewish life with the law?

Although it is impossible to extract the "commonplaces of Judaism" where the Torah is concerned "simply from a reading of Romans and Corinthians,"[41] Paul himself witnesses to the flimsiness of assertions about the "end of the law." For in the passage in question (Rom. 10:4) he actually talks about Jesus Christ as "the *fulfillment* of the law for everyone who has faith." For it is only with this presupposition that it makes sense for him to maintain in the same letter that "[W]e uphold the law through faith" (Rom. 3:31) and that the love through which he believes faith proves its efficacy (Gal. 5:7) is the "fulfillment of the law" (Rom. 13:8).

Paul brings out the positive character of the Torah on the foundation of his faith in Jesus Christ; for Jesus makes accessible to the Gentiles too the One God of Israel (Rom. 3:29), though without imposing on them the obligation to follow Israel's specific way as it is manifested in Jewish halakhah. I observed above that Israel lives out its relationship to God with the help of the Torah, just as the Christian church lives out its own relationship with the help of Jesus Christ—a parallel brought out by 2 Cor. 4:7–8—and we have now seen that Paul does in fact take a positive view of the Torah. All this may encourage us to take a different, less disparaging view of the law from the traditional one and may induce us to put polemic aside where the Torah is concerned and instead to take the first steps in a common learning process.[42]

Workers in Worship

Life with the Torah in exile is still very largely, as it was in ancient Israel, what Paul sums up as *latreia* (*avodah*). What is meant here is "the cult" or—since the destruction of the second temple—everything that is included under the synagogue's *tefillah*—its prayer or worship. We need only remember what the wealth of the biblical psalms alone means for Jews and Christians alike; and these psalms had their origin in the cult. We may think too of the impress of Jewish worship on the developing worship of the church. And we may remember the numerous liturgical features Jews and Christians have in common, here and there, even today. All this deserves a more detailed discussion than we can give it here.[43] We shall therefore concentrate our attention on one single complex: the connection between the Torah as halakhah, or religious instruction, and this very sphere of worship. For it is here above all that essential aspects of the Torah's function as halakhah emerge.

In this framework a considerable part is played by the laws about Sabbath observance, which Christians often feel to be particularly legalistic. From the Jewish side, these injunctions are designed to mark the sanctification, or setting apart, of this day for God. Their existential significance has been described by the most widely varying Jewish writers. Some sentences from Erich Fromm may represent them all:

> On the Shabbat one lives as if one *has* nothing, pursuing no aim except *being*, that is, expressing one's essential powers: praying, studying, eating, drinking, singing, making love.
> The Shabbat is a day of joy because on that one day one is fully oneself. This is the reason the Talmud calls a Shabbat the anticipation of the Messianic Time, and the Messianic Time the unending Shabbat: the day on which property and money as well as mourning and sadness are tabu; a day on which time is defeated and pure being rules.[44]

In the context of the encounter between Christians and Jews particularly, a point of preeminent interest is undoubtedly the view that the Sabbath is an anticipation of the messianic era (*Mekhilta* on Exod. 31:13), an idea that reaches back into Jewish antiquity. Another important and related point is that the Torah or the halakhah is designed to serve the fulfillment of this anticipation. Christians can surely learn something essential from this particular interpretation of the law.[45] On the one hand, the halakhah is a reflection about ways of living in faithfulness to God and what this means in any given case. In this sense it continually seeks to smooth the ways to repentance and is a guide to specific obedience. On the other hand, it also helps to let something of the prereflection of the promised end-time kingdom of God shine out here and now.

This leads us to some additional reflections. In the framework of the Jewish-Christian dialogue, we frequently hear the objection from the Jewish side that there is as yet no sign that redemption has taken place or is taking place. But the interpretation of the Sabbath I have described should suggest that differentiation is necessary. Whether it is possible to talk now, in the present, about messianic signs is a question that has acquired additional contemporary force through the founding of the state of Israel and the return to the land of the fathers which that means. Israel as state sees itself in the context of the Bible's messianic promises. It is therefore directly faced with the problem of acknowledging the beginning of redemption on the one hand and of yet being confronted with facts that speak in the strongest terms against any such beginning. Perhaps this difficulty could help toward a better understanding of Christian tradition at this point. Gershom Scholem formulates the problem in succinct form:

> The readiness for irrevocable commitment to what is concrete, which will no longer be put off, is a readiness, born out of horror and extinction, that Jewish history found in our generation for the first time when it entered upon the utopian retreat to Zion. It is no wonder if this readiness is accompanied by overtones of messianism, even though it is unable to surrender itself to that messianism, since it is pledged to history itself and not to metahistory. Whether it can endure this commitment without being annihilated in the crisis of the messianic claim it has (at least virtually) evoked—that is the question the Jew of our time has to ask. He has to put the question to his present and his future; but it is a question that comes to him out of the great and dangerous past.[46]

Heirs of the Land

Our last reflections have brought us to something that is noticeably absent from the catalogue in Romans 9:4–5, although we might perhaps expect to find it there: the land of Israel (*eretz Yisrael*) as God's gift. It is true that we may perhaps see it as included in the terms *diathēkai* or *epangeliai*. Romans 9—11 apart, Jerusalem was for Paul the center from which he took his bearings (the collections he made for the church there make that clear); and this may be seen not least as a sign of the importance the apostle tacitly ascribed to "the land."[47] As I have already stressed, the destruction of the second temple and its political consequences for the Jewish community in the land of Israel were something Paul could not envisage. On the contrary, for the apostle, the temple and the Jewish settlements in the northern and southern parts of the land of Israel, Galilee and Judea, were facts he took as a matter of course. But ever since 70 A.D. Israel's history has had its centers of gravity in the Diaspora, even though there have always been Jewish communities in the land itself. The turning point came only in our own century, with successive returns to the land and the foundation of the state of Israel, a foundation accelerated by the horrors of the Nazi era. This turning point now puts a challenging question to Christian theology, since for centuries that theology has assiduously offered theological interpretations for the historical event of the destruction of the temple and Jerusalem. In this context Christian theology may find it hard, on the one hand, to accept the interpretation of Israel as a messianic—or at least a messianically colored—event. And yet it is Paul especially who sees Jesus Christ as the yes to all God's promises (2 Cor. 1:20), and it is he who promises that all Israel will be saved (Rom. 11:26). It is therefore Paul above all who in this way smooths the path for an understanding of Israel in its political existence as a place where God's people are preserved and kept under the sign of the promise; so that in this sense the state may be seen as the token of God's faithfulness.[48]

Partakers of the Spirit

In his catalogue the apostle lists a series of splendid gifts. He speaks of the earthly origin of the Messiah. But he avoids mentioning the power of the Spirit, the *pneuma*, in this connection, although this was essential for the communities of Jesus Christ. In contrast, all that I have said up to now implies the interpretation that Israel, the Jewish people, has certainly not been deserted by the Spirit for almost two thousand years and is not "Spiritless" now. On the contrary, it is full of demonstrations of the Spirit and power, to use a Pauline phrase (1 Cor. 2:4). The very reality Paul has in mind when he uses this phrase—the reality of suffering—offers countless examples of this ever since the days of the Maccabees, down to our own time.

It must, however, be said that, although it may seem that Paul neither can nor will call the gift of the Spirit one of Israel's privileges, we can still find some degree of evidence in what the apostle says to suggest that he presupposes that the Spirit is present among the Jewish people. The close connection between the concepts *doxa* and *pneuma*, particularly, points in this direction. More strikingly still, the gifts that the apostle attributes to the Israelites in Rom. 9:4–5 are in Rom. 11:29 called *charismata*, or gifts of grace. And for Paul *charismata* are always efficacies of the divine Spirit, as 1 Corinthians 12 shows.

At the same time, however, there is a significant difference between Jews and Christians in the way they conceive the presence of the Spirit. This difference is intimately linked with the Jewish no to Jesus as Messiah, and the Christian yes. It is true that, according to a widespread rabbinic interpretation, the era of the divine Spirit, as a power shared by the whole people, came to an end with the destruction of the first temple.[49] But parallel to this we find the view that individuals can be endowed with the Spirit as a reward. Indeed there are even traditions that suggest that this link between the Spirit and individuals could be extended further.[50] In spite of this, however, it is undoubtedly true that in the Jewish view the pouring out of the Spirit on all flesh—which the Book of Joel promises for the end time (3:1–5)—is at least no more than a future event.[51] The Christian church, in contrast, lives from the certainty that it already partakes of the Spirit of God as an eschatological gift, in the sense of an earnest or pledge of what will be in the future; and the Spirit is alive in the church as the power sustaining it. As the phrase "eschatological gift" suggests, the pouring out of the Spirit in which Christians believe has its origin in the resurrection and exaltation of Jesus Christ, whose presence with those who are his own is guaranteed by the Spirit, according to earliest Christian interpretation.

This link between Jesus Christ and the Spirit means that the pneumatological dispute between Jews and Christians is a variant of the dispute over Christology. But again it would be a misunderstanding to deduce from the fact that the Jewish community waits for the end-time Spirit of God that it lacks the manifestations of God's presence now. A recollection of what was said about the *shekhinah* especially, ought to be a sufficient warning against any such conclusion.

Jesus' Brothers and Sisters

". . . and of their race, according to the flesh, is the Messiah [*christos*]." With this statement Paul brings to a close his whole inventory in Romans 9:4–5, before he adds the blessing. The next chapter—which represents the main section of our investigations—will be devoted to an inquiry into what this assertion means, and especially the question of who Jesus Christ is or can be for the Jewish people, from a Christian perspective. But we should be detaching Jesus quite illegitimately from the Jewish people if we were not to ask first, as we did with the other gifts, who he is for Jews according to their own view. It is true that by including this question in the attempt to describe Israel's identity we are faced with a problem. For from the Jewish standpoint, a relationship to Jesus (however that relationship may be defined) is by no means an essential element in Israel's understanding of itself as God's people.[52] The lack of interest in Jesus and the church that is shown by very many Orthodox Jewish circles is evidence of this. Nonetheless, it is worth pursuing the question at this point. It would seem possible to do so without violating Israel's identity; and the attempt seems necessary both for Israel's sake and for the sake of the church. For one thing, the Jewish people has, since Jesus, always de facto taken up *some* position or other toward Jesus and the church—whether its no was tacit or explicit, bluntly extreme or more cautiously differentiated. And this means that, indirectly at least, this no has become part of the people of God's interpretation of its own self. For another thing, the question about Jesus is present among the Jewish people in latent form simply because Jesus was a Jew, which is to say a member of the body of "all Israel," so that his life—like the life of any other controversial Jew—casts up the problem, In what sense does he belong to the Jewish people? Even if, according to the Jewish perspective, Jesus is "a lost sheep of the house of Israel," that too implies a tacit relationship to his Jewish brothers and sisters—and perhaps a question to them. Again, what we shall go on to say can do no more than indicate a few guidelines, even though we shall be developing them a little further than in the earlier sections of this book.

Some people, we are told, took Jesus for the returning Elijah, others for a prophet, like the prophets in the Scriptures; still others thought he was John the Baptist, raised from the dead (Mark 6:14–16; 8:28). But these contemporary views fall silent later on. Instead, the acknowledgment of Jesus as Messiah on the one hand (Mark 8:29) was balanced on the other by the interpretation that he was possessed (Mark 3:21). The polemical work *Toledot Yeshu* is representative of the condemnation of Jesus among the Jewish people from the beginning until the Enlightenment.[53] The *Toledot* is certainly no older than the tenth century, but it contains earlier material and passes on an interpretation of Jesus that in general accords with the reproach of possession that is already suggested in Mark 3.

The *Toledot Yeshu* is in general a kind of antigospel. (The title itself may perhaps be a play on Matt. 1:1: *genesis Iēsou*.) The narrators draw on the Gospels among other things but interpret their traditions in a diametrically opposite sense to the one transmitted. According to the *Toledot*, Jesus is the son of Miriam of Bethlehem and "the handsome but wicked"[54] Pandera (or ben Pandera). Miriam was betrothed, but not to Pandera. The child was conceived during Miriam's menstruation. Since in Judaism menstruation is regarded as unclean, Jesus was accordingly conceived not by the Holy Spirit but out of the spirit of impurity. The *Toledot* does not dispute his miracles, but these are again ascribed not to divine authority but to Jesus' misuse of the name of God, that is to say, to magic, which he was said to have learned in Egypt. Jesus' resurrection, finally, is explained in the *Toledot* on the lines of the polemic already passed down in Matt. 28:11–15: the gardener took away the body of Jesus, whereupon the disciples, being unable to find it, proclaimed that Jesus had risen from the dead. Moreover, it is understandable that, according to the *Toledot*, Judas Iscariot is not without merit. What is surprising is the judgment about Simon Peter. He is termed one of Israel's sages, who—in order to save the Jews from being harrassed by the apostles—severed the Christians from the Jewish people and gave them ethical precepts. After he had completed his work, Peter—who had only pretended to be one of Jesus' supporters—withdrew into solitude, writing hymns that, generally distributed, were still sung in the synagogues.

There is unanimity among Jewish scholars as well that the book has no historical relevance for the time of Jesus. Nonetheless, it is of the greatest importance for an understanding of the medieval relations between the Jewish people and the Christian church, or to be more precise, as a reflection of the oppression of the Jews by Christians. Klausner points this out in a few terse words: "The Jews were unable to revenge themselves on their enemies through deeds, so they revenged themselves on them through the written and spoken word."[55] The *Toledot Yeshu* is therefore both untrue and true. As a historical account it is untrue. But it is true inasmuch as the Jesus of Christians could hardly have been seen in any other way through Jewish eyes, in view of Jewish experiences with the church.[56] So in a certain sense the secret authors of the book are the Christians themselves, not Jews. The only positive feature the *Toledot* is indirectly able to note is the existence of commandments in the church, and these, of course, derive from Jewish tradition.

It is only against the background of this medieval Jewish picture of Jesus that we can judge appropriately the modes of interpreting Jesus that have developed since then among the Jewish people.[57] An important change came about in central Europe with the Enlightenment. At that time the social and political situation of the Jews slowly began to change. The "study of Judaism" soon started to develop, in the framework of which Jewish scholars researched into their own traditions, thereby playing their part in the historical—and in this sense critical—studies that dominated the nineteenth century. In this context, in 1839, the French doctor and philosopher Josef Salvador (1779–1873) published, in two volumes, the first Jewish life of Jesus since the *Toledot*. Entitled *Jésus Christ et sa doctrine*, it tried to explain the rise of Christianity and the figure of Jesus historically. Like many later Jewish books about Jesus, and even the *Toledot* in its muted way, Salvador recognized Jesus' ethic as the bond linking him to Judaism, whereas he viewed Christianity as a synthesis of Judaism and paganism. The difference between Jesus and traditional Judaism was solely that Jesus moved the religious and ethical life of the individual into the foreground and laid no stress on the social precepts and ceremonial laws of the Torah.

Jewish research on Jesus in the present day still draws on the breakthrough we have described, though it cannot be reduced to the single denominator of being a repetition of Salvador's position. Some of the work done in succeeding years and some of the positions assumed were marked especially by the attempt to arrive at a constructive religious and theological evaluation of Jesus. The frequently quoted passage about Jesus in Martin Buber's *Two Kinds of Faith* belongs to this group of writings:

> Ever since I was a boy I have felt that Jesus was my elder brother. That Christians saw Jesus and see him still as God and Redeemer always seemed to me a fact to be taken immensely seriously. It was something I had to try to understand, for Jesus' sake and my own. . . . I am more certain than ever that he has an important place in the history of Israel's faith and that this place cannot be described through any of the usual categories.[58]

Almost thirty years before that book, Buber wrote in *I and Thou*, the book which above all brought him fame:

> How powerful, even to being overpowering, and how legitimate, even to being self-evident, is the saying of *I* by Jesus! For it is the *I* of unconditional relation in which the man calls his *Thou* Father in such a way that he himself is simply Son, and nothing else but Son. . . . *I* and *Thou* abide; every man can say *Thou* and is then *I*, every man can say Father and is then Son.[59]

Buber is not alone in seeing Jesus as the elder Jewish brother. Buber's pupil Schalom Ben-Chorin speaks similarly about Jesus in his writings. Ben-Chorin defines his viewpoint more precisely by saying that although he does not believe in Jesus, he does, like Jesus and with him, believe in the one God of Israel.[60] Another book that must be mentioned in this context is the book on Jesus written by the Jerusalem scholar David Flusser, whose work is in the field of religious studies. Flusser stresses as one of Jesus of Nazareth's main characteristics his commitment to the outcasts and the dispossessed—a characteristic that he considers is today particularly likely to arouse people's interest in the Nazarene.[61]

We meet what is perhaps the most exciting position, as far as the Jewish question about Jesus is concerned, in an essay written by Jochanan Bloch. Like Flusser, Bloch was engaged in religious studies, until his early death, and the standpoint of the two men is similar. What Bloch says is based particularly on his interpretation of the parable of the seed that springs up of itself (Mark 4:26–29), and the parable of the talents (Matt. 25:14–30; Luke 19:11–27). The heart of his interpretation of these parables, and thereby of Jesus himself, is this:

> God has prepared the ground for the Kingdom and wants it to come. What is more he is sure that come it will. But "he went away." He has left human beings to themselves. Human "forsakenness" is part of God's "hardness." Can we call God hard? We only have to cast a glance at the earth and at humanity. Do things look as if they were not "Godforsaken"? But it is not quite like that. The mystery is that in the foresakenness the coming is prepared. And it is the very people who are forsaken who, strangely, are the ones who are given the task of helping to bring about that coming. "Forsakenness" means a positive "closeness" to the Kingdom. It is like a way of serving the Kingdom. Isn't that why Jesus says that he has been sent to the "lost sheep" of

Israel, to the sick? Isn't that why he tells us that the poor are blessed, because the Kingdom is *theirs*? At all events, in their forsakenness human beings are to help in bringing the Kingdom. More—they are to hurry on its coming: just as the earth "itself" brings forth fruits, and just as the servants practice usury with their master's property. . . . By beseeching and insisting, by repenting, by fulfilling the law, by loving God and our neighbor? Yes, but above all, and in it all, through self-denial, self-sacrifice. "My God, my God, why hast thou forsaken me?" The last word on the cross is like an endorsement of faith in the human forsakenness that will bring about the Kingdom. Even in its despair, it is a cry of triumph—the triumph that is still possible. For Jesus is quoting. He is quoting (Psalm 22) the cry of the desolate man whom God does not answer but who is certain, in spite of that, that God is not hiding his face from him. So the cry itself is a secret sign that the Kingdom of his Father is coming.[62]

This Jewish interpretation of Jesus sees and says very much more than many a Christian book about Jesus. Bloch gathers together three things that are of fundamental importance if we are to understand Jesus: his commitment to those who were lost; his words and acts, under the sign of the coming divine sovereignty in which he believed; and his death on the cross. The power that sees and interprets all these three aspects as a unity can hardly be called simply a historian's power. It would seem rather as if here the successively initiated interpretation of Jesus as the *enduringly* Jewish brother itself created the premise for this profound view. We may compare it to Marc Chagall's picture the *White Crucifixion*, which moves in the same direction.

These few examples of positive Jewish interpretations of Jesus today may suffice; for our purpose here is not to survey them in all their different colorings. The point is to illustrate the revolution that has taken place since the Enlightenment and to consider its consequences.

In this chapter we have continually returned to our starting point in Rom. 9:4–5. Immediately before his catalogue, Paul calls the Jews who do not believe in the gospel "my brethren, my kinsmen by race." When a little later he says that the Messiah "is of their race, according to the flesh," he—indirectly at least—calls the Jews who do not recognize Jesus as the Messiah, Christ's brothers. This gives *Christians* the right to talk about the Jewish people as Jesus' brothers and sisters. But the Jewish views we have cited take us an important step further. Even if these voices are not the voice of "all Israel" but only represent a part, they justify us in thinking that it may be possible for us to describe the Jewish people as Jesus' brothers and sisters with Jewish consent.

But the Jewish interpretations we have described, again block access for Christians to the well-trodden paths of the traditional relationship between Christians and Jews. Anyone who, in spite of the revolution we have mentioned, still today judges the Jewish people according to the rigidly dogmatic yardstick of confession of Jesus as the Christ, would simply proclaim a mind closed—in defiance of history—to changes of any kind. That person's aim would be to dictate, where the essential thing is *to listen*.

The result would be to stifle the germ of what has just begun to grow, in the form of a new encounter between Christians and Jews. But this encounter can surely only become fruitful if Christians reckon with the possibility that both they themselves and Jews, through their own different ways of understanding, go some way toward grasping an authentic aspect of Jesus; and that these different understandings are therefore not to be thought of as a threat. On the contrary, each is an enrichment of the other.[63]

However far this understanding of Jesus goes, the frontier between the Christian and the Jewish interpretation still remains, since it is rooted in these interpretations themselves. The demarcation line can be shown precisely by another glance at Flusser's book on Jesus. It includes a section the author once called the "confession of faith" in Jesus that he "smuggled into" his little book:

> The very enormity of his life appeals to us today: from his call at his baptism, from the breaking of his ties with the family that was alien to him and his discovery of a new, higher sonship, down into the pandemonium of the sick and the possessed, and on to his death on the cross. That is why the words attributed by Matthew to the risen Jesus (28:20) take on for us a new meaning, which has nothing to do with the church: "And lo, I am with you alway, even unto the end of the world."[64]

This "confession of faith" may shame many a Christian for whom the earthly Jesus is little more than a silhouette, and whose faith is reduced to the mere "fact that" he existed. And yet the difference between what Flusser says and Christian belief becomes clear if we compare his statements with the statements of the Apostles' Creed. Or if we look at the very end of Flusser's book. It is significant that he concludes with the words that for Christians are anything but the last thing to be said about the Nazarene: "And Jesus yielded up his spirit."[65]

3

Jesus Christ, the Son of Israel and Firstborn from the Dead
Guidelines for a Christology Affirmative of Israel

THE SIGNS OF THE TIMES AND THE REQUIREMENT
TO BE TRUE TO THE GOSPEL

The attempt to find an interpretation of Jesus that is not by definition anti-Jewish is an inescapable part of the task described in the first chapter—the task of overcoming anti-Judaism in Christian theology. We cannot arrive at a Christology of this kind simply by describing the way in which one or several of the New Testament witnesses interpreted Christ. For one thing, anti-Jewish elements do not crop up for the first time only, in the later Christologies of the church. We already find them in the New Testament itself. We only have to think of the way in which Matthew described Jesus' attitude toward "the scribes and Pharisees" and the way he talks to them and about them according to the evangelist (chap. 23); or John's account of Jesus' dispute with "the Jews" (whoever may be *meant* by that; chap. 8). These are particularly glaring examples, but they are not the only ones. On the other hand, nothing is more improbable than the assumption that if the New Testament witnesses were writing today, in the situation we described at the beginning, they would simply repeat what they wrote two thousand years ago. The Gospels and epistles were written down in the course of a few decades, but even in this short period the traditions the writers took over were handled with considerable freedom. If we remember this, we shall hardly be able to stress too heavily the indirect demand the biblical testimonies make on us to hear and interpret what even they say in a "modern" sense—which means in accordance with the "signs of the times."

This task has already in part determined what we said in the previous chapter. There we took as our premise an interpretation of Jesus Christ that we shall develop here on the basis of New Testament statements. It will then be possible to consider objectively, and not destructively, the question whether we can call Jesus the Messiah, and in what sense—which means also whether we can talk about him as someone who has soteriological relevance for Israel too.

These christological questions will have to be put to two different sections of the tradition: on the one hand, to those writings which give an account of Jesus' teaching and ministry; and on the other, to the writings that expound his significance as the One who was crucified, raised, and is to come.

As we all know, it is difficult to build up anything more than a fragmentary picture of Jesus of Nazareth. But in spite of that, almost any attempt to do so seems less arbitrary than the assertion made by Rudolf Bultmann and maintained by some of his pupils—the postulate that for the New Testament witnesses of faith the important thing is not the how and what of Jesus and his proclamation; the only thing that matters is *the fact that* he came or preached.[1] The evangelist Luke could not see even the risen Jesus as so ghostly a figure as this (Luke 24:36–42).[2] Luther reminds us "that Jesus Christ was born a Jew."[3] This fact, with all its historical and theological importance, is the first thing that is lost if the figure of Jesus is emptied of content in this way. This loss has almost inevitably docetic consequences,[4] and therefore anti-Jewish ones as well. Of course we do not eliminate this danger simply by turning to "the Jesus of history." Here too everything depends on the questions we ask. For a long time attempts at a reconstruction were based on the criterion that we can only be more or less certain that material about Jesus is authentic if this can be attributed neither to Judaism nor to the early church.[5] But—if we look at the first point—the Jesus that then emerges is theologically from the very outset, whether intentionally or not, the "first Christian." Historically he is a shadow. We must emphasize first of all that the *vere homo*—the true man—of dogma means specifically (i.e., historically) the son of Israel, with all that this implies: his birth of a Jewish mother, his circumcision, his Jewish upbringing, his Jewish life, and his Jewish death. In saying this we are only endorsing the work that has reminded us of the "Jewishness of Jesus" or "Jesus the Jew."[6]

Of course the recognition of these things and the emphasis laid on them is unquestionably due in part to the events between 1933 and 1945. The Nazi persecution of the Jews, with its aim to murder all of them, contributed through that very aim—and in spite of it—to the founding of the state of Israel (and therefore helped towards the reconstitution of the Jewish Christian congregations in that country as well). But that same persecution was an insistent reminder that Jesus was a Jew,[7] a reminder that could not be ignored in spite of countertendencies toward Germanizing Jesus on the part of Nazi aiders and abettors. Here another aspect is implicit too. The return of a large section of the Jewish people to the land of Israel has apparently contributed essentially to the attempts of Jews today to understand Jesus as a child of the Jewish people and its land. A considerable number of the books about Jesus written by Jews—

for example, all the modern works I have cited—come from authors who were or are Israelis.[8]

In order to pursue these preliminary christological and hermeneutical reflections further, we must, however, first of all go back to an essay written in the Diaspora period. A number of years before Martin Buber, at the beginning of the twentieth century, Leo Baeck published a notable appreciation of Jesus that—in accordance with the writer's Diaspora situation—especially considers his significance for the relation between Israel and the Gentiles. In Baeck's judgment, Jesus brought Israel's teaching—monotheism and the ethic of love—to the gentile nations.[9] From the Jewish side, this interpretation is being developed and deepened at the present time by Pinchas Lapide, in particular.[10] But among Christians too, it is also beginning to win more and more supporters.[11] There is no doubt that it is in line with one of the main threads of the New Testament testimony, since this part of the canon lives essentially from the certainty that through Jesus Christ the God of Israel has turned in saving mercy to the Gentiles. In spite of this, a simple acceptance of this christological viewpoint by Christians poses its own problems, theologically speaking, for it means a clear curtailment of certain dimensions of the New Testament message —dimensions that are both essential to the message itself and of fundamental importance for the relationship between Jews and Christians today. The requirement to be faithful to the gospel is certainly a command that has to be obeyed critically and vigilantly, not in unconditional obedience. But it nonetheless requires the particular acceptance of those special aspects of the gospel which made it a revolutionary proclamation in its own time.

Thus, unquestionably at the center of the New Testament message is the assurance that Jesus Christ died "for us" or "for all." This belongs together with his resurrection, which was proclaimed and believed. Both these assurances are attested by the saying in Mark 10:45 that the Son of man was come "to give his life as a ransom for many," by the reminder in 2 Cor. 5:14 that Jesus is the One who "died for all . . . and was raised," and by many other similar statements. As long as these aspects are not constructively included, a theology in Christian-Jewish dialogue is like a ship that avoids the harbor in which its cargo is going to be scrutinized. The question is all the more important because faithfulness to the gospel also means faithfulness to the men and women who in that early period believed in the gospel, and lived with it, as Jews—as a few still do today. It is only if these people are included as brothers and sisters that theology and the church will be prevented from viewing them as an inconvenient burden and treating them accordingly, as has so often been the case in the past. It is only then, too, that theology and the church will be able to profit from these people to whom they owe their own existence, and yet still be able to dispute with them legitimately, where particular questions or observances require it.

The christological point I have stressed must be considered first of all. In Paul's proclamation, Jesus' "for us" or "for all" is interpreted solely in the light of his cross, his resurrection, and his Parousia.[12] It is essentially in Jesus' love that Paul finds the identity of the crucified and raised Lord. As we know, apart from his death, the life of the earthly Jesus does not enter Paul's orbit. If we go beyond this limitation in the light of what we have already said, and on the basis of the Gospels, so that the connection between Jesus of Nazareth and Jesus the Christ is actually emphasized, this immediately determines the trend of the questions we have to put to the traditions about the ministry of the earthly Jesus. These traditions have to be examined for traces of the "for" structure of Jesus' existence, which Paul develops especially with the help of statements about his cross and resurrection. To define our task in this way is not arbitrary, for the Gospels—at least in their final form—interpret the existence of the earthly Jesus as a "being-there for us" or "for all." We can see this, for example, in Mark 10:45, which I have already cited. Moreover, this is not a mere complement to the Pauline view of Jesus. It is also an essential corrective to what Paul says. For if the death of Jesus is not understood as the end of his life in its full, concrete reality, there is a danger, at the very least, that his death will be seen in a merely spiritualized sense.

JESUS OF NAZARETH: THE SEARCH FOR THE LOST

The Uniqueness of the One God

The history of New Testament Christology is determined by the ever-widening significance that is given to Jesus Christ. At the end of this process we find statements like the words of the Jesus of the Gospel of John: "I and the Father are one" (John 10:30), or "I am *the* way, *the* truth and *the* life; no one comes to the Father but by me" (John 14:6). Since this is the general direction of the church's confession of faith in Jesus Christ, it will be hard to confute the general textual principle that the further what Jesus says about himself (or what other people say about him) diverges from this general trend, the more probable it is that this statement belongs to the earliest—and hence authentic—stratum of the Jesus tradition.

In this sense, Jesus' relation to God is described particularly concisely in the introduction to the story of the young man "who had great possessions": "And as he was setting out on his journey, a man ran up and knelt before him, and asked him, 'Good Teacher, what must I do to inherit eternal life?' And Jesus said to him 'Why do you call me good? No one is good but God alone'" (Mark 10:17–18; cf. Luke 18:18–19).[13] The answer, with its echo of the "Hear, O Israel" (Deut. 6:4) (". . . the Lord is one") assumes with radical seriousness that there is only one God. In the form of a rebuke, it emphasizes the difference not only between God and human beings in general but between God and Jesus as well. Matthew already found the question and answer in the version transmitted by Mark to be no longer tenable (cf. Matt. 19:16–17).[14]

The Mission to Sinners and Tax Collectors

Jesus saw himself entrusted with a task that was in line with the pastoral office as it is seen in Ezekiel 34 and that was in full agreement with the criterion we have named his "being there *for* . . ." This task is particularly appropriately defined in the saying with which he defends his fellowship with tax collectors and sinners in the synoptic tradition: "Those who are well have no need of a physician, but those who are sick; I came not to call the righteous, but sinners" (Mark 2:17; Matt. 9:13; Luke 5:31–32). This personal account of the way he interprets his ministry among his people agrees substantially with the saying with which he first of all rejects the plea of the Canaanite woman (Matt. 15:24). It also matches the saying in Matt. 10:6, which also provides the yardstick for the activity of his disciples as they accompanied him on his way through Israel: "I was sent only to the lost sheep of the house [in the house] of Israel." We shall see that a whole series of parables have the same structure. That is to say, they are determined by a distinction between sinners and the righteous—a distinction that was later to prove awkward in the light of the further history of the early Christian proclamation. Even if this distinction becomes somewhat blurred through Jesus' already cited protest that no one can be called good but God, it is certainly not eliminated, for after all, Jesus himself is not presented as a sinner just because he makes this objection.

Openness to Strangers

In the Gospels, Jesus' commitment to groups on the fringes of society—sinners and tax collectors, the sick and the unclean—is understood and interpreted as a prefiguration of the inclusion of the Gentiles in the proclamation of the gospel. It is this, for example, to which Lukan tradition testifies in the parable of the great supper (Luke 14:16–24), but the same applies to a number of other passages. Jesus fundamentally confined his ministry to the land and people of Israel, and the early Christian preachers and teachers, ignoring that, were here certainly interpreting his activity from a post-Easter perspective. But at the same time this interpretation was not without support in what Jesus actually said and did. The exemplary story of the good Samaritan (Luke 10:30–37) is particularly important in this context. The people who listened to the parable undoubtedly expected the third person in the story, who followed the priest and the Levite—as hero, so to speak—to be an Israelite. Instead the narrator makes his chief actor a foreigner. The way the man behaves shows that he is righteous, and yet he does not belong to the Jewish people. On the contrary, he is one of the Samaritans, who in Jesus' time were on extremely hostile terms with their Jewish neighbors;[15] he was an enemy and in this sense a representative of the gentile world.

Teaching in the Mirror of Prayer

Although, then, Jesus basically confined his ministry to Israel, he did not exclude its neighbors even in his own day. Nor did the distinction he made between sinners and the righteous mean that what he said and did had no relevance for the group of the righteous. But this second aspect in particular can only be grasped in the proper sense if his ministry is first of all interpreted strictly in the context of his complete—one might say, bodily—community with sinners and tax collectors, which is to say his commitment to "the lost" in Israel.

The Lord's Prayer may serve as one example among many. In this context its meaning becomes clear, and it offers an exemplary insight into the teaching that accompanied Jesus' actions. In Luke, who offers the shorter version, it is introduced as a prayer that Jesuʒ teaches his disciples (Luke 11:1–4). In Matthew, it is passed down as part of the Sermon on the Mount (Matt. 6:9–13), which means that it was given both to the disciples and to the "multitude" (see Matt. 5:1–2; 7:28–29). But it seems doubtful whether it was originally intended solely for the group of disciples and restricted to them. When Jesus healed, shared meals with people, or told parables, these things too were not restricted to this group of followers, and the Lord's prayer was most probably a prayer meant for the particular groups he especially sought out in his search for the lost, with whom he continually associated, even though he did not confine himself to them exclusively.

Abba. It is important to avoid the misunderstanding that Jesus' purpose was to promise to the groups described as sinners and tax collectors the love of God without conditions or consequences. On the contrary, his ministry aimed at repentance, and that meant leading these groups back into the "total self" of God's people. But what is unique was the way in which he brought them under the end-time rule of God, which he preached and which he believed was imminent. He did not wait until those who were lost turned back, and he did not teach solely at the places that were intended for this purpose. Rather, he went "into the highways and by-ways," eating with people who were unclean, without being afraid of contamination, thus giving physical form to the invitation he proclaimed in his preaching and teaching about the rule of God that was not dawning. It is from this aspect that the Lord's prayer acquires its full meaning. If the original word behind the address Father (Luke 11:2) was really Abba[16]—the familiar name used by a boy to his father—then Jesus' prayer is an encouragement to the men and women who were lost, This is how you too, you especially, are permitted to pray, full of trust and confidence: Abba. On the other hand, it would certainly be mistaken to play off this form of address against the understanding of God held by other teachers in Jesus' time, or against "Judaism" in general. But since this is still common practice,[17] some reasons why it is inadmissible may be given.

Even if Jewish tradition provides no evidence for "abba" as a word used in *addressing* God, God was talked *about* as Abba (see *b. Taanit* 23b).[18] Moreover, it is undisputed that ever since biblical times there have been countless examples in Jewish tradition of prayers addressed to God as Father or as our Father (*avinu*). Now, there is every reason for inferring that the address Abba is the reflection of a warmly loving relationship to God. But it would be arbitrary to conclude from the *absence* of this address that the relationship to God was cold or stiff or fearful—just as arbitrary as it would be to assume that a boy who called his father Father instead of Dad had a less intimate relationship to him. In actual fact, conclusions of this kind are due to a reluctance to listen with proper attention to Jewish tradition, and this reluctance is based on theological prejudice.

We may take only one example. It would surely be impossible to talk more warmly, even tenderly, about God's relationship to Israel than does the rabbinic parable that describes the way God accompanied the children of Israel at the exodus, in the form of a pillar of cloud and a pillar of fire (Deut. 1:31, 33):

> Like a man who went along the road and let his son walk in front of him. Then robbers came along and wanted to take the son captive. So the father took his son and placed him behind him. Then a wolf came from behind. So he took the child from behind him and put him in front. Then robbers came from the front and wolves from behind. So the father picked his son up and carried him in his arms. The son began to suffer from the sun; so the father spread his garment over him. He was hungry, and his father gave him food. He was thirsty, and his father gave him something to drink.[19]

Abba probably really was Jesus' own special way of addressing God, and it is certainly an address suggesting a relationship of mutual love. But the parable I have just quoted shows that this does not differentiate Jesus from his people. More, the Jewish tradition may help us to understand why Jesus invited people in the main field of his ministry to use this particular form of address. For example, a tradition from the Babylonian Talmud says (*b. Berakhot* 34b), "In the place where the repentant stand, the righteous cannot stand." This conviction corresponds substantially to Jesus' certainty that there is more joy in heaven over one sinner who repents than over the ninety-nine righteous persons who need no repentance (Luke 15:7). This is, first, another example of the distinction Jesus makes between sinners and the righteous. But it also shows why, when he goes out to meet sinners in order to bring them to repentance, he talks to God as Abba and encourages his listeners to do the same; for this form of address reflects God's special love for and commitment to the lost.

The Sanctification of the Name and the Kingdom of God. How little reason there is for refusing to interpret the Lord's Prayer in the context of the Jewish devotional tradition is proved especially by its first two petitions. "*Magnified and sanctified be his great Name* in the world which he has cre-

ated according to his will. *May he establish his kingdom* during your life
and during your days and during the life of all the house of Israel, even
speedily and at a near time, and say ye, Amen!"[20] This is the oldest part
of one of the chief Jewish prayers, the Kaddish. And even scholars whose
interpretations are anti-Jewish in tendency do not deny that Jesus was
probably following the Kaddish in the first two petitions of the Lord's
Prayer.[21] Again differences are obvious, but these do not detract from the
bond of similarity. Jesus invites people on the fringes of society to join in
the prayer of all Israel, with its supreme petition for the sanctification of
the divine name—that is, God himself—and for the coming of his sov-
ereign rule. The most important aspects of what these petitions mean can
hardly be more aptly brought out than by the words of yet another ancient
Jewish prayer, the Alenu:

> . . . He is our God; there is none else: in truth he is our King; there is none
> besides him; as it is written in his Torah, And thou shalt know this day, and
> lay it to thine heart, that the Lord he is God in heaven above and upon the
> earth beneath: there is none else.
>
> We therefore hope in thee, O Lord our God, that we may speedily behold
> the glory of thy might, when thou wilt remove the abominations from the
> earth, and heathendom will be utterly destroyed, when the world will be per-
> fected under the kingdom of the Almighty, and all the children of flesh will
> call upon thy Name, when thou wilt turn unto thyself all the evil-doers upon
> the earth. Let all the inhabitants of the world perceive and know that unto
> thee every knee must bow, every tongue must swear allegiance. Before thee,
> O Lord our God, let them bow and worship; and unto thy glorious Name let
> them give honour; let them all accept the yoke of thy kingdom, and do thou
> reign over them speedily, and for ever and ever. For the kingdom is thine,
> and to all eternity thou wilt reign in glory; as it is written in thy Torah, The
> Lord shall reign for ever and ever. And it is said, And the Lord shall be king
> over all the earth: in that day shall the Lord be One, and his Name One.[22]

The prayers for the sanctification of the divine name and for the coming
of the kingdom of God are eschatologically aligned in the Lord's Prayer,
as they are in the Kaddish and the Alenu.[23] This common ground teaches
us again to understand Jesus' teaching and ministry as Jewish and not as
anti-Jewish. It is only within this common framework that the specific
contours of his proclamation and ministry emerge. In the certainty that the
end-time rule of God was at hand, he cut himself off from his family—
apparently in disharmony—and set out first of all to spend a short time in
the group surrounding John the Baptist, and then through his words and
acts to manifest signs of the kingdom's near approach. These signs let the
imminence of the kingdom be felt, and guided other people in their faith,
hope and love along the way that corresponded to it. The two parables of
the treasure hidden in the field and the pearl of great price (Matt. 13:44–
46) bring out in tersest form the importance that the imminence of the
eschatological rule of God has for the beginning of Jesus' ministry and for
the dynamic force of what he did and taught. It is joy over the kingdom's

almost palpable presence that determines what now has to be done. In accordance with biblical tradition, the search for the lost is the result of the kingdom's imminence, for what is expected to happen with the coming of God at the eschaton is the reform of conditions and the restitution of the whole of Israel—and this is proclaimed and to some extent already proleptically realized in the commitment to the lost: "The blind receive their sight and the lame walk, lepers are cleansed and the deaf hear, and the dead are raised up, and the poor have good news preached to them" (Matt. 11:5; Luke 7:22; cf. Isa. 35:5–6).

It is true that when the Christian church thinks of the coming of God it thinks simultaneously of the coming of Jesus Christ, and it is in line with this expectation that the hymn in Phil. 2:6–11 applies the Isaiah quotation (Isa. 45:23) to the enthronement of Jesus at God's side. But on the one hand, even Paul (who passed the hymn down to us) understands the oneness of God as the goal and end of all his ways (1 Cor. 15:28), and on the other, the prayer for the coming of the kingdom, on Jesus' lips especially, seems unambiguous. The subject of the prayer is not his own kingdom but God's, as it is in the Kaddish tradition on which Jesus probably drew. The two prayers have another point in common, which can easily be overlooked but which is equally significant. Jesus prays first of all for the sanctification of the divine name without uttering that name itself, and the whole of the New Testament follows him. So Jesus himself, like his earliest witnesses, conforms to the age-old Jewish custom of leaving inviolate the name of God, the tetragrammaton YHWH. It is sanctified through its nonutterance, metaphorical paraphrases being used for God in teaching, preaching, and prayer. This practice, more than almost anything else, shows how deeply rooted Jesus was in the religious life of his people.

However, *one* difference leaps to the eye when we compare the Lord's Prayer with the Kaddish. The Kaddish names the house of Israel, identifying Israel as the author of the prayer. But there is no corresponding phrase in the prayer of Jesus. We cannot conclude from this that the Lord's Prayer is not concerned about the coming of God for the peace of Israel. But the lack of a specific application to God's people no doubt contributed in no small measure to making the Lord's Prayer what it has become: Jesus' prayer not only for the tax collectors and sinners in Israel but for the *goyim* too—the Gentiles, the unclean outside Israel. But the moment the prayer is prayed by people belonging to the gentile world, a further difference emerges—a difference from the Jewish prayer and a difference also from the Jewish hope for the coming of God's rule. For then a piece of the Alenu's petition and expectation begins to be fulfilled—that "all the children of flesh will call upon thy Name"—though this does not mean that the prayer and the hope have now become groundless.

The Forgiveness of Sins. The point from which we started in our present reflections was the question about the fundamental "for us" or "for all" structure of Jesus of Nazareth's words and ministry. We have seen that his commitment to sinners and tax collectors was its special characteristic. He lived for them and with them by opening up access to God and to fellowship with him—either again or for the very first time. He achieved this by what he did and what he said, in his own way and on his own responsibility. His acts are two things at once: they are on God's behalf (since he was calling God's lost children to him), but they are at the same time and by the same token for the benefit of the "outsiders" themselves. If we stop thinking of the Lord's Prayer merely as a prayer meant for other people (either the disciples or the tax collectors and sinners) and if we see it as being Jesus' own prayer as well, then the "we" petitions of the second half make a new impact, and especially in connection with the prayer for the forgiveness of sins.

According to Matt. 11:19, Jesus' contemporaries rebuked him for being "a glutton and a drunkard, a friend of tax collectors and sinners." This reproach is another reminder of his main sphere of activity. But it also brings out a new dimension of his ministry. His fellowship with that particular group of people was participation in the real conditions in which they lived. When he assured them of God's love, this was a risky intervention in their behalf in God's name, and in tendency it meant sharing their guilt. For their guilt was only taken from them *through* his fellowship with them. Because he participated in their guilt by practicing forgiveness, like the unjust steward in Luke 16:1–8,[24] the petition even in his mouth takes on full harmony: "And forgive *us our* debts. . . ."—sinners their own guilt, he himself the guilt he has assumed for other people, the guilt he has helped to carry in the life he has shared with them, the guilt he has forgiven. Matthew's Gospel later brought out this dimension of Jesus' ministry when it related Jesus' exorcisms and his healing acts to the prophetic saying about the Servant of God: "He took upon himself our weaknesses and carried our sicknesses" (Isa. 53:4 LXX; Matt. 8:16–17).

The center of Jesus' ministry was his search for the lost in Israel, so that he might lead them back into the "total self" of the nation, as *God's* people. The parables of the lost sheep, the lost coin, and the prodigal son in Luke 15 provide perhaps the most cogent evidence. Heinz David Leuner and Franz Schnider have independently proved that it is this restoration of the whole that is the hidden center of all these parables.[25] This is what the shepherd and the woman are searching for, and it can be precisely shown how both of them illustrate in parable form Jesus' own activity, which in its turn represents the will of God. In the same way, the return of the prodigal son and his reacceptance by the father ends in the restitution of the family. In their parable form all three stories are intended to impel the lost joyfully along the path of conversion to God, the Father who hastens to meet them. The parable of the laborers in the vineyard has a very similar structure, with its disturbing, scandalous ending, in which the last to be employed are put on the same level as those who "have borne the burden and heat of the day" (Matt 20:1–16, AV).

Conflicts with the Righteous

The implication of the reproach that Jesus was "a glutton and a drunkard, the friend of tax collectors and sinners" is sometimes expressed in the parables themselves, sometimes even more strongly in their introductions: Jesus' unconventional search for the lost in Israel is a reason for protest and gives rise to conflicts. It implies questions to other "shepherds" of the people; more, criticism of them. And it therefore touches the group of the "righteous" and challenges them to opposition.

For Israel's Sake: The Restoration of the Whole. An example of what I have just said is the second part of the parable of the prodigal son, which tells of the elder brother's reaction and his encounter with his father. When the son who had remained at home reminds his father that he had never disobeyed any of his commands, this characterizes him as a righteous man. In the same way, when the son reproaches his father with never having shown him similar tokens of love, the father's answer "Son, you *are* always with me and all that *is* mine *is* yours" contradicts the interpretation that Jesus means to show the elder brother as the one who is really lost.[26] Rather, the elder brother is surrounded by the father's loving care. But this loving care applies to both sons, and the father's joy is only complete when they are not merely sons but also brothers. So he points out to the elder of the two what the proper behavior would really be: "You should rejoice. . . ." So in his search for the lost, the only thing that Jesus requires from the people to whom he is not sent is participation in God's joy over the restoration of the whole, a restoration not just sometime or other but now, in the form of his ministry, which witnesses to the imminence of the eschatological rule of God.[27] Implicit in this demand of Jesus' is virtually the reproach that the righteous should already have done what he has now begun to do. It implies the claim that in what he does he is acting as their substitute or representative. And in some groups of the righteous, such as the Pharisees (the most important group at that time), Jesus' demand may have met with both assent and disagreement all the more because in a sense Jesus took over the Pharisaic heritage.

As their name suggests, the special characteristic of the Pharisees was their separateness. But this was not an end in itself. It was a struggle to make the whole of Israel, not merely a part of it, conform to the will of God. It is an acceptance of God's decree "You [i.e., all of you, not just those officiating in the temple] shall be holy; for I the Lord your God am holy" (Lev. 19:2). This was the reason that this lay group took over the Levitical laws about what was clean and unclean, and this was why they developed an oral Torah of equal status with the written one. Their aim was to make obedience to the word of Sinai possible in changing times.[28]

There was certainly an inherent antagonism between the goal and the content of the movement which was difficult to master. The aim was to reach as many sections of the population as possible—ideally the whole nation—and to lead people to a life in accordance with the will of God, the purpose of which was holiness and sanctification. The supporters of this movement therefore had to give a particular form to their lives and the lives of the people they won. They had to cut themselves off from everything that was not holy, everything that was unclean according to the norm provided by God's commandments. The borderline between holy and profane, and between clean and unclean, was extended and at the same time accentuated, so that it became a frontier between the righteous and sinners.

The fact that there were *also* hypocrites among the Pharisees is hardly worth mentioning, for there are always hypocrites in any group, whether it is religious or nonreligious. Nor is it a problem that the Pharisaic edicts should have included a number of regulations that seemed to outsiders absurd. Here again there are parallels enough in all other societies. And the church has least of all reason to stumble over this or that atypical accompanying phenomenon, for the church has its roots, essentially, in the Jewish people, who took their stamp from Pharisaism. And one of its founders was Paul, a former Pharisee, whose existence as apostle was very largely molded by his Pharisaic past. The really essential point about the conflict between Jesus and the Pharisees seems to have been simply the antagonism I have already described. In that light, Jesus' search for the lost seemed, understandably enough, commitment to people who were theoretically, perhaps, included in the Pharisaic movement (since the Pharisees were certainly aware of the way to repentance) but who were no longer reached in practical terms.

Here too, however, this antagonism is no reason for proclaiming the end of Pharisaism under appeal to Jesus, or even, later, to Paul. In modified form, the Christian church undoubtedly still shared the same structure a considerable time later. The church extended the concept of the—holy—people of God to the Gentiles but was itself able·to live out this extension only in the form of separation from the world. Paul's letters are evidence of this, and the First Epistle of Peter is another particularly vivid and explicit witness. The writer exhorts the Christian congregation to whom he is writing to show themselves holy in their way of living, in conformity with the Holy One who has called them. As scriptural evidence, he adds the instruction in Lev. 19:2, which he has indirectly absorbed into his admonition. In this way he gives Christians in Asia Minor the same motto that determined the Pharisaic movement (1 Pet. 1:15–16).

This is the background against which we have to see Jesus' commitment to sinners and tax collectors preeminently: it was an act that in no way "abrogated" Israel but that was designed to restore it to its full totality. For in this unconventional, "shocking" way, by seeking the society of the lost, Jesus drew them into the loving sovereignty of God, which was to be finally manifested in the imminent future. In this sense Jesus' ministry is in conformity with Paul's fundamental conviction that "all Israel will be saved" (Rom. 11:26).[29] But inasmuch as Jesus, in what he did, fulfilled the task given to Israel to subject itself to the rule of God as *entire* nation, his loving commitment to the poor was vicarious activity for God's people.

For the Sake of Israel and the Gentiles: Doubts About the Clean and the Unclean. As we saw from the parable of the good Samaritan, Jesus' commitment widened out—here in story form—to include strangers and foreigners, so that his ministry provides starting points for the later interpretation that saw the turning to the Gentiles as a further development of his commitment to the unclean in Israel. In this sense, Jesus' intervention on Israel's behalf for the benefit of tax collectors and sinners was in tendency an intervention in behalf of the Gentiles. This aspect of the "for us" or "for all" structure of his ministry can also be understood theologically in the framework of Jesus' representative activity on Israel's behalf—as the fulfillment of the promise and charge given to Israel in the Hebrew Bible with the assurance that God made her a "light to the nations" (Isa. 49:6).

But what Jesus has to say about the distinction between clean and unclean illustrates his indirect trend in the direction of the Gentiles even more clearly than the story of the good Samaritan. The Gospel of Mark already brings out the connection between the two things by following up the debate and instruction about cleanness and uncleanness (Mark 7:1–23) with the story about Jesus' conversation with the Syro-Phoenician woman. The woman was a Gentile and therefore unclean, but at the end of the conversation Jesus heals her possessed daughter even though the child was not present (Mark 7:24–30). The central statement in the whole complex of Mark 7:1–23 is quite evidently Jesus' saying in v. 15, "There is nothing outside a man which by going into him can defile him; but the things which come out of a man are what defile him." Correspondingly, scholars have found in this saying the authentic core of Mark 7:1–23, which as a whole goes back to the post-Easter church or to the evangelist Mark. If one remembers how difficult Jesus himself finds it to listen to the plea of the gentile woman in the story that follows (Mark 7:24–30)—indeed how bluntly he initially draws the line between Israel and the Gentiles ("children" and "dogs")—one may certainly doubt with some reason whether a saying so far-reaching in its implications can go back to him; and Peter's hesitation (reported in Acts 10) about giving up the traditional distinction between clean and unclean would also suggest considerable forgetfulness, at least, of the Master's teaching.

On the other hand, there are certainly good reasons for accepting the saying as genuine. For one thing, it is in line with one broad strand of the Jesus tradition when it calls "what is within"—i.e., a person's heart—the fundamental anthropological entity in relation to God. Moreover, the attitude that prompts this saying could explain the ease with which Jesus overcame the barriers that cut him off from the cultically unclean. And not least, it helps to explain why he came into conflict with some of his contemporaries.[30]

At the same time, to view the saying as authentic tradition means that all the more caution is called for in its interpretation. There is no occasion for wholesale judgments, such as the assertion that what Jesus says about clean and unclean (like his alleged attitude to the Sabbath and the temple) means that he "actually *replaces* Judaism, from its very roots, by something new."[31] A whole number of reasons speak against any such generalization.

The first evidence for this is the immediate context in which the saying is transmitted in the Gospel of Mark, for here Jesus replies to the questioner's objection with a word of Scripture—that is, he answers out of the Jewish tradition itself—attacking the "tradition of the elders" (Mark 7:1ff.). A second point is that rabbinic tradition is also familiar with a related view of purity and impurity. A saying of Rabban Johanan ben Zakkai to his pupils has been passed down according to which the dead body (which counted as incontestably unclean) does not pollute and water does not purify, but that all the same the particular edict about what is clean and what is unclean was to be obeyed because it was a divine ordinance.[32] It may rightly be pointed out that in his saying in Mark 7:15, it is precisely the binding nature of the halakhah which Jesus is disputing—that is to say, the edicts which Mark 7 calls the tradition of the elders, and which according to the Jewish view are, like Scripture itself, (oral) Torah from Sinai and therefore have the rank of divine commandments. But even if the saying is to be interpreted in this sense, it must still be seen as a judgment made *on the foundations* of Judaism itself, not a judgment from outside. For a parallel we may turn to the Mishnah tractate *Berakhot* (9.5) and the exposition of Ps. 119:126[33] by Rabbi Nathan, which is passed down there. It is an explanation that deviates significantly from the text: "They broke thy [God's] law *because* it was time for the Lord to act." That is to say, "In times of emergency it may be right to set aside or amend the commandments of God enjoined in his law [*torah*]: the law [*torah*] may best be served by breaking it."[34] It would be hard to find any statement through which Jesus' ministry could be more authentically interpreted—as a ministry in conflict—as a critical and eminently Jewish struggle, on the foundation of the Torah and not outside it, in the midst of Jesus' own Jewish nation and not beyond it, for the sake of that nation's life in its relation to God and not with the goal of its abolition. It is only under this premise that what is inherent in the saying in Mark 7:15 applies to the Gentiles too.

*Excursus: The So-Called Abolition
of Judaism by Jesus*

Throughout the ages, Jesus' saying in Mark 7:15 has counted as one of *the* chief witnesses for the Christian view that Jesus "broke with," "abolished," etc.,[35] nothing less than *all* Judaism's traditional ways of thinking about religion. It would therefore seem appropriate not to leave the question merely to the particular interests of Christian theologians but rather to look at it in the mirror of Jewish testimony. Thanks to Claude G. Montefiore's great commentary on the Synoptic Gospels, this is directly possible under the best possible hermeneutical presuppositions, and we can avoid the cumbersome procedure of comparison and deduction.[36] Montefiore's detailed exposition of Mark 7:15 combines deep respect for what Jesus says and a sense of its explosive power, with a clear differentiation between the place of the saying in its own era and its meaning for modern times, in a context molded by orthopraxy and "liberalism." Montefiore interprets the saying very widely. He does not see it merely in the context of the conflict with the (purity) halakhah[37] but views it in the light of the written Torah. The high esteem for Jesus' saying which he nonetheless evidences belongs within the framework of his own *Jewish* existence. And this shows all the more cogently how inappropriate it is to base talk about the "abolition" of Judaism on sayings such as Mark 7:15.[38]

The special strength of Montefiore's interpretation is that, unlike customary Christian exegesis, he knows how to weigh up both sides—Jesus' saying and the no of most of his contemporaries. He affirms the weight that Jesus puts on the impure human heart as the source of all pollution and also agrees with the implicit rejection of the idea that a person can be defiled by things. But he also includes the fact that Christians often forget: that the observance of injunctions about outward purity and the simultaneous orientation of life towards purity of heart and life are by no means mutually exclusive,[39] even though in practice alternatives can arise that distort this fact. Not least, Montefiore makes the no of Jesus' opponents understandable, since this no was determined by the conviction that ethical injunctions *and* injunctions about what is clean and what is unclean are alike commandments rooted in the Bible and are therefore equally binding.

The only problem would seem to be the solution Montefiore offers for what he thinks to be Jesus' inconsistency: the tension between his yes to the whole Torah as a binding divine instruction, on the one hand, and his implicit no to the laws about cleanness and uncleanness, on the other. Montefiore thinks that at the moment when Jesus formulated his saying, he was probably not fully aware of its actual far-reaching implications. One important point in this connection is Montefiore's own contention, first of all, that it is entirely possible for a "modern"— that is, liberal—Jew to keep the dietary laws and to give good reasons for doing so, and yet to recognize the truth of Jesus' saying. This position certainly shows how questionable it is, in the light of modern liberal Judaism, to make Mark 7:15 the basis for talk about the abolition of Judaism as such. But the aim cannot of course be tacitly to impute to Jesus a view similar to that held by liberal Judaism. The example Montefiore provides, however, makes it entirely plausible that what was possible for Montefiore in his time was in principle just as possible for Jesus in *his*—even though the justification was different. Again, here too Jesus' conviction about the immediate imminence of the eschatological rule of God was probably the reason for his doubt about the importance of the commandments about purity[40] and for his stress on the pure heart as the decisive human factor in the relationship to God. Whenever people really believe, body and soul, that the end-time sovereignty of God is immediately impending—and when they are not merely clinging to a traditional doctrine about its imminence—they have at other times too left house and home, broken through conventions, and stressed values other than the traditional ones. And they have done this not in order to abolish their own world but in order to encounter it as the impending *kairos* demands, according to their view.[41]

It is therefore quite logical that, when time extends and the imminent divine kingdom that has been proclaimed and believed is still a far-off event, the traditional ordinances take on new importance, even though it may be in another form. The church, both past and present, offers examples enough, with its consecrated rooms and sacred vessels, or the form given to the Lord's Supper, even down to the handling of the bread and wine or wafers. But the apostle Paul provides an even earlier example, though in another sector: Jesus' prohibition of divorce (Mark 10:1–9), which is an accentuation of the Mosaic Torah, is—horribile dictu—casuistically relativized by him (1 Cor. 7:10–11), although he knows that it was a saying of the Lord's and reminds his readers of the fact.

But to return more directly to my attempt to lay the exegetical ghost of Jesus' abolition of Judaism or the Torah, which is all too readily proclaimed on the evidence of sayings such as Mark 7:15: it is surely hardly possible to doubt the tradition passed down by the evangelists according to which Jesus evidently celebrated the Passover before his death, quite as a matter of course, just as he previously visited the synagogue in accordance with the precepts of the Mosaic Torah. There is no sign here that he so much as dreamed of destroying all Jewish religious categories. The early church gratefully took sayings like Mark 7:15 to be a pointer to the inclusion of the Gentiles. And this attitude is probably not merely more salutary but also truer to the spirit in which Jesus spoke.

If we look at the Gospels as a whole, and if we except Mark in his seventh chapter, Jesus' attitude to the Torah has probably been transmitted most accurately by Matthew in the Sermon on the Mount (Matthew 5—7). The antitheses in chapter 5 have a very similar structure to the statements in Mark 7:1–23: in both passages Jesus' words, which are directed toward the human heart, are set against the "tradition of the elders," but what Jesus says is declared to be the *fulfillment* of Torah and prophets, *not* their abolition (Matt. 5:17). Finally, a further point is surely important if we are to understand Jesus' actions as being actions on the foundation of Judaism. The critical treatment of commandments, down to the actual abrogation even of a biblical precept of the Torah, for the sake of obedience, was a practical reality in rabbinic Judaism. It was not merely a doctrinal tenet, as it is in *Berakhot* 9.5. Rabbi Eliezer's abrogation of the divine judgment in Num. 5:11–31 is one example among many (*Sotah* 9.9).[42]

Death at the Hands of a Roman

According to a well-known tradition of the Babylonian Talmud (b. *Bava Metzia* 59b), about the turn of the first century Rabbi Eliezer ben Hyrcanos was banished and excluded from the school in Jabneh because of his deviating halakhic decisions, in spite of signs and wonders that he was able to adduce as proof of his authority. The ministry of Jesus was undoubtedly accompanied by conflicts in a similar way. In many passages in the Gospels these disputes are described in highly colored terms because of later conflicts between the early congregations and their coldly disapproving Jewish brothers. In spite of this, they may certainly have been more acrimonious, here and there, than the previous account has suggested. Even then, however, they would still fall far short of the polemic that has come down to us from some of the biblical prophets.[43] Another point of discontinuity seems much more important than this question, because it is of fundamental importance. None of the disputes that took place between Jesus and his contemporaries before he went up to Jerusalem have any bearing on his end. Their link with the crucifixion, which is found in Mark first of all and was stressed more and more in the succeeding Gospels, is a construction of the evangelists. The behavior of the Pharisees is the clearest evidence for this. In the accounts of the first three Gospels, we do not meet with a single representative of this group as actor in the events surrounding the Passion. According to statements in the Gospel of John—which was about thirty years later than the Gospel of Mark—the Pharisees were the main force behind these events; but this is not borne out by conditions as they really were.[44]

It was Jesus himself who took the decisive step towards the end in Jerusalem, according to the Synoptic Gospels. His entry into the city was apparently surrounded by all the glamour of a messianic claimant. This, together with his provocative actions in the forecourt of the temple, was reason enough for the two different authorities to intervene, although these interventions then in fact partially coincided. The one authority was the supreme council, the Sanhedrin (or at least, more probably, its Sadducean groups, which were concerned with temple matters); the other was the Roman prefect Pontius Pilate.[45] The Sanhedrin, probably assisted from the beginning by the Roman occupying power in Jerusalem, had him arrested and after cross-examining him (which was the most the Sanhedrin could do), passed him on to the Roman governor. The Roman condemned him and had him crucified. The statement in the "Old Roman" version of the Apostles' Creed "crucified under Pontius Pilate" is a precise statement of the facts, but the baseless accusation that "the Jews" killed him is apparently ineradicable, even though this accusation is simply dictated by what one can only term hate of our neighbor. We cannot even say that "the Jews" had him arrested and delivered him over to Pilate. Here, if anywhere, exactitude is required of us. If we follow that requirement, we can at most say that the Sanhedrin played a part in his arrest and surrender to the Romans—and probably only parts of the Sanhedrin at that. To talk here about "the Jews" is just as logical as it would be to say that "the Romans" or "all the Romans" or even—since the accusation against the Jews is maintained by certain groups even today—that "the Italians" killed him. And all this is quite irrespective of the fact that, according to what the Gospel of Luke tells us, the dying Jesus already forgave those who *really were* involved (Luke 23:34). Tested against that criterion alone, the church's hostility to the Jews is an age-long, continued act of disobedience to the Lord of the church, even though it justifies its enmity by an appeal to Jesus' Passion. The same may be said about statements by so-called Christians today who interpret the crime committed against the Jewish people as a punishment for Jesus' crucifixion: from this aspect alone, these accusations must be defined objectively as theological lies, quite apart from the appalling nature of the picture of the God that these Christians adore—these people themselves are often the victims of unteachable teachers.

Even if there is no causal relation between disputes in which Jesus was involved during his ministry up to his entry into Jerusalem, and his death, this does not mean that there was no connection between these two stages of his activity. On the contrary, it is precisely the background of his ministry that I have described—his fellowship with sinners and tax collectors —which is also the background against which his dying and his death are theologically to be understood and interpreted. According to the evidence of the Synoptic Gospels, Jesus no longer performed healings in Jerusalem; his ministry was now a ministry of teaching only. The community in which he lived was the community of the disciples, the germ of the wider circle of "sinners and tax collectors" and its enduring form. The Gospels depict Jesus' relationship to the group of disciples in the days of the Passion as one in which Jesus was increasingly forsaken, although he himself had lived chiefly in order to take the part of other people. The opening chord is struck by the faithlessness of the Iscariot (Mark 14:10). This is followed by the prayer in the loneliness of Gethsemane, which is thrown into sharp contrast by the sleeping disciples (Mark 14:32–42). Finally comes the denial of Jesus by the only person who still followed him, Peter (Mark 14:53–72). In the rapid sequence of cross-examination by the Sanhedrin, condemnation by Pilate, and crucifixion, Jesus is alone. It is only when he has been left in the lurch by everyone else and is at the mercy of the jibes of the mocking bystanders (Mark 15:30–32)—only in the isolation of complete solitariness—that he utters the cry that is the last thing he said, an utterance at once despairing and full of trust: "My God, my God, why hast thou forsaken me?" (Mark 15:34 = Ps. 22:2).[46] The balanced antithesis of the two periods of his life can hardly be overlooked: through his fellowship with sinners and tax collectors, Jesus brings God close to these people; in the solitariness that closes round the end of a life that bears all the marks of failure, comes his cry ". . . why hast thou forsaken me?"[47] The end—or more than the end?

Christian belief answers this question with its confession of faith in Jesus' resurrection and with the development of what this confession of faith means. This pegs out in advance the path that our future reflections have to follow. "And Jesus yielded up his spirit": this is the last sentence in the book about Jesus written by the Jewish scholar David Flusser,[48] and it shows with sufficient clarity that this is the parting of the ways for the Jewish and Christian understandings of the man from Nazareth. This, then, may be the appropriate place to consider once again the essential question, Does Jesus have a meaning for Israel, a meaning that goes beyond the view that he was one of Israel's sons but that it was only his relationship to the Gentiles that was significant?

A Good Thing from Nazareth

What has already been said permits a differentiated answer to the question of which I have just reminded readers. For sinners and tax collectors, for the unclean in Israel and—in tendency—for the Gentiles, Jesus is the mediator who brings them into fellowship with God, or under his sovereignty. This is evident from his ministry. For Jews, who already follow the way of God through their life with the Torah, Jesus does not have this function. But if Jews are able to recognize in Jesus the one who brings sinners and tax collectors and the goyim into the kingdom of God, or under God's rule, then they are really seeing him in the very way he is seen by "sinners and tax collectors" and by Gentiles. Jews are then rejoicing in the repentance of the lost, though without entering the discipleship of the one who calls them. They are recognizing him as the one who, at least in part, is vicariously taking on himself Israel's task to be a light to those who sit "in the shadows and darkness of death" (Isa. 9:2; Matt. 4:16).

An interpretation of this kind leaves the identity of Israel and the identity of the Christian church unviolated and yet understands them both in their indissoluble mutual relation to each other, which Jesus mediated. In this way, therefore, the traditional "anti" structure of the relation between Christians and Jews is transformed into a "co" structure, where the understanding of Jesus is concerned; and yet this interpretation avoids the danger that the two will proceed parallel to one another but without meeting. As I hope to show, this by no means puts an end to Israel's task to be herself "a light to the Gentiles."[49] But it may perhaps be cautiously suggested that such an interpretation provides the necessary presupposition if Jews are to find more in Jesus than is suggested by Nathanael's skeptical question "Can anything good come out of Nazareth?" (John 1:46).

JESUS CHRIST: THE FIRST FRUITS OF THOSE WHO HAVE FALLEN ASLEEP

Of all the titles that have been applied to Jesus of Nazareth since his death, and of all the postulates that have been made about him, the most important of all is, perhaps, that he is *aparchē tōn kekoimēmenōn*, "the first fruits of those who have fallen asleep" (1 Cor. 15:20). This statement picks up the assurance that was fundamental for the whole history of the early church: that Jesus has been raised from the dead and was alive. The declaration also indicates a second dimension of this assurance: that the raising of Jesus Christ is part of a whole, that it is directed to "all" (1 Cor. 15:22)—Israel, the Gentiles, and nonhuman creation.

The Identity of the One Who Is Alive

Because the raising of Jesus only arrives at its goal with the whole, and stands in the service of that whole, it is the beginning of redemption, but is not redemption itself in all its fullness and completeness. The raised Jesus, therefore, inasmuch as he is seen in a complex of events that is oriented toward time, is himself interpreted temporally, or historically. With this historical understanding, Paul maintains that this Jesus is none other than the Jesus who was crucified, the man from Nazareth whose humanly verifiable life ended on the cross, and Paul is followed in prin-

ciple by the whole of the New Testament in what it says about the raised
Jesus. For Paul, this identity is of such fundamental importance that he can
assert to the Corinthians: "I have claimed to know nothing among you
except Jesus Christ and him crucified" (1 Cor. 2:2). And the evangelist
Mark—to take one example—very like Paul, considers that he can testify
to the raised Jesus only by narrating earthly events. Mark breaks off his
Gospel at the very moment when the reader or listener expects the disciples to encounter the raised Jesus. So the evangelist compels us to begin
the Gospel again from the start if we want to learn who the risen One is.[50]
All this shows that, in the framework of our present reflections too, the
following attempt to interpret the proclamation of Jesus' resurrection has
to have one particular structure: it has to cast back, with the strictest reference, to what we are told about the life and death of Jesus of Nazareth.

The Return to the Lost

Jesus' ministry—what we see of it from his life in the land of Israel—
appears largely in the form of his community with tax collectors and sinners. It ends in a loneliness that, on the evidence of the Passion narrative
(Mark 15:27–37), finds its authentic description in Psalm 22:[51]

> All who see me mock at me,
>   they make mouths at me, they wag their heads;
> "He committed his cause to the Lord;
>   let him deliver him,
> let him rescue him,
>   for he delights in him!"
>
> (Ps. 22:7–8)

The enmity and the torment endured lead to the physical end:

> I am poured out like water,
>   and all my bones are out of joint;
> my heart is like wax,
>   it is melted within my breast;
> my throat is dried up like a potsherd,
>   and my tongue cleaves to the roof of my mouth;
>   thou dost lay me in the dust of death.
> (Ps. 22:14–15)

The experience of suffering and death in forsakenness by all others is the
reason for the complaint "My God, my God, why hast thou forsaken me?"
(Ps. 22:1), with its implicit petition "But thou, O Lord, be not far off!
O thou my help, hasten to my aid!" (Ps. 22:19).

The church's acknowledgment of Jesus' resurrection testifies in the context of this psalm that it is not the complaint over forsakenness by God
that is the final word; it is the prayer for God's nearness. So resurrection
means the transformation of forsakenness into a fellowship that can never
be forfeited with the God who is called upon. In this sense it means the
overcoming of the death whose closeness evokes the cry. But just as the
complaint at being forsaken by God breaks out when the sufferer is for-

saken by human beings, so life at the side of God, participation in his life, includes new community with human beings and surmounts the situation of forsakenness. Jesus' fellowship with the people to whom he had devoted himself begins anew. According to the witness of his resurrection he is the "first-born among many brethren" (Rom. 8:29), the Son, but not alone—only together with the other sons and daughters, brothers and sisters. He is at home, newly at home, surrounded by those who were in fellowship with him and who are now newly constituted as the fellowship of the church.

The presence of Jesus in the group of sinners and tax collectors, represented by the disciples and his followers from the *am haaretz*, the common people, is thus the center of the message of the resurrection of the One forsaken on the cross. Because Jesus shows himself as alive to the disciples he left behind, and because they experience his closeness, in this group of people what the psalm sums up becomes reality:

> I will tell of thy name to my brethren [the name of
>   the One who raises from the dead];
>   in the midst of the congregation I will praise thee:
> You who fear the Lord, praise Him!
>   all you sons of Jacob, glorify him,
>   and stand in awe of him, all you sons of Israel!
> For he has not despised,
>   has not abhorred the affliction of the poor;
> he has not hid his face from him,
>   but has heard, when he cried to him.
> I praise thy faithfulness in the great congregation. . . .
> The poor shall eat and be satisfied;
>   those who seek him shall praise the Lord!
> Your hearts shall live again for ever!
>   (Ps. 22:22–26)

The fellowship of disciples that has been newly formed out of the experience of Jesus' nearness responds to his deliverance from death in two different ways especially. It proclaims the resurrection; and it awaits his coming presence in praise and thanksgiving, in the renewed breaking of bread together.[52]

The Setting Forth to the Gentile Nations

It was only for a certain time that the presence of Jesus was limited to that small circle, for from there his search for the lost continued. Impelled by the experience of his living presence, the church began to interpret his death as a death on their behalf—"for us," indeed "for all," not merely in Israel but among the Gentiles too. Accompanied by conflicts and internal struggles, the first steps were taken in the direction of the gentile world. The door to that world was opened slowly, hesitantly, in a conflict of viewpoints, some people appealing to Jesus' confinement of his mission to Israel, others pleading his trend to the goyim, the Gentiles.

Through the proclamation of the gospel, the presence of Jesus began to extend into the pagan world, and—since it depended on the proclamation of the God of Israel in the world of the Gentiles[53]—the words of the psalm took on a further dimension, one which diverged from Israel's previous missionary activity and yet cannot be separated from that:

> All the ends of the earth shall remember
> and will turn to the Lord;
> all the families of the nations
> shall cast themselves down before him.
> (Ps. 22:27)

Up to now Israel had brought people from the gentile nations into the people of God only by changing them into Jews. Now a group from Israel, appealing to Jesus Christ for their legitimation, set out to live together with Gentiles, no longer requiring them to obey the commandment to be circumcised or other ritual precepts, and in this sense to become converted. They could remain non-Jews, just as that first missionizing community, for its part, continued to feel that it was a part of the Jewish people. In this extension of the presence of Jesus, a fundamental biblical theme takes on a new form.

Excursus: Israel and the Gentile Nations

This theme acquired increasing importance, at least from the period of the Babylonian exile onwards.[54] Separation from the gentile nations, on the one hand, and a solicitous approach to them, on the other (especially in the Diaspora), are the determining factors in the relationship of the people of God to the nations who surrounded, or even dominated, them. Which of these two aspects was dominant at any given time depended on the political circumstances of the moment. For example, according to the testimony of Deutero-Isaiah, toward the end of the exile God could address the Persian king Cyrus (who liberated the Jewish community, among others, from Babylonian rule) as his anointed one (Isa. 45:1). On the other hand, according to the testimony of the Book of Daniel, in the second century B.C., all that God had in store for the kingdoms of this world was annihilation (Dan. 2:44). It was above all in the period of the Maccabees that the relationship of Israel and its God to the Gentiles took this excessively destructive form. This indicates that the attitude of Israel's God to the nations of the world was given an aggressive definition especially when Israel's identity as people of God was endangered—that is, when obedience to the Torah and temple worship were encroached upon.[55] Essential preconditions for Israel's succeeding history, down to the destruction of the second temple, were created in this period. The struggle of Jews faithful to their tradition against the Hellenistic-Syrian rulers and against the Hellenized aristocracy of their own nation certainly ended victoriously, but it did not bring peace. Hardly had the Maccabees gained the upper hand and reached out beyond their original goal of restoration of the temple worship, when we come across a number of sometimes crassly conflicting groups in the country which contended for the interpretation and presentation of an obedient Israel. In this way they testified to the permanent discrepancy between what Israel was supposed to be and what it actually was under the Maccabean or Hasmonean rulers, with their illegitimate grab for the dignity of the high-priestly office. Among these groups were the Dead Sea community, the Pharisees, perhaps also the Sadducees, though the last two groups were involved in shifting coalitions with the rulers. Later other groups were added: the Zealots, the disciples of John the Baptist, and the people surrounding Jesus of Nazareth.

For a considerable time the disputed rule of the Hasmoneans preserved Israel's political independence yet once more, but this rule lasted for a bare century. Then, from 63 B.C., the Romans became the lords of this region of the Near East too. Part of the time they exerted their authority indirectly (e.g., through Herod and his sons), part of the time directly (in the province of Judea, for instance, from 6 A.D. onwards). In rabbinic tradition, the Roman occupiers are later, after the destruction of the temple, called the "iniquitous rule."[56] They were probably viewed in the same light even earlier by most of the people, with the possible exception of the Sadducees, the people who had retained a degree of power. If a Christian interpreter of our own day paints a picture of the life of the Jewish people in the land of Israel at the time of Jesus, showing it to be "sick and full of conflicts,"[57] the second epithet may well be apt enough, for the same may be said, more or less, about every period and society. But to call it sick is to miss the heart of the conflict. It ignores the determining mark of that period—the oppression of the people by the alien power of Rome. The Jewish War against the Romans (66–70 and 74) makes this especially evident. So the disappointed sigh of the disciples on the road to Emmaus, "But we had hoped that he was the one to redeem Israel" (Luke 24:21), is probably a far more accurate record of what extensive circles in the Jewish nation hoped for at the time of Jesus and of what they accordingly suffered in day-to-day terms. Central prayers, such as the Eighteen Benedictions, the Kaddish, and the Alenu, confirm this, as do other testimonies that clearly go back to this period.

Moreover, hostility towards Israel was not confined to people living in the country itself. In 38 A.D., the large Jewish community in Alexandria was subjected to a pogrom engineered by the pagans surrounding the Jews. Even if enmity did not take this extreme a form every day, remarks passed down by Roman writers suggest that anyone in the Diaspora who adhered to the synagogue and acknowledged that he was a Jew had on occasion to reckon with scorn and calumny.[58] And yet, in spite of that, the Jewish community exercised an extraordinary fascination. Apart from proselytes in the strict sense, there was a group of "God-fearing" people—people attracted by the life of the Jewish community—who adhered to the synagogue though without joining it in the official sense.

In the framework of Israel's relationship to the Gentiles, therefore, in the first century A.D., at the time when the congregations of Jesus Christ were growing up, the following aspects must be registered above all: a fervent hope for liberation from the Roman occupying power; rejection of heathen idolatry; and a witness to the one God, the God of Israel, which was designed to woo others. In this framework, certain possibilities emerged for overcoming either hostile antitheses or the actual difference between Israel and the gentile nations. These possibilities were, first, the hope for a divine liberating intervention (with or without the help of the Jewish people) and, second, the courting of the Gentiles (goyim) in an attempt to convert them to the faith of the Jewish people, or at least to persuade them to participate sympathetically in the life of the Jewish community though without the further step of full integration.

It was therefore only this last-mentioned group of sympathizers who, *as*

Gentiles, *as* goyim, enjoyed a relationship of commitment or friendship towards the Jewish people without renouncing their status as non-Jews. But—since they continued to adhere simultaneously to their previous status—welcome though they were, they had only the rank of guests and did not belong to the Jewish community in the full sense.

It was at this precise point that the Christian congregations took a further step. This step was not initiated by Paul, but it was decisively encouraged and indeed pushed forward by the apostle to the Gentiles. "There is neither Jew nor Greek, there is neither slave nor free, there is neither male nor female; for you are all one in Christ Jesus" (Gal. 3:28; cf. 1 Cor. 12:13). What counts is not whether one is circumcised or uncircumcised; the only thing that matters is the trust with which the "word of faith" is met—the proclamation of Jesus' resurrection and his position as *kyrios*, which has its foundation in that resurrection (Rom. 10:9). Jesus Christ and the believing acceptance by Jews and Gentiles of the gospel that makes him present are both initial messianic phenomena; Paul sees them both as implementations of the promises with which the Scriptures describe the goal of the way of God: Jews praise God among the Gentiles (Rom. 15:9 = Ps.18:49) and the Gentiles in their turn rejoice with the people of God (Rom. 15:10 = Deut. 32:43 LXX). In this unity, in which the opposition of Jews and Gentiles is overcome, Paul is convinced that Jesus Christ also manifests himself as the "servant to the circumcised" (Rom. 15:8) and as the one "in whom the Gentiles shall hope" (Rom. 15:12 = Isa. 11:10).

Paul is therefore convinced that Jesus Christ has made it possible for Jews and Gentiles to go hand in hand. And because this is the center of his message, he attaches the utmost importance to the acceptance of his gospel by the Jewish community of Jesus Christ in Jerusalem, thinking it vital that the church there should not put an end to the community of Jews and Gentiles, for that would mean nothing less than that he had labored in vain (Gal. 2:2). His various journeys to Jerusalem and the collection made for the original congregation there show that for him, as for every other Jew, Jerusalem was the center of the world, and the proclamation of the gospel to the Gentiles in accordance with the Scriptures means that now they too are included in the orientation toward Jerusalem through the form of ties with the first congregation there. The Gentiles are debtors of the saints in Jerusalem, partakers in their spiritual blessings, and hence in duty bound to offer them service in the form of material help (Rom. 15:27): this is the clear trend of the relationship between Israel and the Gentiles as it has been established through Jesus Christ.

The End of Hostility

Reconciler of the Church of Jews and Gentiles. Although the author of the Epistle to the Ephesians was one of Paul's pupils, he undoubtedly found it difficult in some respects to follow in the footsteps of his master. But he grasped like no one else the essential features of what was the center of the Pauline proclamation: the unity of Jews and Gentiles.[59] Once—without Jesus Christ—the Gentiles' relationship to the community of Israel had been one of estrangement. They were untouched by the promises of the covenant, without hope or ties with God. But now these people, who had once been far off, have been brought near through his blood: "For he is our peace, who has made us both [Israel and the Gentiles] one, and has broken down the dividing wall of hostility" (Eph. 2:14), killing it on the cross (Eph. 2:16). So "he has come and has proclaimed peace to you who were far off and peace to those who were near; for through him we both have access in one spirit to the Father" (Eph. 2:17–18). When the author sees the abolition of hostility on the cross as being due to the fact that Jesus Christ "abolished [katargein] the law of commandments and ordinances" (Eph. 2:15), he is certainly using a highly problematical expression for which he can hardly appeal to Paul. The apostle answers this very question (whether the law would be abolished—katargein— through Jesus Christ or through faith) with a categorical no, going on to assert the precise opposite (Rom. 3:31). But if one sees this phrase as a way of expressing the fact that obedience to the ritual commandments of the Jewish people is no longer the constitutive element for nearness to God, then the connection with the Pauline proclamation is maintained.

At all events, it is the strength of the Epistle to the Ephesians that, unlike some modern interpreters, it does not indulge in any kind of abstract talk about Jesus Christ as the "end of the law."[60] It confines itself to speaking about the "law of commandments," and moreover, before it mentions this aspect at all, already points forward positively to the fruits of Jesus' death: as "our peace" he has put an end to the hostility between Israel and the Gentiles. The formula "Christ the end of the law" permits a complacent theological existence, with its suggestion that polemic against the Torah is the first Christian duty, but things are different if—as in Ephesians—the gospel really finds expression as good news, as the proclamation of peace, and hence the end of enmity. For then it is not primarily the Jewish people who are challenged about their dealings with the Torah, it is the Christian church that has to face the question about *its* dealings with the gospel it claims for itself, the gospel of peace, reconciliation, and the end of hostility. Both theology and church history teach the relevance of this question. And tested against the gospel as it is presented by Paul and, with especial pregnancy, by one of his pupils, both theology and church history can be read largely as the witnesses not of obedience but of disobedience. Israel's no becomes all too understandable if the proclamation of peace is lived in the form of anti-Judaism and if, even among the people who acknowledge its claim on them, the messianic event (whether we see it from a christological or an ecclesiological perspective) is allowed to show so little of what it should, surely, preeminently include—peace, not merely for a small group but for everyone, and for others most of all.

The whole complex therefore already has two dimensions, even in the

New Testament, one dimension affecting the church itself, the other affecting those outside. It has, indeed, been suggested that the Epistle to the Ephesians is not thinking, in chapter 2, about the relationship in the church between Jewish Christians and gentile Christians but is talking about Jews and Gentiles generally, quite apart from their particular attitude to the proclamation of Jesus Christ.[61] It would certainly be helpful if this interpretation were correct. But it is as untenable[62] as the same author's thesis that the Epistle to the Ephesians was probably written by Paul himself, not by one of his pupils.[63] In the case of both propositions, the wish is father to the thought. But if Eph. 2:11–22 is an interpretation designed for the information of gentile Christians (see Eph. 2:11 and frequently elsewhere), showing that Israel (the Jews) and the nations (the Gentiles) belong together *in* the community of Jesus Christ, then the very fact that this teaching was necessary shows how, even at this period, even in the first century, it was not at all clear to Gentiles in the church who they really were—strangers brought near through Jesus Christ—and that if they had not gone hand in hand with the community of Israel, represented by the Jews in the church, they would have been strangers to the promises of the covenant, without hope and without God in the world (Eph. 2:12).

It is difficult to discover whether the author of the letter intended to exert his influence on some actual conflict between Gentiles and Jews in the church or churches of his time, or whether he wanted to offer more general instruction about the essential orientation of the Gentiles toward the community of Israel in the church as well. Whichever it was, it is obvious that even a few decades after the founding of the first congregations in the Diaspora, Christians had lost their awareness that "it is not you that support the root, but the root that supports you" (Rom. 11:18). In fact the Epistle to the Ephesians did not have any permanent success either, in its attempt to create this awareness. One might even say that in a certain sense, in spite of this attempt, it did not merely witness to a development that narrowed down the full gospel, it actually participated in that development. For emphatically though the writer stresses in chapter 2 that for Jews and Gentiles to go hand in hand in the congregation of Jesus Christ is one of the essential marks of the church, to the extent to which Israel did not believe the gospel, it had little place in the writer's proclamation, according to the evidence of the whole epistle.[64] Here the author of Ephesians differs from Paul, whom he purports to represent.

Reconciler of the Church with Israel. The passage in the Epistle to the Romans that explains that Israel (represented by the Jews in the church) are the roots and the Gentiles are the (grafted) branches is evidence that there was already lack of clarity about the true relationship of Jews and Gentiles in the church years earlier, at the time of Paul himself. But in that particular context (Romans 9—11), Paul, unlike the Epistle to the Ephesians, was not primarily concentrating on conditions inside the church; he was concerned with the relationship of the church of Jews and Gentiles to

Israel insofar as it rejected the gospel. In his letter to the church in Rome, Paul was already—in the 50s—trying to combat the opinion that was later accepted largely as a matter of course and was assumed by Christians to be the scriptural view: the arrogant standpoint, hostile to Israel, that God had rejected his people because of their no to Jesus Christ (Rom. 11:1–2). The fact that this attitude existed among gentile Christians in Rome shows how far back we can trace the phenomenon that churches of Jesus Christ do not merely show themselves incapable of softening or transforming the hostile relationship between the Gentiles and Israel, they actually present themselves as Israel's gentile enemies. In addition, they even probably won new enemies for the Jews through their missionary activities: many of the "God-fearing"—that is, friends of the Jewish community—may well have been drawn into the vortex of anti-Jewish Christian attitudes once they had turned to the church of Jesus Christ.

The Pauline struggle against behavior of this kind makes it obvious that these attitudes depended on a fundamental misunderstanding of the relationship between Israel and the Gentiles as this appears in the light of the gospel. In fact Paul even makes it clear that the final result of this attitude is a surrender of the gospel itself. For only this can explain why the apostle threatens those who look down on Israel with nothing less than the divine judgment (Rom. 11:21–22). Correspondingly, according to Paul's interpretation, the gospel and its obedient acceptance do not merely imply the messianically defined phenomenon of a united church of Jews and Gentiles, they also enjoin an attitude to Israel as a whole which is determined by the certainty of the people's continuing election and the saving mercy of God toward his people both now and in the future. If, then, the binding nature of the Scriptures for theology and church has any meaning at all, what Scripture has to say at this point must be listened to with particular attention.

It is only in relatively few passages that Paul formulates his message with the help of the theme of reconciliation and the terms belonging to it.[65] But to draw qualitative conclusions from this quantitative observation would be mistaken for a number of reasons. First of all, when Paul takes up and partially develops this theme, it is always at key points in his letters (Rom. 5:1–11; 2 Cor. 5:17–21). Second, the statements about reconciliation in these passages are worked out theologically in the context of the proclamation of justification, which was indisputably central for Paul, and are closely woven into that proclamation, so they do not appear in isolation like what the geologists call an erratic block.[66] And third, important individual concepts relating to the proclamation of reconciliation (e.g., the proclamation of peace in particular) are widely dispersed throughout the epistles and are again to be found at especially illuminating points. So it would seem to be really chance—conditioned by the specific matters Paul had to discuss—that he did not develop his message about the reconciliation of enemies in the same breadth as his proclamation about the justification of sinners. The essential starting point of his theological reflections in this context is in each case the same: the assurance of the death and resurrection of Jesus Christ "for us," "for the many," that is to say, for the benefit of all, as proof of his love, or of God's love in him. This is brought out particularly impressively in the whole passage Rom. 5:8–10:

> But God showed his love to us in that while we were yet sinners Christ died for us. Since, therefore, we are now justified by his blood, how much more shall we be saved by him from the wrath [judgment] of God.
> For if while we were [still] enemies we were reconciled to God by the death of his Son, how much more, now that we are reconciled, shall we be saved [from the wrath] by his life.

The passage 2 Cor. 5:17–21 is similar:

> If any one is in Christ, he is a new creation; the old has passed away, behold, the new has come. All this is from God, who through Christ reconciled us to himself and gave us the ministry of reconciliation; that is, in Christ God was reconciling the world to himself, not counting their trespasses against them, and entrusting to us the message of reconciliation.
> So we are ambassadors for Christ, God making his appeal through us. We beseech you on behalf of Christ, be reconciled to God.
> For our sake he made him to be sin who knew no sin, so that in him we might become the righteousness of God.

The statements about reconciliation in 2 Corinthians 5 differ from those in Rom. 5:8–10: on the one hand they are more comprehensively formulated, it being expressly stressed that the goal of the divine activity is the reconciliation of the *world*; moreover, the context of the verses makes it clear that, as a second aspect, emphasis lies on the presence of the reconciling act of God in the apostolic ministry. It is only in the final sentence that Paul leads over to the style of the congregational creed that marks the parallel passage in Rom. 5:8–10.

From both contexts, and especially in their links with Paul's proclamation of justification, a thread can be traced back to Romans 11, which we have already touched on, and which is of such determinative importance with regard to Israel. Having confuted the assumption or assertion that God had repudiated his people Israel (Rom. 11:1–10), Paul then in Romans 11:11ff. refuses to accept the possibility that the part of Israel that does not believe the gospel has rejected the message of Jesus Christ and has consequently stumbled *in order that* it should fall. To bear out what he says, he demonstrates the positive function of the no of the people of God. That is, he shows how the Gentiles themselves (who are always in danger of arrogance towards God's people) profit from Israel's no. Paul makes his fundamental assertion at the very beginning. Through the recusancy (the "fall") of Israel, the essential content of the gospel, salvation (*sōtēria*) has reached the Gentiles. Admittedly this is not solely for the sake of the Gentiles themselves; the purpose is to make the part of Israel that did not believe in the gospel jealous, because of the presence of *sōtēria* among the goyim

(Rom. 11:11; cf. 10:19). But then this incentive, in its turn, does not have significance solely for Israel either; in the perspective of the future it will be a renewed gain for the Gentiles. For "if their trespass [already] means riches for the world, and if their failure has become riches for the Gentiles" because it has led to the gift of God's mercy to them (see Rom. 11:30–31, 33), "how much more will their [Israel's] full inclusion [mean riches for the Gentiles]." Without Israel, the Gentiles will cheat themselves of their own future.

For Paul, this perspective is of such decisive importance, both for Israel's sake and for the sake of the Gentiles, that he goes on to put his whole ministry as apostle to the Gentiles under the heading of making his fellow Jews "jealous, and thus to save some of them" (Rom. 11:13). Paul wishes to make it unmistakably clear that this viewpoint is not the outcome of his own private problem as Jew, so to speak, but that it is the authentic element of his existence as apostle and his charge to minister to *the Gentiles*. So he repeats yet again the deduction from the lesser to the greater which he already made in Rom. 11:12 when he expounded the indissoluble ties binding together the future of Israel and the future of the church: "For if their rejection [of the gospel][67] has become the reconciliation of the world, what will their acceptance [then] mean [for the world] but life from the dead?" (Rom. 11:15). The Gentiles have already had the gift of *sōtēria* bestowed on them (in hope, Rom. 8:24). But the resurrection of the dead, for which, even so, they still hope, depends on what Paul a little later calls the salvation of all Israel (Rom. 11:26). It is as closely and as inextricably as this that the fate of Israel remains intertwined with that of the Gentiles, until the real end of history.

The whole weight of these assertions, particularly the last, only emerges when we compare them with the statements we have already looked at, especially Romans 5. The gift of the reconciliation of the world, which 2 Corinthians 5 declares is the center of God's act in Jesus Christ, comes to the Gentiles through Israel's help—through its no, which God uses for the benefit of the goyim. When, in Rom. 5:10, Paul describes the status of the church as "reconciled to God by the death of his Son," this demonstrably includes what is said in Rom. 11:15: that it is thanks to Israel's no to the death of Christ as redeeming act that the Gentiles have been saved. But this by no means exhausts the inner connection of the two passages. In Rom. 5:10, Paul links the reconciliation that has taken place to the death of Jesus Christ and deduces from that saving act the future, all the more certain salvation through the life (resurrection) of the Son of God, which can only mean the resurrection of the dead, as a positive way of describing redemption (from judgment). In Rom. 11:15, he sees in Israel's no the basis for the reconciliation of the world, and deduces from Israel's yes, which he confidently expects, an all the more certain resurrection from the dead for the Gentiles.

The two statements therefore show a noticeable parallelism. In both passages reconciliation is something that belongs to the present, whereas (final) salvation, or the resurrection of the dead, is reserved for the future. But according to Rom. 5:10, both events are brought about by the death and life of Jesus Christ—and according to Rom. 11:15, by the no and yes of the Israel that does not believe in the gospel. Paul therefore dares in Romans 11 to make statements about Israel in its relationship to the Gentiles that bring it extraordinarily close to Jesus Christ. With its no, Israel makes it possible for the reconciliation effected by God through Jesus Christ to come to the Gentiles; with its yes (which Paul hopes for, and of which he is certain) it enables God to complete his saving acts through the resurrection from the dead. So it is precisely in Israel's no that God's saving acts in Jesus Christ coincide with the behavior of his people.

In the face of this common perspective, which draws into a single viewpoint the work of Jesus Christ and Israel's behavior, every injury done to Israel is an injury to Jesus Christ himself as the one who died for the reconciliation of the world. So whenever gentile Christians behave not as men and women who have been reconciled but as the enemies of God's people of Israel, they testify that not only is Israel's no in vain but that at the same time the death of Jesus Christ as the work of reconciliation is vain as well.[68] In Rom. 11:28 Paul sums up his description of the people in Israel who do not believe in the gospel, calling them "[a]s regards the gospel . . . enemies for your sake," and the parallel formula for the Gentiles who are indebted to the message could only be "judged by the gospel, friends for Jesus Christ's sake." The Christian organizations that have been concerned, and still are, to find an appropriate expression for the relationship between the church and God's people of Israel, and who have included the word "friendship" in their description of themselves, have grasped a good deal about this whole complex, whether consciously or not.[69] It must, however, be said that in Germany any strivings after a friendly relationship with Israel, on the theological level too—a relationship, that is, which departs from the well-worn paths of theological hostility toward the Jews —are all too swiftly written off with the very simple and very convenient exonerating reproach of philo-Semitism.[70]

So according to Romans 9—11, the most important thing that Christians have to discern about Israel as part of their own faith, and that they have to recognize and live out in their relationship to this people, is that Israel's election as the people of God endures from the beginning to the end. Paul says of no other people that it has been chosen *as people* (Rom. 11:1–2). Nor does he say of any other people that it will be saved *as a whole* in the end time (Rom. 11:26). On the contrary, this is the special thing about Israel, the exceptional characteristic, which has its foundation in God himself and in his act of election. It is only if we grasp that these "bracketing" statements (9:1–5 and 11:25–32) surround and encompass Romans 9—11 as a whole complex, that we can evaluate adequately the other statements too: that although Israel has pursued the "righteousness which is based on law," it has not succeeded in fulfilling that law (9:31); and its zeal for God is not "enlightened"—not guided by knowledge—because it has tried to establish its own righteousness and has not been obedient to the righteousness of God (10:2–3); that these are a disobedient and contrary people (10:21); that they are hardened, have stumbled and fallen (11:7, 11, 22); that some of the branches on the olive tree of Israel have been broken off because of their unbelief (11:17, 20). There is no doubt at all that Paul means just what he says here. So it is all the more important to note three things.

First, as we have seen, everything he says falls *within* the encompassing brackets I have mentioned, and in the whole of chapter 11 he is intent on emphasizing that these statements cannot and may not be played off by the church against Israel (cf. 11:1–2, 11ff., 18ff., 25). Instead, the church has to remember that Israel's no has been for *the church's own benefit.*

Second, it must be asked whether we can today simply take over what the apostle says in condemnation of Israel's behavior or whether we do not rather have to look for a different kind of language. Many people are very well aware of this problem. That is evident, for example, when someone, echoing Romans 11, talks about Israel's having been "hardened," but always uses the expression in quotation marks. In this case the person in question wants to use the phrase but does not feel unreservedly free to do so. So the quotation marks express something like an inhibition or perhaps even a bad conscience. However that may be, *this*, at least, is the worst possible solution. One can either use the expression or—in view of its fateful effects in history—feel unable to use it. But if its use is impossible, then another expression must simply be chosen in its place.

The following reflection may perhaps also be helpful here. Today it is not merely the Jewish people who say no to the gospel. In many cases it is our own relatives or members of our family in the closer sense, to say nothing of ourselves. Is it our usual practice in these cases to say that this or that member of our family has been "hardened" by God? And if not, why do we want to go on talking like this when it is Israel that is in question?

Of course the problem involved here is a more far-reaching one. It raises a more general question. How far can we today talk about God's acting in judgment, and especially in connection with the rejection of the gospel? This problem cannot be pursued here in any detail. All that can be done is to show, with Israel as example, what the general outline of an approach to the question might be. If, instead of talking about Israel's being "hardened," we talk about the gospel's being *closed* to the Jewish people, we may well have taken an essential step toward preserving what the apostle says from misuse. Indeed, this word "closed" has another great advantage too, for it immediately raises the question, *Why* is it closed to the Jewish people? And this question in its turn must be directed to the church at least as much as to Israel. What this phrase makes evident applies correspondingly to all Paul's other critical statements about Israel in Romans 9—11. It is also true, above all, of the apostle's assertion that Israel was trying to become righteous through "works of the law" (9:31–32) and was seeking to establish its "own righteousness" (10:3). The final chapter of this English edition of the present study will offer an opportunity for a further consideration of this complex.

I have first of all reminded readers of the "bracketing" statements that embrace all the others in Romans 9—11, and I have then gone on to raise a few hermeneutical questions about how far Paul's language can still be taken over today. A third point is equally important. We must again note a specific characteristic of Paul's assertions about judgment in Romans 9— 11. These contrast noticeably with the dominating statements about salvation. For whereas Paul says that *some* of the branches have been broken off (11:17), what he says about salvation applies to *all* Israel. This mention of "some of the branches" is extremely significant, for there is no doubt at all that the apostle is perfectly aware that the number of Jews who reject the gospel is anything but merely some. If, in spite of this, he still talks about "some," his interpreters have no right to expand the "some" and to turn it into "all" or "most." The apostle's distinction here between the some who have been broken off, and "all Israel," which is going to be saved, represents a pattern of thought that is the diametrical opposite of what hostility toward the Jews has been at all times and in all its gradations. For both religiously motivated enmity and politically active enmity toward the Jews are determined by the same view: that there are individual "good Jews" (everyone knows a few), but that "the Jews," the Jews as a whole, are this or that—and then there follow the negative characterizations in their particular coloring. This way of thinking is the basic law of hostility toward the Jews, and it is precisely here that the pattern of ideas put forward by Paul may offer a bulwark of defense. For Paul's argument shows that it is *the whole* that deserves protection. The single thing or the single person can always be faulty or open to criticism. But the criticism must be specific and precise, not wholesale. That is why this bulwark is also far removed from any kind of philo-Semitism.

The Practice of Reconciliation: The End of Mission to the Jews. It would seem as if the exegesis of Rom. 11:11–15 that I have put forward would be a positive incitement to a relationship to God's people of Israel based on a mission-to-the-Jews mentality, contrary to the theological insights so laboriously arrived at in recent years.[71] But in fact there can be no question of this. Paul himself makes it abundantly clear what his attitude to his people is in this regard. The apostolic service *to the Gentiles* is the way in which Israel is to be made "jealous." But if this is already true for the apostle to the Gentiles, who is himself a Jew or an Israelite (Rom. 11:2), how much more is it true for the goyim of his own time and ours. Paul certainly then expects Israel's future yes to Jesus Christ. But, on the one hand, he is silent about the how and when of this yes, and on the other, toward the end of the chapter he leaves this yes unmentioned at the very point where we should perhaps expect to find it—in just that statement into which it is often read (Rom. 11:26): "And so all Israel will be saved."[72] The connecting words "And so" do not refer to a condition of faith that Israel has to fulfill; the reference is to the gathering together of the fullness of the gentile nations.[73] The two dimensions in which Christians are to lend authentic expression to their "zeal for Israel" are hence, first of all, credible, convincing existence as a Christian community—that is, as men and women who have been reconciled—and second, a struggle for the fullness of the Gentiles. By behaving to God's people of Israel as those who have been reconciled— which means believingly, lovingly, and hopefully—their witness will be in keeping with the gospel, testifying that Jesus Christ died "for us," or that "in Christ God was reconciling the world *to himself,*" which is to say, especially, also, with his unfathomable, scandalous, and yet incontestable and irrevocable love for his people Israel, to which Paul bears a witness in Romans 9—11.

This means that, in the light of Paul's gospel, where theology and the church (as institutions of gentile origin) have a bearing on Israel, they are called simply and solely to recognize God's enduring relationship of love for his people. It is this they have to affirm, and it is from this that they have to draw conclusions *for themselves* in their theological and practical relationship to the Jewish people. Here, if anywhere, the Pauline gospel must prove itself.[74]

A relationship of this kind is all the more urgently required, the more difficult the trend of the times makes it appear. Today an important section of the Jewish people lives in the state of Israel, and it is often hard for outsiders to perceive the reasonableness, let alone the salutariness, of various political actions on the part of their present government. Certain things can be explained from the history of fear the Jewish people have endured in the gentile world, especially in the Christian west, and Christians should therefore be exceedingly reserved about any form of condemnation. At the same time, the point cannot be to palliate questionable acts and decisions. Theologically, however, nothing could be more mistaken than to draw any conclusions from problematic present-day circumstances that would release the Christian church from its commitment to the Jewish people in Israel. This emerges from the very heart of the proclamation of justification *sola gratia* (by grace alone), and.this is still central for both theology and the church. For if Christians were to think that the Jewish people in the country of Israel had first to earn the commitment of God or the commitment of Christians through their political actions, this would mean departing from this proclamation, in terms of theology and doctrine, and also existentially. And theologically speaking it can be no more than a rhetorical question to ask who could maintain that *he* stood in a more attractive position before God on any grounds whatsoever, even where his political behavior is concerned.

The implications of Paul's gospel that I developed before this political excursus, and in its context, are also especially important because the situation of the Christian churches has changed fundamentally at a number of points since the time of the apostle. We must first of all remember the complexes touched on at the beginning (in chap. 1), when we were trying to define the contemporary preconditions that are necessary for a new thinking-through of the relationship between the Christian church and the Jewish people. A second point to be mentioned is the serious change of structure that the Christian proclamation went through in the period after Paul, which also helped to determine the reception (the acceptance and interpretation) of Pauline theology.

Paul's activity, like that of the early Christian congregations, is shaped by his expectation of the imminent coming of Jesus Christ (which was thought to be a daily possibility) and, with that, the end of the world. Most people today can hardly form any picture, probably, of the intensity of this expectation. Every sympathetic approach is of necessity an intellectually mediated attempt to enter understandingly into this expectation, since this assurance of the imminent Parousia by no means now stamps the whole of existence as it did for Paul and others in his time. It makes a fundamental difference whether we expect the possible Parousia of Jesus Christ in the time of *every* generation, or whether we definitely expect its coming in the imminent future, at latest within the period of a single generation. In Romans 11 this immediate expectation on the part of the apostle found expression in the summary phrase that God has acted towards Israel and the Gentiles in the way Paul describes in this chapter "so that they [the Israel that rejects Jesus Christ] also may receive mercy *now*"—that is, when God's plan for the world is consummated in Jesus' Parousia. The expected "now" of God's mercy touches the present existence of God's people so intimately that it is possible to talk about the presence of God's mercy to Israel in the literal sense. But insofar as the "now" is related to the Parousia, when the church's conscious expectation grew fainter the assurance of mercy also shifted from the present into the undefined future. In the same measure Israel's presence is viewed solely in the light of her no to the gospel, and the no itself at once ceases to be understood soteriologically (as it was by Paul) but is seen under the foretoken of judgment on the people of God. The consequence of this, in its turn, is that the church and theology grind to a halt on their obsession with the "guilt of the Jews" (which was completely irrelevant for Paul), making this the main subject of their theology of Israel.[75]

Observers who have no ties with the Christian faith can speak only of *the nonappearance* of the Parousia if they take their bearings from the original expectation, even if they are thinking about the end of the first century, let alone the twentieth. Theology and the church, on the other hand, have to view the matter in the light of faith and can only admit to the Parousia's *delay*; anything else would mean surrendering their assurance that their definitive tie with Jesus Christ belongs to the future also. But the concept of the delay of the Parousia is wrongly used if it serves to conceal the fact that its delay, and the church's movement into history that is conditioned by that delay, have brought about fundamental changes in the church's situation and structures, as well as in its theological thinking. These changes mean that the mere repetition of the New Testament proclamation is often the most certain guarantee that it will be ideologized or falsified.

Where Romans 9—11 is concerned, this means that the purely didactic recapitulation that Israel will find mercy at the end of history leads de facto—as church history shows—to lack of mercy in the present and, second, means practically that Israel is deprived of the "now" which for Paul is the positive signature and identifying mark of his gospel. According to Paul, this "now" is not dependent on Israel's acceptance of the gospel; it depends on the flocking in of the Gentiles (Rom. 11:26). Israel will experience the "now" (provided that the church really lives in a Christian way) through the appropriate behavior, which Paul indicates in his prohibition "Do not become proud!" (Rom. 11:20). Jesus' parousia is no more in the hands of the church than is the gathering of the gentile nations, which has long since stagnated. But what is given to it as the church of Jesus Christ is the power to live this "Do not become proud"— that is, to spell it out as the practical way of expressing commitment, and in *this* way to testify that God is *now* showing Israel mercy, with and through the Gentiles, and insofar through Jesus Christ.

Both Romans 11 and the largely gloomy history of the relationship of the Christian churches to the Jewish people are evidence that this commitment must primarily take the form of an affirmation and support of the right of members of God's people to live as the people they are and should be—Jews, the children of Israel. And this applies especially to their obedient no to Jesus Christ, which is determined by their zeal for God (Rom. 10:2).[76]

Paul did not merely guard Israel in its no with the protective shield of the prohibition to the Gentiles "Do not become proud!" Even before that, he worked out the salvific effect of that no for the Gentiles, that is, its soteriological function. At the time of the apostle, in view of the swiftly approaching end of the world that was anticipated, it might well have seemed appropriate to be content with that prohibition, as a negative commandment, and to consider the fact of Israel's no simply in the light of its formal effect, the turning to the Gentiles. The delay of the Parousia does not only constrain theology to ask about the meaning of this delay for Christology and ecclesiology. It also imposes the question about the significance of Israel's no, which is prolonged through this delay. But if, then, the nonarrival of the Parousia in the early period of the church meant that the Christian community has become bound anew into the history of this world and saturated with this world's content and tenor, it would seem no more than consistent to understand Israel's no after that delay, not merely in its formal effect but in its substantial character. Church history teaches that from time to time there have been Christians who have at least sensed, probably, that this context makes a substantial encounter with the Jewish people necessary, even though specific encounters were as a rule accompanied by an unbiblical feeling of superiority, if they were not actually under duress.[77] If the encounter remains free of these things, the significance of Israel's no to the gospel in its actual content may emerge. For according to Paul, the no leads formally *to the fact that* goyim become

Christians; the profit of an encounter with the reasons for that no—that is, with its content—is to be understood primarily, in the movement of Pauline theology, simply as a chance (and challenge) for the baptized goyim, the existing Christian church, to understand *that they should become* Christians. Pierre Lenhardt remarks that, in relation to the Jewish people, the Christian must "primarily, if not exclusively, testify to his own conversion to the God of Abraham, Isaac, and Jacob, the God of Jesus Christ";[78] and this remark suddenly brings out an essential dimension of this complex.

To realize the necessity for a substantial encounter with the Jewish people in this sense, for the sake of the gospel and for the sake of the Christian church itself, means a change of direction to a degree that can hardly be overestimated. It means a readiness to allow the depressingly large number of prejudices to be shaken, especially prejudices determined by dogma; it means listening anew to what we can still, down the centuries and at the present day, hear from the oral, scripturally based tradition of the Jewish people, as testimony to the God of Abraham, Isaac, and Jacob, the God of Israel; and it means not merely registering this but listening to it with the attention that, as the Jewish and the Christian Bible both tell us, is the behavior to our neighbor that God himself desires.[79]

This aspect will have to be taken up again when we consider the close connection between Christology and ecclesiology. But in the framework of the christological and soteriological emphasis of the present chapter, we must first listen to another New Testament witness.

Unfulfilled Hope

Paul was a solitary voice in his proclamation of the principles by which he determined the relationship between the church and the Jewish people, Israel and the Gentiles, in the light of the gospel—and a solitary voice not only in his own time. As the Epistle to the Ephesians already shows, even Paul's pupils seem to have lost sight of the hope for Israel. Where Ephesians is concerned, this is, largely speaking, a deduction drawn from the writer's silence on the subject. But in Luke, for example, the fact becomes plainly evident. In Acts 13, the evangelist transmits a scene that reads like a story illustrating what Paul states in abstract terms in Romans 11: that the result of Israel's no to the gospel is that God (through his messengers) turns in saving grace to the Gentiles.[80] In Paul, however, Israel's no is reduced to merely relative importance because of the enduring faithfulness of God, for Israel's hope is founded on that faithfulness and there too the church's relationship to Israel finds its orientation. But according to Luke, Israel through its no is robbing itself of this very future. With their rejection of the apostle's message, "the Jews" (Acts 13:45) show themselves "unworthy of eternal life" (Acts 13:46). They thereby lose the commitment of the Christian church, whose messengers shake off the dust from their feet as a sign that their fellowship with Israel has been canceled (Acts 13:51).

It is true that in the succeeding parts of his work Luke makes the apostles, especially Paul, continue to seek dialogue with the Jews, before turning to the Gentiles, in spite of the announcement in chapter 13: immediately afterwards in Iconium (Acts 14:2), later in Philippi (Acts 16:13), in Beroea (Acts 17:1ff.), in Corinth (Acts 18:4) and finally also—and this is again especially stressed—in Rome (Acts 28:17ff.). But these reiterations of the movement from Israel to the Gentiles can hardly be interpreted as a revision of the scene in chapter 13. On the contrary, they reveal its programmatic character. The incident in Antioch, on Paul's first missionary journey, makes clear what was happening in this period of Paul's missionary work as a whole and what reached its conclusion with the apostle's arrival in Rome. Acts 13:42–52, at the beginning of the missionary journeys, is like the opening bracket that finds it correspondence in the closing bracket in Acts 28:17–28 at the journeys' end. Thus Paul's final words to the leader of the Jewish congregation(s) in Rome at the end of the Book of Acts seems like a seal to the programmatic prelude in Antioch: "Let it be known to you then that this salvation of God has been sent to the Gentiles; they will also accept it obediently" (Acts 28:28; cf. Acts 13:47–48). After Paul has earlier (with an eye to his discussion partners) cited Isaiah 6:9–10, with its announcement of the divine denial of salvation to Israel, the final sentence shows the trend even more clearly: the future belongs to the Gentiles, not Israel.[81] It would seem that Paul could not have been more gravely misunderstood, on the evidence of Romans 11, for it is, after all, Paul who is talking here, and it is Paul to whom Luke devotes almost two-thirds of his Acts of the Apostles.

The curtailed, and hence mistaken, account of Paul's activity that Luke gives us in the final scene of Acts is all the more important because this evangelist—here comparable only to Matthew—seeks in a specially intensive way for the link with biblical language and tradition, in order to characterize and establish the identity of the Christian church. Just because he tries to depict the church as the heir of the Scriptures and of the promises to which the Scriptures testify, there is an increased danger that the relationship to Israel implied (as this is exemplified in Acts 13 and 28) will be considered to be legitimated by Scripture and by the divine activity, which is interpreted with scriptural help. Luke, as the "theologian of salvation history"[82] does not try to leap aside from history but tries rather to mediate between history and the scriptural word, reconciling the two through the theme of fulfillment. And this, on the other hand, encourages us, in the framework of the reception of his double work—its subsequent interpretation—to pick up the discussion with him and to ask where we can perhaps find statements that make it possible to think further theologically and that lead to different perspectives. Once again, it is itself the theme of Israel that offers starting points here, though not so much, initially, in the framework of what is said on the subject in the Book of Acts as in the context of Luke's Gospel.

One of the texts where Luke works out with particular concentration the scriptural character of the way of Jesus Christ, in its divergent particularity, is the story of the meeting of the risen Jesus with the two disciples on the road from Jerusalem to Emmaus (Luke 24:13–35). The positive evidence provided with the help of Scripture that "it was necessary that the Messiah should suffer these things and enter into his glory" (Luke 24:26) is contrasted with the disappointed expectation of the disciples "that he was the one to redeem Israel" (Luke 24:21). The tension lying in this contrast stands out when this resurrection story at the end of the Gospel is compared with the childhood story at its beginning. For right at the start, at the birth of John the Baptist and in view of the impending birth of Jesus, Zechariah praises as fulfilled the very expectation that is presented at the end as disappointed:

> Blessed be the Lord, the God of Israel,
> that he has visited and brought about liberation [lytrōsis]
> for his people,
> and has raised up a power [horn] of salvation for us in the
> house of David his servant,
> as he promised it through the mouth of his holy prophets from
> of old—
> salvation from our enemies and from the hand of all who
> hate us—
> to show mercy to our fathers and to remember his holy covenant,
> to fulfil the oath which he swore to our father Abraham,
> [so that we] being delivered out of the hand of our enemies,
> may serve him fearlessly
> in holiness and righteousness before him all our days long.
> (Luke 1:68–75)

It would seem as if this central expectation of the liberation of Israel, with the goal that it might serve God fearlessly in holiness and righteousness, was being fulfilled through the precursor, John. But in fact, according to Luke in the verses quoted, Zechariah is talking about the coming of the Messiah Jesus. For as Zechariah's son, John is of priestly descent, not Davidic. It is therefore only at the close of the Benedictus (vv. 76–79) that the evangelist also makes Zechariah address the Baptist—here too in his role as precursor. And correspondingly, in the stories that follow about the child Jesus, he also links the fulfillment of the expectation of peace (which he has called to mind in 1:68–75) with the name of Jesus. At Jesus' birth the angels proclaim peace on earth among the chosen, that is, in the first place, Israel (Luke 2:14). Simeon, who looks for the "consolation of Israel," can die in peace now that he has seen "God's salvation" (Luke 2:25–26). The aged prophetess Anna (Hannah) jumps up at the sight of the boy, praises God, and speaks about Jesus "to all who were looking for the deliverance [lytrōsis] of Jerusalem" (Luke 2:38). It is true that in his whole Gospel Luke is concerned to mediate both things: on the one hand, the certainty that Jesus Christ has begun to fulfill what was promised to the patriarchs; and on the other hand, the fact that now, after all—compared with Luke 1:68–75, for example—this fulfillment has taken place in a very different way from what was promised and hoped for.[83] The final point of this mediating process is the answer of the risen Jesus to the Emmaus disciples: "Was it not necessary [in accordance with the Scriptures; see Luke 24:25, 27] that the Christ should suffer these things and enter into his glory?" (Luke 24:26). The fulfillment of the expectation therefore takes place in a modified way and, through the form the fulfillment takes, the expectation itself is transformed. But it is by no means thereby abrogated.

An important indication of this is offered by the beginning of the Book of Acts. It is all the more remarkable because Luke, in chapter 24, gives the impression that the tension between messianic expectation and the actual history of Christ has been resolved in favor of the latter. In spite of what happened on the road to Emmaus, the disciples remain true to their expectation, according to Acts 1, for at the end of the period of teaching and learning about the "kingdom of God" that they share between Easter and the ascension (Acts 1:3), they ask the risen Jesus, "Lord, will you at this time [now] restore [apokathistanein] the kingdom to Israel?" (Acts 1:6). But anyone who is led by Luke's Gospel (esp. chap. 24) to expect Jesus' response to be a correction of the question, in the light of the theme of Israel's kingdom (of peace), will be disappointed. Jesus' answer merely repulses the curiosity about the chronology and points to the receiving of the Spirit and to witness, as the marks of the era that is now beginning (Acts 1:7–8). The biblical vision that brings together the rule of God and the rule of Israel remains unaffected. The provisos and modifications merely concern the way of Christ and the communities of his people until the time when the kingdom of God comes in glory.

This passage is not simply a mistake on Luke's part or perhaps a piece of carelessness: the author of the Acts of the Apostles makes this quite clear a little later, in Peter's great address to the people (Israel) in front of Solomon's porch, in the temple precincts. It is still true that with the fate of the Christ, the Messiah, and his suffering, God has fulfilled "what he foretold by the mouth of all the prophets of old" (Acts 3:18). But this fulfillment is really more of a beginning, a reason for repentance and turning to the forgiveness of sins (Acts 3:19) to which Peter summons, "that times of refreshing may come from the presence of the Lord, and that he may send the Messiah appointed for you, Jesus, whom heaven must receive until the time for the establishment [apokatastasis] of all that God spoke by the mouth of his holy prophets from of old" (Acts 3:20–21). Not only is here repentance interpreted as the precondition for the coming of the messianic era, in true Jewish fashion. The use of derivatives of the same word —in Acts 1:6 to describe the future establishment of the rule of Israel [apokathistanein], in Acts 3:21 for the future establishment [apokatastasis] of the prophetic promises—rather suggests in the first place that the two statements illuminate one another, and that the things which according to Acts 3:21 are still outstanding therefore include that kingdom (of peace) for Israel. The statement in Luke 21:24, that Jerusalem will be trodden down by the Gentiles until the times of the (mission to the) Gentiles have been fulfilled—that is, not forever—fits in excellently with this interpretation.[84]

So in spite of his marked fulfillment terminology and all his many statements about fulfillment, Luke shows a clear awareness that up to now only a fraction of what the prophets have promised has been fulfilled. In this sense both history and Scripture remain in Luke relatively open to the future. And even if, in his Acts of the Apostles, the evangelist steers toward that scene in Rome in which he seems to make the invitation to Israel a phenomenon of the apostolic era, yet, according to the structure of his Gospel, Israel retains a legitimate place in the prolongation of the times, in the form of that openness of Scripture and history. Luke may write with almost monotonous persistence that "Israel" did not accept Jesus because of its lack of knowledge, but in the context of the Lukan viewpoint we have outlined, this suggests the presentiment or awareness that it could by no means be expected as a matter of course that a biblically oriented Jew should recognize along the path of Jesus Christ the footprints of the Messiah. Luke's "Was it not necessary that the Christ . . ." in no way contradicts this conclusion. On the contrary, it lends it extra force. It makes clear yet again the point at which Luke himself thought he had to work on tradition with particular intensity—that is to say, the point where he came up against a difficult problem. Apart from any other observations, the sensitive understanding of the Jewish biblical tradition and its expectation that is evident in all the passages we have discussed would, incidentally, suffice to show that the common assumption that Luke was a gentile Christian deserves to be expelled into the wilderness of exegetical legends.

The result of this interrogative discussion with Luke brings us back to the path that—as we already discovered in the framework of our reflections on Romans 9—11—provides the only approach to the Jewish people that is appropriate for the Christian church. Where Christians really take seriously the gospel that has been told to them and laid upon them, they are inescapably faced with the question, What about the fulfillment of God's oath to Abraham, which Zechariah acclaimed right at the beginning of Luke's Gospel—his promise to grant to his people that "being delivered out of the hand of their enemies, they might serve him fearlessly in holiness and righteousness" (Luke 1:74–75)? It is true that, as I have just shown, according to Luke himself so many promises are as yet unfulfilled that in actual fact it is only possible to talk about the beginning of the fulfillment, at most: complete peace between Israel and the hostile nations is unquestionably still the subject of expectation. But then if God's oath counts for anything at all and if the Christian church lives from the assurance that the fulfillment has already begun in Jesus Christ, there is surely no other way open to the church than to let the Jewish people sense, from its own specific behavior, through the way it lives, something of the fact that a fractional part of the time might really have come for Israel, "delivered out of the hand of its enemies, to serve him fearlessly in holiness and righteousness." But in fact the history of the way the Christian churches have behaved to God's people of Israel has run in so diametrically opposite a direction that, throughout the centuries, the Jewish congregations have been delivered *into* the hand of their (Christian) enemies and have had to serve God in fear and trembling—not because of the behavior of some random gentile nations but because of the acts of nations specifically "Christian." And if, even then, this service has still been joyful, fearless, and in holiness and righteousness, then it is certainly only in exceptional cases that this has been due to the behavior of Christians. The Jewish no to Jesus Christ, and even more to the church, has therefore been legitimated countless times by the obedient behavior of Jews and the disobedient behavior of Christians. The Christian churches will only be what they are called to be for the people of God, as far as is humanly possible, when they have testified convincingly through their life and behavior for just as long a period as they filled the Jewish people with apprehension, that for Israel they are a reason not for fear but for fearlessness and perhaps even for confidence. That is to say, the churches will only be what they should be for the Jews when they have testified convincingly that they are reconciled to God's unshakable and "scandalous" love for Israel. Until then, everything we can see in the way of signs of common ground, reconciliation, and a new beginning from the Jewish side can—like the possibility of a new relationship to the Jewish people in general[85]—only be adequately described, theologically speaking, in the category of miracle.

Israel's Messiah?

". . . and of their race, according to the flesh, is the Messiah [the Christ]." Picking up this statement in Rom. 9:5, we have already tried in this third chapter to find answers to the question of who this Christ is for the Jewish people, the Christ who for Paul and the other early witnesses to the gospel bears an unequivocal name—who he is, or who he can be, for Jews, according to the Christian perspective, if we take what was said in the first two chapters as our premise.

Of decisive importance, first of all, is the closer definition of the question we have already arrived at, for both the discussion of essential aspects in Romans 9—11 and the inclusion of Lukan texts force us to make an important correction to the usual treatment and interpretation of the acknowledgment of Jesus Christ as Messiah. According to the evidence of Romans 9—11, the whole trend of this confession of faith, as part of gentile Christian testimony, is directed not initially toward the Jewish people but at the church itself. The church is asked whether it is living out this confession of faith in such a way that the Jewish people can recognize—in whatever way—that in Jesus Christ God has acted for the benefit of Israel also. As long as the Jewish people are not able to feel this from the total behavior of the Christian churches, from the way they listen, learn, understand, and act, anything else that theology and the church may have to say about Israel is of little importance.

In the framework of this fundamental provision, the following recognitions may well be of particular importance. If the wealth of aspects involved in this provision is preserved, then the possible meaning of Jesus Christ for God's people of Israel can be understood as being precisely his position as God's mediator (or even reconciler) between Israel and the Gentiles. After Easter, or on this universal level, this function corresponds exactly to the function the parables about the lost showed to be the purpose of the ministry of Jesus of Nazareth *within* Israel in the period before his death.[86] This description of Jesus' function after Easter potentially implies the recognition that in the relationship to the Jewish people Jesus Christ mediates ecclesiologically and soteriologically, that is, through the concrete existence of the church. The prevalent definition of the church's task, given through the command to carry the gospel to the Gentiles (Matt. 28:18–20), not only illegitimately extends this task to Israel, it means at the same time a restriction of what the church of Jesus Christ should be, according to God's will. And this is a restriction that can hardly be maintained. This is again evident if we remember that the christological definitions we have named by no means point away from the theological center (the center, for example, of the proclamation that originated with Paul). On the contrary, they actually emphasize it.

In the center of this proclamation, whether it is Paul's own or the message of the early deutero-Pauline writer of Ephesians, stands the evidence that by virtue of Jesus Christ's death and the resurrection in which the church believes, the relationship of enmity between the Gentiles and Israel has been transformed into a relationship of peace. This promise and certainty is represented physically, so to speak, in the church of Jews and Greeks. But precisely because this gift of peace has its origin in God and, mediated through Jesus Christ, signifies the concrete form of reconciliation with God (2 Cor. 5:19), it is not restricted to the inner Christian sphere. Fundamentally speaking, it extends as far as the will of the reconciling God itself and can only be the reflection of what Paul reminds his readers: that "while we were enemies we were reconciled to God by the death of his Son" (Rom. 5:10). This means that in relation to Israel, the people so reconciled have laid upon them the all-embracing lived—or to-be-lived—testimony *that* as people who have been reconciled they have become reconciled to God's yes to the Jewish people, for this yes endures in spite of the no to Jesus Christ. And it therefore endures also in spite of the Jewish no to the church as a messianically founded phenomenon. Since this reconciliation is related to God's yes, it does not let hope for the future full community of Israel and the nations die away; it animates and strengthens that hope in an entirely new way. In this sense it is the church of Jesus Christ that has to show that, on the basis of God's acts in Jesus Christ, it has been liberated for life with God's people of Israel in a relationship of surmounted enmity, that is to say, a relationship of peace. Consequently, attempts to make this physical, concrete, comprehensive witness (which therefore also includes theology) dependent either on a previous verbal testimony or on the Jewish acceptance of Jesus Christ as Messiah amount to a flat ideologizing of the gospel.[87]

If friendship is justified for Christ's sake in this way and if this is the reason the enmity of the Gentiles towards God's people of Israel should end, then the original Christian proclamation of Jesus Christ's death for Jews and Christians becomes effective, provided that friendship and the abolition of enmity are lived by the Christian church for the sake of the Jewish people. In this sense the fundamental, central christological and kerygmatic statement of the New Testament can be taken up in a pro-Jewish sense and not in an anti-Jewish one—that is, not in the sense of denying Israel's right to live before God and in its own relationship to God. And in this sense too we can even say that Jesus is Israel's Messiah and can say it with a healing intention, in accordance with the character of the gospel. This assertion can then be made for the benefit of the Jewish people and not in order to destroy it. Once a Christian testimony like this has been uttered for a long period of time—a period that cannot yet be determined—then, one may even venture to add, the children of Israel themselves will come to understand, perhaps tacitly, perhaps joyfully, that the acts of Jesus Christ, or of his church, as "Gentiles" and in relation to the Gentiles, are acts for their benefit and vicarious acts made on their behalf. And they will understand this *without* therefore becoming Christians.[88]

Lived Reconciliation: The Handling of Guilt

It must be said that at present the Christian churches have clearly failed to take up the venture I have suggested. They are at most concerned with their first steps along a new path, after the years from 1933 to 1945, in which they for the most part kept silent when their representatives at all levels were accessories and only a few protested as inconceivable numbers of Jewish communities were persecuted and murdered. How to cope with this period and the guilt accumulated during it is a question that stands implacably at the center of reflections about the implications for the relationship between Christians and Jews of the New Testament message of reconciliation.

At the beginning of what he has to say about reconciliation in 2 Corinthians 5, Paul throws open the perspective of the reconciling acts of God: "If any one is in Christ, he is a new creation; the old has passed away, behold the new has come" (v. 17). Throughout the ages the Christian church has unquestionably lived from the assurance that this promise does not apply merely to the first period of the church but that the forgiveness of sins meant here (see 2 Cor. 5:19, 21) can be conferred anew at all times. And inasmuch as the second statement finds its equivalent in Isa. 43:18, the permanent encouragement to life lived from the promised new creation applies in a corresponding sense to the Jewish community too.

Certainly the cry "the old has passed away" is open to considerable misunderstanding. According to the biblical view there is no forgiveness of sins unless a person acknowledges his sins and therefore takes the path of repentance. But it is difficult for any individual or any community to acknowledge guilt specifically and openly. And it seems as if this would be true once more and to a special degree for the guilt of the years 1933 to 1945.

From the first days after liberation from Nazi rule down to the present day we can observe a striking phraseology, especially in confessions of sin or statements about guilt made by the official churches. For example, the frequently quoted Protestant "Stuttgart acknowledgment of guilt" of 1945[89] begins as follows:

> It is with great pain that we say that through us infinite suffering has been brought on many peoples and countries.

But the sentences that follow contrast quite remarkably with this introductory statement ("through *us infinite* suffering . . ."):

> We now say in the name of the whole church what we have often testified to our congregations: we certainly struggled for long years in the name of Jesus Christ against the spirit which found its terrible expression in the National Socialist rule of violence; but we accuse ourselves of not having confessed our faith more courageously, of not having prayed more faithfully, of not having believed more joyfully, and of not having loved more ardently.

Here, in the first place, the introduction is extremely hard to understand, for how, in the face of conformist regional churches and assenting Lutheran church leaders, can it seriously be said "in the name of the *whole* church" that "we"—that is, the whole church—"certainly struggled for long years against the spirit. . ."? Moreover the self-accusation that follows is also lacking in biblical orientation: the representatives of the "whole church" who are speaking here are indirectly testifying, through the form of their self-accusation, first that they *did* confess their faith courageously, pray faithfully, believe joyfully, and love ardently; they see themselves as guilty only because more did not happen. I have certainly no intention of casting the faintest shade of doubt on the behavior the declaration describes. We can only be grateful for everything that was actually done, and those who were born later cannot know how they themselves would have behaved. But the question remains whether *this* is the appropriate way for the church to confess its guilt, if we compare this declaration with confessions of sin in the Bible, such as Dan. 9:4–7. As has often been stressed, the Stuttgart acknowledgment of guilt does not explicitly mention the crime committed against the Jewish people. The declaration of the German Evangelical Church (EKD), made on the fortieth anniversary of the pogrom of November 9–10, 1938, which mentions the crime, is nevertheless similarly worded and goes back to this earlier Stuttgart acknowledgment.[90] A Catholic declaration of 1975 is also strikingly close to the Stuttgart confession:

> We are the country whose recent political history has been darkened by the systematic attempt to eradicate the Jewish people. And in this period of Na-

tional Socialism, we were as a whole, in spite of the exemplary behavior of individuals and groups, a church that as community continued to live *too much* with its back turned to the fate of this persecuted Jewish people, a community whose gaze was fixed *too firmly* on the threat to its institutions, and which was silent about the crimes committed against Jews and Judaism.[91]

For all its "acknowledgment of guilt and co-responsibility," a very much more serious detachment from the question of guilt is to be found in the "considerations as to ways in which the church can help towards a renewal of the relationship between Christians and Jews," which was published in 1980 by thirteen professors of theology at Bonn. Point 7 runs:

> The acknowledgment of guilt and co-responsibility [i.e., for the murderous persecution of the Jews] should not, either, misinterpret the National Socialist ideology and its crimes as Christian or as committed by Christians or the fault of Christians as such. The National Socialist ideology was just as openly un-Christian as it was anti-Christian and anti-Jewish.[92]

It is not difficult to detect the purpose behind this. Christians, theology, and the church are to be freed of culpability for what happened by way of the abstraction "Christians as such" and by putting the anti-Christian and the anti-Jewish character of Nazi ideology on the same level—which is really tantamount to a leveling down of actual events.[93] In this way the utterances in which Christians or churches, precisely "as such," thought they were obligated to tolerate, welcome, or support National Socialist endeavors were to be suppressed and consigned to oblivion.[94] This suppression may perhaps be understandable enough, but it must be resisted, for theological reasons above all. Churches that put the preaching of the *forgiveness* of sins at their center, and theologies that (like the Bonn professors in point 9 of their considerations) cannot do enough to stress the subjection of us all to sin, are doing the worst possible service to this proclamation if they are so reluctantly hesitant in what they say when they themselves are asked about guilt in the churches and the guilt of the churches. It would almost seem as if they are not prepared to trust their own gospel. Where the declaration of the Bonn theologians is concerned, the statement quoted is all the more regrettable because it is directed against a church resolution in which the matter of guilt is dealt with in a way that breaks new ground theologically.[95]

The examples we have discussed would seem to be most easily explicable theologically as manifestations of a highly questionable way of dealing with the cry "The old has passed away, behold the new has come!" The proclamation of the distance between old and new is either accepted in such a way that the declarations of guilt are played down. (We see this, for example, in church statements in which the very structure of the declarations implicitly testifies—and deliberately so—to the existing, if limited, reality of the "new creation.") Or it is so adopted that Christian guilt is suppressed—as in the Bonn statement, with its distinction between "people" or "Germans" and "Christians as such."

But the forgiveness of sins and reconciliation are quite distinct from this or any similar way of handling guilt. Where the forgiveness of guilt is promised, or where the plea to "be reconciled to God!" (2 Cor. 5:20) is heard, people are affected by the transforming power of God's word precisely because they *are* guilty, and without denying, shuffling off, or limiting that guilt. A gate of hope is broken open in the wall of guilt, and this hope confers the strength to recognize the guilt of the past but to see it also as exorcised, as it were, by this transforming assurance, so that it becomes endurable.

The connection between guilt and forgiveness is important, first, for the integrity of the people who call on God's mercy. For if the forgiveness of guilt is misunderstood as the right to suppress guilt, this means that the guilt is not accepted and that the very "forgiveness" is preventing people from being liberated from their internal mechanisms of suppressing guilt. On the other hand, the confession of guilt is the prerequisite for true liberation from the entanglements of guilt. Moreover, it ensures that whatever knowledge is implicit in the forgiveness of guilt, or can be won from that forgiveness, may be preserved and serve as orientation in the progress of history.

Second, this relation between guilt and forgiveness is just as important, if not more so, for the victims of guilt.[96] The suppression of guilt—that is, of injustice—always goes hand in hand with a suppressed awareness of the victims. But forgiveness and reconciliation are misused if the victims are no longer remembered because forgiveness of sins has been granted. Theologically speaking, people lose sight of the fact that the target of God's reconciling acts is the world—all human beings. Once this "all" is requisitioned solely on behalf of the living or the survivors, it has already been distorted. "All" does not only mean people today, it also means people yesterday and people tomorrow. But among yesterday's people are especially the victims. Where they are no longer remembered, so that the paths that led to their victimization are no longer retraced, they rise up as witnesses that the first steps along the path of reconciliation have already been taken under the banner of a sham peace. Thus, hearing and accepting reconciliation includes a recollection of the victims, both dead and surviving—a recollection that accepts guilt and guilty involvements. This is the possibility open to men and women on earth of carrying the victims with them on that path of reconciliation. In this connection it is particularly important that not merely individuals but also communities or congregations find a place for the victims in their remembrance. The crimes committed against the Jewish people in the years between 1933 and 1945, and the consequent accumulated guilt of the perpetrators, direct and indirect, as well as of the people who looked on and did nothing, are of such dimensions that the accepting recollection of individuals can meet no more than a fraction.

Both attitude and behavior are especially at stake in the context of the message of reconciliation, and both these are illuminated in sharpest outline by one of the few texts about reconciliation in the gospel traditions. Matthew 5:23–24 passes this saying down to us as Jesus' admonition on the subject: "If you are offering your gift at the altar, and there remember that your brother has something against you, leave your gift there before the altar and go; first be reconciled to your brother, and then come and offer your gift." The remembrance that is brought to bear on the guilt and works on it is the way in which the Christian churches can meet—and have to meet—this admonition of Jesus', where the victims are concerned. This is the practical application of what it means to live from the word of reconciliation in respect of the past, a past made present through the victims who have survived. Today's frequently heard appeal to make an end of remembering the victims, the injustice, and the guilt is therefore the expression of a bad conscience, not a conscience that has been reconciled. And the consequence of this appeal is that the people to whom infinite wrong was done in the past are shut out yet again.

The last text quoted from the Sermon on the Mount is to be found in a context that is of hardly less importance for the questions we are discussing here. In six antithetical sections (Matt. 5:21–48), Jesus expounds what fulfillment of the Torah (and hence righteousness) means, as behavior in accordance with God's will. The first of these antitheses may serve as example to show the trend of all the rest. The prohibition, You shall not kill, does not apply merely to the act of killing in the literal sense. More than that, the very first beginnings of a hostile attitude that finds expression in insulting words and anger are already forbidden; or rather, these beginnings are condemned as the beginning of the path that ends in murder.[97]

It is true that the interpretation of the Sermon on the Mount is disputed. Some scholars hold the view that the commands of Jesus were serious and literally meant instructions. A contrasting interpretation—which leans more heavily on the Pauline understanding of the law—maintains that the antitheses are supposed to show how incapable of fulfillment God's commandments are for human beings; they are therefore supposed to demonstrate human sinfulness. But this diverging overall view does not affect the general trend "not just . . . but already . . ." If this is really taken seriously (whether in the one sense or the other), the result has far-reaching consequences both for the way the church's history is interpreted and for its present tasks. For this cuts the ground from under the feet of every attempt to play down the involvement of Christendom, or the churches, congregations, and individual Christians "as such" (or even not "as such"), in the history of violence under National Socialism. It will also especially rebut every endeavor to resist the recognition that a thousand years of hostility toward the Jews on the part of the church was an essential precondition for the National Socialist persecution and murder of the Jews. On the contrary, in the light of Matt. 5:21–22, the churches, and their theologians especially—and most particularly those of them who write the history of the churches—must be more, if not totally, concerned to detect the first traces of a feeling of revenge or anger toward the Jewish people in the history of the Christian churches.

This search will not be able to stop short even of the New Testament, for its testimonies date from a period of sometimes violent disputes, and they are by no means free of hostile attitudes such as are condemned in the Sermon on the Mount. It is a search that can find its positive correspondence only in the attempt to find a way of theological thinking, a form of proclamation and education, and a readiness to listen, learn, and understand that make every effort to absorb what has been learned from past events and all their immediate and more remote ramifications, for the benefit of Jews, Christians, and other people.

The period into which theology and the church are therefore entering in their relationship to the Jewish people can be theologically defined only as a period of repentance,[98] or as the time of God's patient waiting for that repentance.

THE ONE WHO IS TO COME

The subjects we have just touched on have not led us away from the christological questions, although it may look like that. On the contrary, the essential step has been taken for a thematic consideration of the third christological topic that is constitutive for the New Testament: the expectation of the coming or Parousia of Jesus Christ as Israel's Messiah and the Savior of the Gentiles at the end of history.

The Parousia, the Delay of the Parousia, and Repentance

The expectation of the Parousia of Jesus Christ is so essential a component of all the New Testament testimonies that the outline of a Christology developed on the foundation of the New Testament that rests solely or principally on the "kerygma" of Jesus' cross and resurrection is a curtailment from the very outset. Rudolf Bultmann's *Theology of the New Testament* is a striking example of just such an abridgment. It shows that the leveling down of the importance of the earthly Jesus and the leveling down of the expectation of his Parousia (because of a one-sided adoption of the kerygma) go hand in hand.

A conception of this kind has far-reaching consequences. One of these is the detachment from history as events in the past: in Bultmann this makes itself felt in his theological relinquishment of the earthly Jesus[99] and in the corresponding depreciation of Israel's history, as a history of failure.[100] But another consequence is a detachment from history as future. This is made clear by the way in which Bultmann dissolves the Parousia into the present[101] and also by his estimation of the salvation of Israel (which goes together with the Parousia, according to Paul) as an expression of "speculative fantasy."[102] But for the Bible, both the Old and the New Testament, history is not simply something abstract, the content of which can be filled in at will, nor is it in essence the history of the individual. It is essentially and decisively the history of specific groups of people, Israel and the Gentiles. Consequently a concept of history for which the path of the people of Israel, past, present, and future, is no longer constitutive has hardly anything in common anymore with the biblical understanding of what history really is.[103] In the framework of this biblical understanding and its reception, however, the theme of repentance and conversion plays an outstanding role, both in the Old and New Testament, as well as in the ancient Judaism that ran parallel to that. Examples are the biblical prophets; the various conversion movements that flourished at the time of Jesus (for example, the Pharisee group, the Dead Sea community, and the group of people around Jesus of Nazareth himself); and also the great importance attached to repentance which finds expression in rabbinic Judaism, for example, in the Eighteen Benedictions or in the tradition about repentance as the second work of creation, after the Torah (b. Pesaḥim 54b). The call to repentance brings to remembrance contours of the divinely willed path of life that have been perceived in the past, but it is at the same time guidance into the future—both these things in the stage of decision that is the present. This connection between repentance and the interpretation of history leads back, first of all, in the direction hitherto taken. Here recourse to the concept of repentance is all the more pressing because the call to return to the path marked out by the will of God is particularly closely linked with the proclamation of the imminent approach of God's decisive act.

However, notwithstanding the constitutive importance of the Parousia of Jesus Christ for the Christology of the New Testament witnesses, the expectations that are linked with the cry "Our Lord, come!" (1 Cor. 16:22) or with the assurance that he will come (1 Cor. 11:26) differ individually. This is true especially of the point in time at which the rule of God or the rule of Jesus Christ is expected. As we know, the witnesses whose voices are heard in the New Testament had already grappled with the problem that the coming of the Messiah, Jesus, was considerably delayed, measured against the original expectation. When knowledge of "the day and the hour" are said to be reserved for the Father alone (Mark 13:32; Acts 1:7), this reflects the struggle with the problem on a small scale, while Luke's outline in his Gospel and in the Acts of the Apostles shows the same difficulty on a wider canvas.[104] The question of the actual time is pushed into the background, and the prolongation of that time is interpreted as the period of witness for the sake of the whole world (Acts 1:8). But whereas the theme of witness is not new but is firmly anchored in the context in which the Parousia is most imminently expected, the theme of repentance, on the other hand, maintains its central position even where the delay is perceived and felt.[105] The call to watch and to be prepared for the coming of the Son of man, as one is prepared for the always possible intrusion of the thief in the night,[106] becomes more urgent in the New Testament with the increasing delay, and it is hardly comprehensible except as encouragement to maintain the reality of the repentance that has begun. But the connection between the delay of the Parousia and repentance emerges even more clearly in 2 Pet. 3:9, where the delay of the expected end is directly traced back to the gracious intention of God who "is forbearing towards you, not wishing that any should perish but that all should reach repentance."[107] This shows yet again the relevance of the theme of repentance in the framework of the subject of the Parousia—here under the foretoken of its delay.

The One Who Has Come and the One Who Will Come: Continuity and Discontinuity

Apart, again, from the variations I have indicated, the New Testament expectation of the Parousia is the expression of a fundamental assurance: Jesus Christ, as the Messiah of Israel and the Savior of the Gentiles, does not determine past and present only, for in spite of many a dogmatic formulation, by no means everything has already been fulfilled. On the contrary, creation still groans and sighs (Rom. 8:22), "all Israel" persists in its justified no, the fullness of the Gentiles has certainly not as yet been attained, and even the community of Jesus Christ can only be described, as Rom. 8:24 tells us, as saved in the mode of hope.

This recollection of the breadth of the New Testament's spectrum of hope and expectation of the Parousia shows how much specific hope is lost if—through an existential misinterpretation—what the New Testament has to say about the future is reduced to the mere concept of the futurity of human or Christian existence. It also makes it possible to specify more closely how an outline of New Testament Christology, viewed solely in the light of the kerygma of cross and resurrection, is an inadmissible constriction of Jesus Christ himself. It is true that for the New Testament tradition the identity between the Jesus of Nazareth who was once crucified and is now raised, and the coming Son of man is the fundamental premise and the specific characteristic of all statements about Jesus. But without impugning this identity, the subject of continuity-discontinuity (which has hitherto been considered largely in the context of the discussion about the connection between the earthly Jesus and the Christ of the proclamation) faces us no less when we consider the relation between Jesus Christ as the One who has already come, and Jesus Christ as the One still to come. The discontinuity between "the come" and "the coming"—that is, the difference in kind of the Christ to come, in spite of his presupposed identity with the Jesus who has already come—can be shown without much difficulty, with the help of the various motifs we can discover in the Parousia texts. But it can already be deduced in principle from the basic expectation itself, as we meet it, for instance, in Mark 8:38.

The coming of the Son of man "in the glory of his Father with the holy angels" is an authentic borrowing of an important contemporary Jewish expectation, which was based on Daniel 7. It contrasts considerably with the ministry of Jesus Christ that is presupposed and emphasized by the Gospels. As we know, in the Gospels Jesus is seen from the outset in his unity as the earthly, crucified, and raised Jesus, so that his "kingdom," as that of the One raised, continues to bear the signature of his service in lowliness and humility. It is true that where Jesus' participation in the "glory of God," now and then, is in question, even the Gospels themselves offer different interpretations of the continuity between the One who has come and the One who is to come. Thus in the Synoptic Gospels the announcement of the coming of the Son of man "in the glory of his Father with the holy angels" is followed by the story of Jesus' transfiguration and his meeting with Moses and Elijah (Mark 9:2–9). This arrangement will hardly have been a matter of chance, and it suggests that this meeting is an intimation and prefiguration of Jesus' coming participation in God's glory and his fellowship with the "holy angels" who are expected together with him.[108] But when all is said and done, the story *is* an anticipation, and the experience it describes is esoterically limited to the disciples (Mark 9:3), the group of the "holy angels" being represented merely by Moses and Elijah. And although the command to tell no one about what they had experienced is intended to apply only until "the Son of man should have risen from the dead" (Mark 9:9), the direct vision remains a part of the past of the three disciples, and if it was subsequently relived, that was dependent on the faith of the church.

The discontinuity between now and then cannot be expressed merely through its reflection on the human level, in the distinction between faith and sight.[109] On the contrary, the distinction is also, and especially, a christological one, as can be shown by a number of other observations, which go beyond the ones already cited. For example, in his version of the saying about the coming of the Son of man, Matthew names a further feature that modifies the picture of the One who is to come when he adds, "And then he will repay every man for what he has done" (Matt. 16:27). In accordance with this, Matthew broke the link between human acknowledgment of Jesus in the present and the Son of man's acknowledgment at his coming of those who confess him. The acknowledgment of Jesus' words and of Jesus himself is not the essential point, as the evangelist has already stressed in the Sermon on the Mount (Matt. 7:21–23) and later in the picture of the last judgment (Matt. 25:36–50). What is decisive is action.

It is true that the connection between the Sermon on the Mount and the last judgment shows that for Matthew's Gospel itself there is initially continuity at this point—continuity, that is, between the teaching of the One who has come and the act of One who will come. But in view of the key position of the acknowledgment of the *kyrios* as criterion of right doctrine and true piety according to Christian understanding, Matthew's view of the Son of man, precisely *through* this continuity, on the one hand introduces something strange or unusual into this commonly accepted picture of the One expected, for what is decisive here is not whether a person acknowledges Jesus as Messiah; the essential point is how he acts. And on the other hand, even Matthew's pictures of the Son of man who has come and the Son of man who is to come are not simply congruent. The features of the Son of man are different when, at the present time, in accord with God's goodness (cf. Matt. 5:45), he lets the wheat and the tares grow together (Matt. 13:24ff, 36ff.), and when he then, as independent agent, divides the righteous from the unrighteous with the help of his angels (Matt. 13:41–43; 25:36–50). Here the ruling orientation everywhere is towards action as the determining criterion. On the basis of the Gospel itself, it potentially secures a future for all those who, like the second of the two sons in the parable in Matthew 21:28–32, say no but then do the Father's will all the same—that will which in Matthew finds its central expression in the command to love one's enemies (Matt. 5:44).

Luke offers no less cogent reasons for considering the continuity and the discontinuity between the One who has come and the One who will come. A reminder of what we have already said may be sufficient. The sufferings of Christ are the sign and token of what is earthly, realized and made present in witness, and is subject to an eschatological proviso. The future of the One to come is unlike the past and present of the One who has already come, since it is characterized by the fact that everything that God has promised through the mouth of the prophets will finally be established (Acts 3:20–21). According to Luke, this everything includes the kingdom or rule of peace for Israel, about which the disciples dream even after Jesus' resurrection. So according to Luke especially, the expected Son of man is not simply a recurrence of the One who has come, and least of all in respect of what is expected of him.[110]

We should at least touch on two further New Testament testimonies in order to expand the field of our observations.

According to Paul in 1 Corinthians 15, the crucified Jesus is characterized as being "the first fruits of those who have fallen asleep." As such he represents, *pars pro toto*, all those who will be made alive at the end of days. Until then the risen Christ, entrusted by God with plenipotentiary sovereignty, is engaged in the struggle with the powers hostile to God who seek to divide creation from its Creator. Chief among these powers is death, the last enemy. So the subjection of death is the purpose and end of the struggle (1 Cor. 15:23–26). It is identical with the resurrection of the dead or the transformation of the living at the Parousia (1 Cor. 15:50–55). In this context too the form in which the raised Christ shows himself in the present (for example, in the apostle's sufferings in patience, 2 Cor. 4:7–15) differs from the form in which he is expected as universal victor over death, in spite of the identity that is presupposed.

The difference is deepened still more if the end of the whole drama is included, as Paul defines it in 1 Cor. 15:28: "When all things are subjected to him, then the Son himself will also be subjected to him who put all things under him, that God may be everything to every one."[111] The charge of representative rule given to the crucified Jesus on the basis of his resurrection from the dead and after that resurrection corresponds to the handing back of this rule at the end of the victorious struggle with death. In this sense the Christ who rules and who struggles in the present is contrasted with the victorious Christ of the future, who will lay down that rule. The complex of ideas in this passage, in which the sole lordship of God is identified as the goal of all his ways, represents the strongest bond linking the Jewish and the Christian hope. As what Paul says shows, this bond is in no way strained to breaking point by the Christology; rather, it is confirmed in its ultimate validity.

The Book of Revelation then impressively teaches the distinction between the Messiah who has come and the Messiah who will come. This can be clearly seen, for example, if we compare Rev. 12:1–6 with Rev. 19:11–16. The two passages are linked together by the theme of the Messiah's rule over the nations. But they make him appear in two completely different forms—in the one passage as child, in the other as victorious commander.

When texts like Rev. 19:11–16 (but the other examples too) show the discontinuity between the One who has come and the One who will come, they first of all bring out the unchanged "rightness" of the biblical and Jewish expectation in its whole material character, as this is illustrated by passages such as Isa. 2:1–4. As *christological* texts they make Israel's no to Jesus as the Christ plausible, since they point to the unredeemed nature of the world. They offer room for an identity between the One who has come and the One who will come that leaves that identity uninfringed for the Christian churches, and yet, in view of the discontinuity I have demonstrated, leaves Israel free, without theological discrimination, to welcome the Messiah only when he shows himself to the people of God in the form in which he is awaited—a form that is reserved for the future and is withheld even from Christians.

If the interpretation of the Messiah's Parousia is given this outline, it is possible for the Christian churches to keep their faith in Jesus Christ as Israel's Messiah in the perspective of the future too, yet it at the same time avoids imposing on Israel in the present time the "must" of a demand for faith in the.crucified and risen Jesus. And in this way it does not infringe the identity that shows itself in the "obedient disobedience" (Karl Kupisch) of Israel's no to Jesus Christ as the Messiah who has already come. In this sense it is also possible to assent to an attempt by Hans-Joachim Schoeps to harmonize Christian and Jewish messianic expectations in a positive way, though what he has to say takes its bearings from a different viewpoint:

> Israel's messianism is directed towards what is to come, while the eschatology of the world-wide church of the Gentiles looks for the return of the One who has already come. The two are united through the common expectation that the decisive event is still ahead, as the goal of God's ways which he is pursuing with humanity, in Israel and in the church. The church of Jesus Christ has preserved no portrait of its Lord and Saviour. If Jesus were to come to-

morrow, probably no Christian would be able to recognise his face. But it could well be that the One who will come at the end of days, who is the expectation of both synagogue and church, will bear the same countenance.[112]

This is the point at which to draw attention to a surprising overlap between the Jewish and the Christian messianic hope—an overlap with a biblical foundation. As is generally known, in the tractate *Sanhedrin* X.1 (XI.1), the Mishnah has passed down a saying that is closely related to Rom. 11:26. "All Israel participates in the coming world." But it is not merely in this assurance that Paul and Jewish tradition agree. The apostle justifies his assertion in Rom. 11:26b–27 with words of Scripture. Most of them are taken from Isa. 59:20–21, and the last line from Isa. 27:9 ("when I take away their sins").

Anyone who studies the Jewish prayer book soon makes an astonishing discovery. The words from Isa. 59:20–21 with which Paul justifies the mystery of all Israel's redemption play a similarly prominent part in Jewish expectation of the future. These words are, among other things, a firm component in the daily morning prayer of Jews where, followed by Ps. 22:4, they introduce a lengthy section given the name u-ba le-Ziyyon (the words that open Isa. 59:20) and containing above all the Kedusha de-Sidra, the form of the trisagion that is prayed toward the end of the service.

The essential common characteristic of the application of the prophetic announcement in Paul and in the prayer book is that in both it is interpreted as pointing to the messianic era. In the apostle this is clear from the context. In the case of the prayer book, it emerges from the original function of the Kedusha de-Sidra and from the corresponding interpretation of Isa. 59:20 in the Babylonian Talmud.[113] The way Paul takes up Isa. 59:20 certainly differs in detail from the way it is applied in the Jewish prayer book. The apostle quotes from the Greek Bible, essentially speaking (LXX or another translation); the prayer book from the Hebrew text. Paul writes that "the Deliverer will come from Zion, he will banish ungodliness from Jacob." In the Siddur version (as in Isa. 59:20) we read that he will come for Zion and for those in Jacob who turn from transgression. Again, Paul breaks off after Isa. 59:21a ("and this will be my covenant with them") and continues with Isa. 27:9b, allowing himself in the true rabbinic way to be guided by the fact that beforehand Isa. 27:9a also talks about Jacob and the forgiveness of its godlessness. The prayer book, on the other hand, quotes Isa. 59:21 right to the end. In spite of these differences in detail, the whole biblical orientation of the hope is still linked with Isa. 59:20–21; that is to say, it is associated with the coming of the Redeemer. And the differences may be most adequately understood if they are seen *in the framework* of this common conception, and not purely antithetically. The form of the text in Paul is determined by the fact that the quotation, like the promise in Rom. 11:26, expresses the conviction that God keeps his word. He, or the Messiah, will redeem Israel-Jacob. He is faithful to his covenant and forgives all sins. The form of the text in the prayer book is closer to the Hebrew text and promises the Redeemer to those who repent and in this way prepare the way for him—whether this Redeemer is God or whether, as is more probable, he is the Messiah.

The way in which, in the context of the Kedusha de-Sidra, Israel pleads for the coming of the Redeemer and, in accordance with this prayer, lives for his coming at the present time, is brought out best by an extract from the prayer itself. The text shows how little the traditional concepts and judgments that we apply to Jewish life with the God of the patriarchs are capable of comprehending that life. It is not least for this reason that the text is also a wholesome corrective.

> And a redeemer shall come to Zion and to them that turn from transgression in Jacob, saith the Lord. And as for me, this is my covenant with them, saith the Lord: my spirit that is upon thee, and my words which I have put in thy mouth, shall not depart out of thy mouth, nor out of the mouth of thy seed, nor out of the mouth of thy seed's seed, saith the Lord, from henceforth and for ever.
>
> But thou art holy, O thou that dwellest amid the praises of Israel. And one cried unto another, and said, Holy, holy, holy is the Lord of hosts: the whole earth is full of his glory. Then a wind lifted me up, and I heard behind me the voice of a great rushing (saying), Blessed be the glory of the Lord from his place. The Lord shall reign for ever and ever.
>
> O Lord, the God of Abraham, of Isaac and of Israel, our fathers, keep this for ever as the inward thought in the heart of thy people, and direct their heart unto thee. And he, being merciful, forgiveth iniquity and destroyeth not: yea, many a time he turned his anger away, and doth not stir up all his wrath. For thou, O Lord, art good and forgiving, and abounding in lovingkindness to all them that call upon thee. Thy righteousness is an everlasting righteousness, and Thy Torah is truth. Thou wilt show truth to Jacob and lovingkindness to Abraham, according as thou hast sworn unto our fathers from the days of old. Blessed be the Lord, day by day he beareth our burden, even the God who is our salvation. (Selah.) The Lord of hosts is with us; the God of Jacob is our stronghold. (Selah.) O Lord of hosts, happy is the man who trusteth in thee. Save, Lord: may the King answer us on the day when we call.

Israel and the Church in the Light of the One Who Is to Come

To some extent the consequences of this point of view have already been indicated. They affect the Jewish people and the Christian church with equal intensity, even though in different ways.

Just because of the discontinuity I have demonstrated, Israel can be taken quite seriously in its no, and its identity is not therefore infringed. And this discontinuity permits the continued power of the shining promise that "the whole of Israel will be saved." At the same time, this promise is not separate from the assurance, equally central for both Israel and the church, that the salvation of the people of God includes the acceptance of its Messiah. If, on the Christian side, the fulfillment of Israel's hope is asserted not *contrary* to the hope that is Israel's own but in awareness of the elements of hope that Christians share with the people of God, this above all will ultimately exclude every form of misunderstanding of the promise that the whole people of God will be saved. Just as Paul's proclamation of justification by faith does not abrogate judgment according to works but includes it,[114] so, equally, we may not conclude from this promise to Israel that it will be saved because of what it does, that is, that everything it does will have a halo conferred on it. It is rather that what Paul establishes in Rom. 2:6 remains valid for the people of God as for all other human beings: that, in the words of Ps. 62:12, "God will requite every man according to his works." It is probably here that "all Israel," unlike many a Christian theologian, would assent to what the apostle says with particular emphasis. The already mentioned parallel to Rom. 11:26 in the Mishnah tractate *Sanhedrin* 10.1 (11.1) is a case in point. After proclaiming that "all Israel will participate in the coming world," the tradition immediately lists the particular children of Israel who are excluded. So this Jewish parallel confirms us in calling in question a nondialectical interpretation of the "Christian" promise in Rom. 11:26.

Because of the discontinuity we have demonstrated between the Messiah who has come and the One to come, the Christian church in its turn is led along the same path that already emerged on the basis of the proclamation of the raising of the crucified Jesus, only now from the perspective of his future. Life as people reconciled with God (which also means life as people reconciled with the unshakable and "scandalous" love of God for Israel, which aims at life and not at death) is the way in which Christians can and must witness to the identity between the Messiah who has come and the Messiah who will come. And it is surely in no other way that the church can testify to the Jewish community that the idea of a possible identity between the One who has come and the One who will come is not a reason for alarm. In Israel the plus sign used in mathematics is represented by a horizontal stroke with a vertical hook instead of the sign otherwise used all over the world, because the latter is reminiscent of a cross. Even this example makes clear how deeply seated that fear is, founded as it is on the centuries-long anti-Jewish life of the church with its "Lord." So from this aspect too the path the church of Jesus Christ has to follow in its relationship to the Jewish people can only be more closely defined as a path of repentance, which means that it is the very way the New Testament testimony envisages as necessary in both situations—for the imminent and for the far-off expectation of the Parousia.

In the face of these facts it can only be viewed as a profound misunderstanding when the revised list of preaching texts issued by the West German Evangelical Church (EKD) and the Federation of Protestant Churches in the German Democratic Republic earmarks Rom. 11:25–32 not merely for the tenth Sunday after Trinity (Israel Sunday) but also as alternative text in series 2 for a special "service of intercession for the spread of the gospel."[115] The interpretation of the relationship between the church and the Jewish people that is manifested here comes down to the conditional clause "Only when Israel believes in Jesus Christ . . ." The only support for this interpretation is its wide dissemination. The appropriation of this text at this particular place certainly betrays the realistic judgment that the church does not reckon with the Parousia in the near future, but that, to use Lukan diction, it is living in the period of witness. But when Rom. 11:25–32 is requisitioned in a missionary sense, the passage completely loses its real point, since according to Paul here the salvation of all Israel is anything but the result of endeavors on the part of the church, even endeavors taking the form of intercession for the spread of the gospel among Jews. On the contrary, Israel's redemption is clearly and unequivocally understood as God's work when "the Deliverer will come from Zion" (Rom. 11:26)—whether this phrase be a way of describing the coming of God himself or a reference to the Parousia of Jesus Christ. In the light of what has been said above, the proper place for Rom. 11:25–32 would not be as text for a sermon to be delivered at a service of intercession of the kind indicated, for that would mean that the Christian church has shifted the text out of its proper context. It would actually be appropriate as the text for a service of repentance, the theme and the context of whose intercessions would be the conversion of the Christian church in its relationship to the Jewish people. In a service of that kind—though not there only—the concepts we have already discussed would find a central place, the ideas, that is, which we considered under the headings of remembrance, guilt, and the forgiveness of guilt.

The Christological Consequences of the Delay of the Parousia

Here it emerges once more that repentance aims at specific consequences, and this comes out in all its indispensability and urgency from christological reflections that, in their turn, result from observations about the Parousia and the delay of the Parousia.

Paul's christological summary in 1 Cor. 15:20–28, which we have already glanced at, teaches that the crucified and raised Jesus has been entrusted by God with plenipotentiary rule, so that in the period between his resurrection and the final end of this world he may conquer the powers opposed to God, and especially death. According to the apostle, this period will be extremely short—he himself reckons with at most a single generation, considerably less rather than more. The reactions of the early congregations and their teachers when the Parousia failed to materialize took varied forms, as we can see from what they taught, preached, and did. But at all events an understanding of Christ won acceptance in the patristic church, which grasping the nettle, in a sense made a virtue of necessity. We already frequently find the beginnings of this approach in the New Testament, for example in Colossians and Ephesians, or in the Gospel of John. A movement began in Christian thought and belief that ascribed increasing power to Jesus Christ and made the lowliness of the Son a phase belonging to the past. The picture of Christ as Pantocrator that we find in the eastern church is as indicative of this as is the denial of Paul's proclamation of the end of Christ's lordship at the Council of Constantinople a good three hundred years later.

In contrast to this christological process, the conclusion drawn about the reason for the delay of the Parousia would seem to be much more plausible: the struggle of the crucified and raised Jesus against the powers hostile to God is much more difficult and prolonged than was originally believed. Here the raised Christ really continues to bear the features of the powerless, earthly, and crucified Jesus. He struggles and, what is more, the struggle is still an open one. His "sphere of sovereignty" is identical with the space occupied by his adherents. But if one tries to determine who he is as "ruler," in relation to the throng of those who are his people, then the inappropriateness, indeed inapplicability, of the common concept of rule emerges at once: "For the Son of man came not to be served but to serve, and to give his life as a ransom for many." And even if this is the formulation of the evangelist Mark (10:45), the statements in 1 Corinthians 15 can hardly be more adequately described than through this saying, since according to this chapter of Paul's on the resurrection, the life of the raised Jesus is at the *service* of the kingdom of God and the liberation of men and women.

At the beginning of the present section on Christology, it was said that this service can be described as a continual search for the lost. At the time of his earthly ministry Jesus needed the disciples, for his mission and for his own sake. And now as then, today and tomorrow, he needs the community of his people, for whom and through whom his service is fulfilled. So Abraham Heschel's insight that God needs man,[116] which I stressed at the beginning, is also true of Jesus Christ in relation to his church.

Matthew's Gospel teaches us to perceive a further correspondence as well. On the one hand, more emphatically than almost any other New Testament writing, it promises that Jesus will be present in the community of his people,[117] and on the other hand, again like hardly any other New Testament writing, it stresses the free independence of the disciples in what they do, and the importance of their actions.[118] Paul van Buren tried to define God's relationship to human beings very similarly, as he entered into the Jewish struggle for God after the Holocaust.[119] These correspondences can surely be adequately understood only as clues to the enduring interdependence of the God of Israel and Jesus Christ. The God of Israel reveals Jesus Christ to the Christian church, and Christ reveals the God of Israel to the church. In this sense, for the church Jesus Christ *represents* the God of Abraham, Isaac, and Jacob-Israel. We can also say that in this sense he is the presence (*shekhinah*) of the God of Israel in the Christian community. And in this perspective the title Son of God also acquires full harmony.

What has been said up to now may therefore be summed up as follows. The delay of the Parousia does not as a whole corroborate the ideas about Jesus Christ that continually ascribe to him more and more of everything that was originally expected only in the future. On the contrary, it confirms the ways of interpretation that, like Paul, take their bearings from the crucified One and, like the Gospels, are oriented toward the earthly Jesus. Following these witnesses—and in view of the still greater prolongation of time—these interpretations develop even more keenly, if possible, the way in which Jesus Christ participates in this world.

In recent theological history (in spite of the central importance it gives to the "word of the cross"), this participation has been less thoroughly thought through by Rudolf Bultmann and his school (with the exception of Ernst Käsemann) than by Karl Barth and his pupils, but it was emphasized by Dietrich Bonhoeffer more than by either group, even though he was not permitted to develop the approaches he recorded as one would have wished. But the basic outline of these approaches is clear enough. Particularly in the years of his imprisonment, Bonhoeffer moved purposefully in the direction of the Old Testament, allowing himself to be led by it into a "this worldly" approach that was in conformity with his own experience of the reality of suffering.[120] Hand in hand with this experience went the key word of participation in God's sufferings in this world—a concept that for him became of constitutive importance.[121] At the same time Bonhoeffer was one of the few people who remembered God's people of Israel when its persecution by the Nazis began.[122] And we have him to thank for the development of that christological and ecclesiological definition of "Christ existent as the community of his people"[123] which has, perhaps unjustly, receded into the background. It is true that the formula can be interpreted in such a way that the difference between Jesus Christ, as the foundation of the church, and the church itself is blurred.[124] On the other hand—and this is where the phrase, essentially speaking, proves so helpful—it brings out more than any other definition that every statement about Jesus Christ is a statement about his church and every statement about his church is a statement about Christ himself. It therefore makes it impossible for the church to acknowledge anything in Jesus Christ to which it does not itself testify *as* Christ's body, and hence in bodily obedience—praying, proclaiming, teaching, and acting.[125] All the approaches I have mentioned belong closely together in substance and find common expression in Bonhoeffer's well-known answer to the question, What has the church of Christ to do in the present?—his answer being, To pray and to do what is right among men and women.[126] Through this specific precept, with these approaches, and in the light of the path he himself followed, Bonhoeffer was able to offer points of orientation, especially in Protestant theology and the Protestant churches, for the way of repentance in the patience of God, with the goal of a different relationship between the church of Jesus Christ and the Jewish people.[127]

THE CENTER OF THE GOSPEL IN THE
CHRISTIAN-JEWISH RELATIONSHIP: THE
CONFESSION OF ONE WHO HAS BEEN RECONCILED

It would go too far if we were to sum up finally, and without justifiable abridgment, all the manifold aspects touched on in this extensive christological section. Instead, and as representing such a summary, let me in this context stress one theme, in the form of a variation—the theme which may perhaps be called the decisively important subject of the complex we have been considering.

Before Paul turns in Romans 9—11 to his development of the relationship of the church of Jesus Christ to the Israel that does not believe in the gospel, he closes what he has said hitherto in his letter with a passage that sounds like a hymn. At the end of it he expresses the assurance given by the gospel in the following words: "For I am sure that neither death, nor life, nor angels, nor principalities, nor things present, nor things to come, nor powers, nor height, nor depth, nor anything else in all creation, will be able to separate us from the love of God in Christ Jesus our Lord" (Rom. 8:38–39). The love of God in Jesus Christ, or even the love of Christ directly, is, according to Paul, the reality that brings about reconciliation with God.[128] Consequently, the passage I have quoted must be termed quite precise, theologically, as the confession of faith of someone who has been reconciled with God through Jesus Christ. In Romans 9—11 Paul demonstrates in the light of the same gospel that Israel's existence is enduringly founded on the love of God. In saying this he testifies that the certainty of the person who is reconciled with God through the gospel includes what we might express in the apostle's own words, in the following variant: "For I am sure that neither death, nor life . . . can separate all Israel from the love of God in Christ Jesus."[129] This includes everything the Christian church has laid upon it in its relationship to the Jewish people—everything that, on its way, it has to learn and to teach, to do and to proclaim.

4

Israel's Presence in the Church
The Jewish Christians

The Gospel of John passes down to us a saying of Jesus in which, referring to himself, he maintains that "salvation comes of the Jews"—not, that is, from the Samaritans or any other nation (John 4:22). In view of such vicious attacks as John 8:44, it would seem doubtful whether in the Fourth Gospel itself this sentence is really grasped sufficiently as a corrective to anti-Jewish statements. But there is no doubt, at all events, that for most of its history the Christian church has not taken the saying nearly enough to heart. Generally speaking, where the saying is remembered theologically at all, it is understood christologically, as it is in the Gospel of John, as a pointer to Jesus' Jewish origin. Yet it applies no less in the ecclesiological sense. Right down to the present day, the Christian church is indebted for its existence to the host of Jews who were the first to pass on the gospel, that is to say, the power for salvation (Rom. 1:16). In this sense too, John 4:22 has enduring validity. But we have, of course, to ask whether the ecclesiological dimension of the saying is exhausted by this historical reminiscence. The question is all the more pressing because the company of Jews who believe in the gospel—that is, the Jewish Christians (or the messianic Jews, as those of them who are Protestants increasingly term themselves)[1]—have in our century become for the churches a reality with unmistakable contours, since they have shared the same path of suffering as the Jewish people as a whole.

ISRAEL'S SHARED PATH

Nazi persecution of the Jews who were citizens of Germany started up fairly soon after Hitler came to power and included Christians who were Jewish in origin. From the time of the pseudo-racist Nuremberg Decrees until they were transported into the Nazi murder camps in the forties, these people were forcibly incorporated into a fellowship of suffering and death with the Jewish people to whom they originally belonged. The reactions of their fellow Christians were divided. On the one hand, individuals (or even whole movements, like the Confessing Church, by way of the "Büro Grüber") helped their persecuted Christian brothers and sisters. But on the other hand, whole regional churches (for example in Thuringia, Saxony, Nassau-Hesse, Mecklenburg, Schleswig-Holstein, Anhalt, and Lübeck) closed their doors against these persecuted men and women.[2]

This experience was one of the main reasons many Jewish Christians became aware for the first time, or at least actively so, that they had a special relationship to God's people of Israel. And it was this that caused them to acknowledge their enduring affiliation to the Jewish people, even as Christians. Of course from the Jewish side, Jewish Christians being regarded as apostates, have ceased to count as a legitimate part of the people ever since the beginning of the second century. Nevertheless, in recent history there have been some paradoxical correspondences. Contrary to the intention of its perpetrators, the persecution and murder of Jewish communities in Europe by the Nazis contributed to the foundation and worldwide recognition of the state of Israel in 1948. Equally paradoxically, murderous persecution and the constitution of this new state then played an essential part in developing an awareness of the Jewishness of Jesus of Nazareth among Christians in Germany and among Jews in the land of Israel.[3] Not least, persecution also led to a strengthening, or to the new birth, of the sense of identity among Jews belonging to the Christian church. And this is true both in the subjective sense of their own self-understanding[4] and in objective and clearly manifest circumstances.

This is most evident from the way in which Jewish Christians play their part in the de facto existence of the state of Israel. It is true that there were Jewish Christian groups in the country even before the founding of the state. But since 1948 the Christian churches have had to come to terms with the fact that, for the first time in almost two thousand years, there are Jewish Christian congregations in the land of Israel (however small and varied in their orientation they may be) who see themselves as part of the state of Israel and hence as belonging within the Jewish context, which they themselves share as far as they can.[5]

The theological significance of these events can hardly be overestimated. Ever since the early period of the church, Jews who came to believe in Jesus Christ were thereupon excluded from the synagogue and practically compelled to give up their Jewish existence unless, indeed, they joined one of the soon ostracized Jewish Christian fringe groups. From the second century onward, the Christian congregations increasingly took their character from gentile Christians and no longer offered any opportunities for "a Jewish life in the bosom of the church."[6] To develop any opportunities of this kind in the context of the Diaspora, in churches that are gentile in provenience, is in any case extremely difficult if not impossible, unless here too purely Jewish Christian congregations are to be formed. But at its meeting in Budapest in 1937, the International Hebrew Christian Alliance, founded in London in 1925, rejected the notion of an independent Jewish Christian church in the Diaspora. It undoubtedly did so for well-considered theological reasons, seeing its own task as the attempt to give effect to the special aspects of the Jewish Christian testimony in the framework of the existing churches, witnessing both to these churches themselves and to Israel.[7] However, I mention this at the moment merely in passing. More important in our present context is the fact that since the founding of the state of Israel, the churches have been confronted, after almost two thousand years, with the fact of Jewish Christian congregations that, first of all, will not permit themselves to be brushed aside wholesale as sects (as was the fate of the successors of the first church); that, second, see themselves both as a part of the Jewish people and as a church of Jesus Christ; and that, third, confute the judgment that Jewish Christianity "was only possible as a phenomenon which, though indispensable, was also restricted to its unique historical function."[8]

THE ROOTS OF THE CHURCH

This new awareness does not suit the views either of Christian theology and the church or of the state of Israel. In accordance with a Jewish tradition going back to the end of the first century,[9] the state of Israel does not recognize Jewish Christians as Jews. It grants them Jewish citizenship in the same way that it does non-Jews who apply for it. Yet for theology and the church since about the same period, Jewish Christianity that is not assimilated to the Christianity of the Gentiles has ceased to exist as a theologically important factor. It is seen only in the perspective of sectaranianism or as a forgotten, indeed often an annoying, minority.[10] As *Jewish* Christians—that is, as Jews who believe in Jesus without thereby ceasing to belong to the Jewish people—they seem to be wanted by no one, neither Israel nor the church.[11]

Of course in saying this about the church I am not talking about a superficial tolerance or about material support for Jewish Christian congregations. But whether the churches really want these people—whether, that is, they see these Jewish Christians as a significant part of themselves—will be decided only as an answer to the question, Are they prepared to accept the theological thinking of the Jewish Christian groups in Israel and in the Diaspora, which in part deviates considerably from traditional dogmas? And are they prepared to see it as a corrective to their own theological views, particularly with regard to Christology and the Torah? How long the road ahead here still is, is shown by the difficulties the Jewish Christian groups have to face when they try to deepen the Jewish side of their worship and liturgical life free from objections from the gentile Christian side.[12]

The purpose here can by no means be to consider all Jewish Christian viewpoints as inviolable simply because they *are* Jewish Christian views. Nor can our aim be to applaud when Jewish Christian groups display an almost fanatical missionary zeal (as is evidently the case here and there in the United States). Like its gentile Christian equivalent in past years (and sometimes even today) this kind of zeal destroys more than it builds up.[13] But apart from any given contemporary situation and discussion, the church does have every reason, for its own sake and for the sake of the gospel, to be alive to the fundamental importance of its Jewish Christian section in the Diaspora and in the land of Israel. Without this awareness—to name only one result—the New Testament, which Martin Kähler called the "charter of the preaching on which the church is based," will remain closed to theology and the church in spite of all the scholarly work devoted to it, particularly where Israel as a whole is concerned.

We must look at three reasons, in particular, for the importance of this section of the church. These reasons differ in weight, but they are related in substance.

1. The first factor to be mentioned has already been touched on, but we must now define it more closely. The nucleus or matrix of the church after Easter was the Jewish community of Jesus in Jerusalem. This grew up out of the group of his adherents soon after his death, in the certainty of his resurrection and in the expectation of his Parousia. Moved by the One who the earthly Jesus was and who he remains as the One who, faith claims, has been raised, this group continued what Jesus had performed vicariously for Israel in his search for the lost. Because of its witness, this group drew new members. They came from the world of the Diaspora, but they were still Jews. At other times too, the land of Israel and the Diaspora have held different views in some matters, even while belonging together in principle. And here also, in the first, rapidly growing congregation, conflicts arose. Soon there were two "original" congregations, the one gathered round Peter, the other round Stephen, a Jew from the Diaspora.[14] In Stephen's congregation there began to be a glimmer of an insight that what Jesus had told them to do led beyond Israel's frontiers into the gentile world. It was members of this group who, after they had been driven out of Jerusalem, began to preach the gospel among the Gentiles. At the council of the apostles held in Jerusalem (probably in the year 48) the question whether Gentiles were bound to the ritual obligations of the Torah was discussed and decided in a group consisting almost exclusively of Jewish Christians. There James, Peter, and John (Jews from Jerusalem) with Paul and Barnabas (Jews from Antioch) sealed an agreement: Christians from Jerusalem were to be entrusted with the proclamation of the "gospel to the circumcised," Christians from Antioch with the preaching of the "gospel to the noncircumcised" (Gal. 2:6–10).

This is not the place to discuss problematical aspects of the decision taken at Jerusalem. But we must remember its fundamental importance for both sides. The Gentiles who believe the gospel are as such—that is, in their very difference—part of the church of Jesus. And the Jews who trust in the gospel are, also as such, part of the church of Jesus—that is, in their ties with the Torah, which are thereby recognized. So on the evidence of this decision, the church in the comprehensive sense was intended to consist of both Israel *and* the Gentiles. On the one hand, the council of the apostles legitimates the turn to the Gentiles as part of Jesus' commission, but conversely, the council also testifies that the Gentiles' bond with Israel is indissoluble, in the form of the enduring bond with the community of Jesus in the land of Israel. Israel and the Gentiles, each with its own identity, form a single unity in the framework of the church of Jesus.

These decisively important aspects of early Christian history make plain the Jewish provenience of much that is all too easily appropriated as "Christian" in the general sense: the living stones that go to make up the structure of the church of Jesus in the initial period, both in the land of Israel and in the Diaspora, are *Jews* who believe in Jesus. In common parlance they are Jewish Christians—messianic Jews, according to the term that is increasingly winning acceptance. They are the ecclesiological bridge joining Israel and the Gentiles, the lack of which is unimaginable. And they have the specific task of witnessing to and emphasizing, in the light of the gospel especially, the indissoluble bond between the two.[15]

2. The Jewish Christian impress on the church's origins is by no means restricted to its preliterary beginnings, as it were, up to the council of the apostles. The earliest of the New Testament writings, the first letter written by the Jewish Christian Paul to the Thessalonians, belongs to the period immediately following the council. And what is true of that, may be said of all or nearly all the New Testament writings: they go back to Jewish Christian authors or editors. Their intellectual positions certainly vary in detail. Furthermore, these are testimonies by writers coming from the Jewish Christian Diaspora: Jewish Christian traditions from the land of Israel are only tangibly present as components, in the Gospels especially. But necessary though these differentiations are, they do not alter the fact that the signature of the proclamation that was the foundation of the church and—in view of the authoritative status of the New Testament—still provides its norm, is Jewish Christian throughout.

And yet it must be said that the unremitting encounter with the deliberately affirmed testimonies by Jewish Christians, in the form of the canonical texts of the New Testament, has not saved theology and the church from a highly questionable relationship to this part of the community of Jesus. On the contrary, the patristic church "commandeered" the Old Testament, thereby severing it from the people who gave it birth. And in the same way the reception of the New Testament writings was such that they were successively detached from the original Jewish messengers of the gospel. By the turn of the second century at latest, the little Jewish Christian groups who still remained in the land of Israel and its adjoining territories were branded as heretics by the growing mainstream church in Rome[16] because they were faithful to the Torah, even though this faithfulness was by no means unified.

Since then the constitutive position of the Jewish Christians has been largely a matter of historical reminiscence associated with the first years of the church. Nothing is so surprising for many Christians as to learn that there are still Jewish Christians at the present day who see themselves not as Christians in the usual sense but actually as *Jewish* Christians. And yet the Jewish Christian dimension of the church is not merely a historical relic from the initial period, nor is it simply the historical signature of the canonical writings. On the contrary, Jewish Christians are still at the present day a part of the church of Jesus Christ. And because of this fact, that part of the New Testament writings which delineates the permanent importance of this group in the church of Jesus both for the church itself and for Israel is particularly important. And here I am again referring to Romans 9—11.

3. In his struggle against the specifically gentile and gentile Christian arrogance that declares that Israel has lost its election, the first fact Paul mentions as argument to confute this hybrid view is the existence of Jewish Christians, and himself above all: "Has God rejected his people? By no means! I myself am an Israelite. . . ." (Rom. 11:1–2), like other Jews who have come to believe in the gospel. Just because this group represents Israel's promised "remnant," there can be no question of God's having rejected his people. But the thing that makes Paul's exposition specifically his own is that, unlike many later commentators, he does not content himself with this "remnant." On the foundation of the gospel he preaches, he sees the remnant rather as the beginning of the whole of Israel, just as Jesus Christ himself is the "first fruits." So according to Paul, there really are two Israels in a certain sense. But it is not a matter of the "false" and the "true" Israel.[17] Rather, the division is between Israel as the holy remnant (the Jewish Christians) and the "others." But the two are so closely related to each other that strictly speaking it is only possible to talk about *one* Israel, though within that unity these two groups have to be distinguished for the period of time that will elapse before the end. The "remnant" is not the end. It is Israel's eschatological beginning, the guarantee of the promised enduring participation of the whole in the eschatological end that God is going to bring about: "If the dough offered as first fruits is holy, so is the whole lump; if the root is holy, so are the branches" (Rom. 11:16).

This interpretation of what Paul says as referring to the Jewish Christians, and in so far to Israel, probably best represents the meaning of the passage. It is unambiguous, on the one hand; on the other, it is open-ended. Inasmuch as the Jewish Christians—the "eschatological remnant"—are treated by Paul in the context of the biblical promises, they themselves are the root through which a relationship can be traced back as far as Abraham. Inasmuch as, through Jesus Christ, they are constituted as eschatological remnant they are, as root, for their part indissolubly embedded in him. But inasmuch as they represent the beginning of the "all Israel" of the end time, this eschatological Israel belongs potentially within the Jewish Christians, as root. It is only this complex and suggestive interpretation of "dough" and "Israel" as pointing to the Jewish Christians that does full justice, ultimately, to the whole trend of Romans 11, to which Paul, in turn, has led up in Romans 9—10. In Rom. 11:1ff.—by pointing to the existence of the "remnant"—he repudiates the assertion that God's people of Israel have been rejected; in Rom. 11:26 he leads over to the promise that "all Israel" will be saved. The statements in 11:16 that I have just quoted provide the link between the two passages. So the existence of the remnant is also in this sense a refutation of the rejection thesis, since this remnant, as earnest, pledge, or first fruits, is the guarantee that the whole of Israel will be saved. There can therefore be no question of a supplanting of God's people, either on a small scale or generally.

This close connection between Jewish Christians and the Jewish people as a whole has emerged historically at very different periods. But it has made itself felt not in the form of promise, as in Romans 11, but in the guise of oppression. We have already touched on the persecutions of Jewish Christians during the Nazi era. But examples go back to the early history of the church. After the destruction of Jerusalem in 70 A.D., Christian estrangement from the Jewish people went hand in hand with a gradual separation from the Jewish Christians. In the eyes of a Jewish Christian belonging to our own time, the development of the church that began at that period looks as follows. The Jewish Christian, he writes,

> looks on appalled and astonished as very soon "his brethren, his kinsmen by race" (Rom. 9:3), the Jewish-Christian "Nazorim" [Nazarenes], continually decreased in numbers, were misunderstood and oppressed by the "Christianoi" [Christians] from other nations who were now in the majority—indeed that the Jewish Christians were actually expelled from the church as heretics. And that later this Gentile Christian majority neither understood nor spoke "the voice of Jacob." Instead—from at least about 120 A.D. onwards—they believed and proclaimed: "The Jews alone are responsible for the suffering and death of Jesus Christ; the Jews, all members of their people and all generations, are stained with the innocent blood of Jesus Christ. The Jews are therefore eternally rejected and cursed. They are now merely a memorial to the wrath of God, evil men, inferior, worthless life, given over to the devil and his angels. All the promises of the Holy Scriptures, the Old and the New Testament both, now belong to the church of Christ. Now only the punishments, threats, and curses are left to the Jews." So, when the Jewish Christian considers the church which has become so full of hate and so lacking in love (and thus so un-Christian), what can he do but think: "The voice is Jacob's voice, but the hands (the nature) are the hands of Esau" (Gen. 27:22)?[18]

THE CHALLENGE TO THE CHURCH

If we take our bearings from what the apostle says in Romans 11, we can only see in this development a radical uprooting of the church, in the period of a single century after its genesis. Tested against Paul's gospel, on which Protestant theology and the Protestant churches lean so heavily, the consequences can hardly be exaggerated: everyone knows the fate of uprooted trees. If we drop the metaphor, we can also describe what happened with the help of the definition of the relationship between gentile Christians and the Jewish Christians in Jerusalem that Paul gives a little later, in Romans 15:27, which is along the same lines: "For if the Gentiles [gentile Christians] have come to share in their [the Jerusalem Christians'] spiritual blessings, they ought also to be of service to them in material blessings." Here Paul stresses where God's gifts for the Gentiles still have their ecclesiological origin; and in doing this he goes so far as to use the profoundly significant term "the gifts of the Spirit." For the apostle, therefore, a purely gentile church, existing for itself and out of itself, without a Jewish Christian section, would quite simply be not conceivable, let alone theologically tenable. Rather, according to his gospel and to the Bible in general, with its clear "Israel *and* the Gentiles," it would be an utterly heretical body. If, in spite of his warning, Paul had ever heard talk about the end of Jewish Christianity, or about the end of the "remnant of Israel" or of "all Israel," he would undoubtedly have spoken about the end of the church (cf. Rom. 11:21–22), and he would have done so with the same vehemence with which, in Rom. 11:1–2, he counters the assertion that God's people has been rejected.

So the church of Jesus Christ has every reason to be grateful that, in individual cases in the Diaspora and in little groups in the land of Israel, there are still Jewish Christians as a sign of God's faithfulness[19]— and especially his faithfulness toward the church itself. And it has every occasion to help to bear, and to overcome, the loneliness that is a "heavy cross" lying on the Jewish Christians. It is a cross in a double sense, for while among his own people the Jewish Christian counts as a renegade, "among his new brothers in faith" he is viewed "very often either as 'a judaizer' or as 'a heretic.' "[20] But just because of this isolation toward both sides and because at the same time the church's attitude to the Jewish Christians is inextricably linked with its attitude to the Jewish people as a whole, attempts to arrive at a new relationship to Jewish Christians and to "all Israel" cannot be separated from each other. Examples from the period of persecution under the Nazis teach us that where Christians (and especially the Jewish Christians among them) advocate and work for a sound and healing attitude to (other) members of the Jewish community, the Jewish community also becomes more open-minded towards its former members as well, and the odium of apostasy begins to disappear.[21]

To see and understand these things is certainly no more than a first step. The more central question is whether (gentile Christian) theology and the church really live *with* the Jewish Christian section of the community of Jesus, instead of regarding it as a prop for absolutist claims that have become questionable.[22] The attitude that genuinely exists will show itself in preparedness to listen to Jewish Christian testimony *in* the Christian church and in a readiness to allow this testimony to call in question the form of Christian doctrine that has for so many centuries been molded exclusively by gentile Christians.

In this respect the signs of the times are not very propitious. For example, the opinion has recently been voiced that the assertion in the synodal resolution of the church of the Rhineland that Jesus Christ is

"Israel's Messiah" is not a christological acknowledgment that is in line with the gospel—indeed that it is "quite simply false."[23] This judgment amounts in substance to a rejection of the Jewish Christian testimony and confession of faith. For this testimony lives precisely from the assurance that Jesus is Israel's Messiah and is as such, at the same time, the Savior of the Gentiles. Without this assurance, fellowship with Christians from the church of the Gentiles would be quite simply impossible for a Jewish Christian, as far as one can see. For the Jesus Christ testified to by Jewish Christians and by Gentiles would scarcely be the same. Consequently this judgment or protest is merely the symptom of the age-old view that Jewish Christians must assimilate themselves to Gentiles—not that, through their own witness, they must offer a corrective to nonbiblical manifestations of the gentile Christian gospel. But contrary to this prevalent view, the purpose and priority of the gentile churches can only be not to abolish the Jewish Christian identity but actually to help the disputed, assailed and (in the sense I have suggested) isolated representatives of Israel in the church of Jesus Christ to *develop* their own identity, for their own sakes, for the sake of Christians from the gentile nations, and for the sake of Israel.

—It will be for their own sakes because, from the point of view of the gospel, they are and should be *as Jews* a part of the church of Jesus Christ.

—It will be for the sake of the Gentiles, because without the Jewish Christian section of the church, they will be cut off from the roots that nourish them in the ecclesiological sense.

—It will be for Israel's sake, because the Jewish Christians, to the extent to which they are true to the gospel, as friends of Israel *and* the Gentiles, witness first of all to what the gospel proclaims as a reality (or the beginning of a reality): the establishment of peace between God's people and the Gentiles, though it is true that the church has all too often made this a utopia.

DIMENSIONS OF THE JEWISH
CHRISTIAN TESTIMONY

This brings us once more to a group of questions that are particularly disputed today and that may be summed up under the headings "witness" and "mission." [24]

The New Testament certainly does not envisage a gentile Christian mission to the Jews. But its writings undoubtedly assume that the gospel is going to be proclaimed among Jews by Jewish Christians. In the light of the New Testament, therefore, this proclamation can be basically justified. But in this context particularly we have to remember the changed circumstances of our own time.

In the first place, it must be said that mission today is to an encouraging degree no longer what it was for many centuries—the expression of a Christian imperialism that was all too often bound up with political colonialism. On the contrary, service and the dialogue that respects the partner's identity have become the essential media of Christian testimony, the motivation being to a considerable degree insight into the need for material help.

Second, the direct relationship between the Christian church and the Jewish people has taken on a form in at least some sections of the church in recent years that is simply not comparable with anything in the New Testament period. This change was triggered by the crimes of Jewish persecution and murder in the Nazi period. The deepest expression of the new relationship are the services of worship in which Christians and Jews occasionally share—for example, in the framework of the general assemblies of the German churches (the *Katholikentage* and the Protestant *Kirchentage*). These can certainly not be viewed as typical of the general relationship between the Christian church and the Jewish people today. But, compared with earlier times, the recognition that synagogue and church share common ground in spite of what divides them has grown considerably.[25]

Facts like these indicate the inappropriate and dubious nature of some of the usual categories and terms used to describe the relationship between Christians and Jews. All the same, the on-going dispute about mission or dialogue shows that in the background other questions still play a role, at least in a more far-reaching sense. One example may serve to make this clear.

Excursus: The Allegedly Exclusive Nature of Salvation in Jesus Christ

Today, the essential point of dissension between supporters of the "mission to the Jews" and supporters of "dialogue" is hardly the question of witness, for this is for both sides the constitutive element of both Christian *and* Jewish existence,[26] even if the stress may be placed differently by Jews and Christians. The distinction that divides the two standpoints is connected with the "absolutist" claim, or the question about the exclusive nature of salvation in Jesus Christ. Arnulf H. Baumann quite rightly stressed this in a recent book deserving of serious consideration.[27] Baumann distinguishes between an appropriate and an inappropriate use of the term "absolute." His diagnosis is as follows:

"The whole biblical heritage and the extrabiblical Jewish tradition were absorbed into, combined and concentrated in the confession of faith in Jesus as the Messiah. All this found expression in the expansion and rounding off of the Bible through the New Testament, in the calendar of Christian Sundays and feast days, and in Christian worship. Everything was directed toward the central acknowledgment of Jesus Christ.

"It is from this point that I see the solution. The error is not the confession that 'there is salvation in no one else' except Jesus Christ (Acts 4:12). Confessions of faith are by their very nature unequivocal and tend toward exclusiveness. They cannot content themselves with a 'both—and.'

"The error is that the absolute confession of faith in Jesus as the Messiah was turned into the absolutist claim of Christianity: the church, that is, put itself in the place of her Lord. This being so, every refusal to join the ranks of Christianity appeared to be an attack on Christ. There is no doubt that this aberration has to be viewed in the context of the development of the Christian faith into the state religion in the patristic period."[28]

Baumann's conclusions include such important viewpoints that they are deserving of full quotation:

"Today—partly because we are still suffering from the shock of the Holocaust—we are in the process of extricating ourselves from the Constantinian era and its structure of thinking, in which Christianity and power were linked and Christian theology came clothed in the garment of triumphalism. If we are totally serious in our recognition that all mission proceeds from God, that it is not we who are the instigators of mission but God himself, and that the salvation and damnation of other people are not ours to decide, then we can testify to our faith in Jesus as Messiah to Jews too, without infringing their self-respect. If we are totally serious in saying that Christianity too is still living in the expectation of the full and perfect manifestation of God, then we can bear it when Jews counter our absolute acknowledgment of Jesus Christ with their equally absolute acknowledgment of the Torah as their way of access to the Father. We can quietly leave it to God to decide what he is going to make of the testimony of Christians and Jews. The result will be the conversion of individual seekers, and a changed relationship between Christianity and Judaism as a whole, which will not permit them to go on seeing one another as mutually exclusive antitheses.

"No Jew needs to feel threatened by a testimony to Christ interpreted in this way. He is free to accept it or to stick to his own confession of faith. But no Christian need fear either that through a testimony to Christ interpreted in this way the heart of his faith will be obscured or enfeebled, because of the Christian-Jewish dialogue. On the contrary, through an encounter which leaves room for the efficacy of the Spirit of God, Christians and Jews will be led into the depths of their own self-understanding and their own testimony of faith."[29]

Of course it is also worthwhile considering the implications of Baumann's remarks more closely. What is the relation between the absolutist confession of faith, on the one hand, with its exclusive insistence that there is "salvation in no one else" (and that this is true not only for the people who make that confession but for everyone) and, on the other, the expected and hoped-for change that will ensure that Jews and Christians will *not* see themselves as "mutually exclusive antitheses [sic]"? This change would really again put a heavy question mark against the exclusive claim already mentioned.

There is another serious point as well. Baumann first contrasts "absolute acknowledgment of Jesus Christ" by Christians with "absolute acknowledgment of the Torah" by Jews. But these positions are not as symmetrical as he seems to believe. For, unlike the Christian confession, the Jewish "absolute acknowledgment" has a gap, a salutary openness. Ever since the period of rabbinic Judaism, there has been an accepted teaching about the "righteous among the Gentiles": because of their righteousness, these Gentiles will participate in the world to come.[30] Jewish tradition, that is to say, contains a "retarding" aspect that prevents statements about Israel's salvation from necessarily becoming unbridled statements about the damnation of the Gentiles.

There is nothing comparable to this in Christian dogmatics. The occasional reference to the saying in John 3:6, that the Spirit blows where it will, could possibly indicate a similar openness, but it would then of course have to be interpreted against the grain of the whole passage and contrary also to the whole Johannine conception (cf. John 14:6). But in discussion the very people who point to John 3:6 are generally the ones who are least of all prepared to take any such step.

A genuine correspondence, on the other hand, can be found in Jesus' differentiation between sinners and the righteous in Israel. This differentiation is fundamental to our present investigation and has already been expounded at some length, so we need do no more than refer to it here. It leaves room for the discipleship of Jesus and for confession of faith in him, but it does not simultaneously evoke the danger of an implicit or explicit absolutism that denies "salvation" to other people in toto (even if perhaps in varying degrees) unless they share the presuppositions of one's own faith. For, emphatically though we may agree with Baumann's final sentences, if "the acknowledgment of the exclusiveness of salvation in Jesus Christ"[31] is not confined to the confessing individual or congregation but if this exclusiveness becomes the subject of doctrine or proclamation, then the first, fateful step has inevitably been taken in the very direction Baumann would rightly like to see closed: toward the decision (which can in actual fact only mean the judgment) about the "salvation and damnation of other people."

In an addendum to the second edition of his book (1983, pp. 34–35), Baumann does indeed go into the questions raised here. But his responses do not reflect the differentiated form in which the questions are asked. It is not merely a matter of avoiding an "insult to" or "denigration of" other people, as Baumann thinks. The real question is, What assertion is being made about Judaism if one does not merely *acknowledge* the "exclusiveness of salvation in Jesus Christ"—if one does not, that is, merely use this formulation as a statement about oneself—but *teaches and proclaims* this exclusiveness? Baumann cites 1 Pet. 2:9 as evidence that in the Bible "the title of honor 'God's own people' is applied to the Christian church without its thereby being denied to Israel." But of course this is not enough, since in this epistle the Jewish people is not under consideration at all. Moreover, it must be asked what a proceeding of this kind could really mean in actual substance. What are we to understand if the exclusiveness of salvation in Jesus Christ is preached on the one hand and yet, on the other, Christians and Jews are not to be interpreted in a relationship of mutually exclusive contrasts? Baumann still leaves this question open.

The connection between the assertion of the "exclusiveness of salvation in Jesus Christ" and statements about the doom of the Jewish people can be demonstrated by a sermon meditation on John 2:13–22 written by Bishop Gerhard Rost for the tenth Sunday after Trinity that recently appeared in the periodical *Friede über Israel*, which Baumann himself edits.[32] Right at the beginning, the writer picks up the catchword about the "exclusiveness of salvation in Christ," seeing this as an expression of the message of his text "to a degree that can hardly be exceeded."[33] According to the author, we have to accept this message. No risk is too great. "But this exclusiveness has always been a stumbling block. For modern tolerance especially, it is out of fashion. Where Judaism and the Jewish religion is concerned it seems completely inappropriate. Under the shock of the Holocaust, we can hardly bring ourselves to utter the message of our text at all. Some people see it as the deepest root of a pernicious anti-Semitism. And anyone who, in spite of that, voices it in unmistakable terms can expect nothing except the cross of Christ. That, and no less, is the cost of preaching this text."[34]

It must be said that it would also be impossible to evade the problems the writer himself touches on, in a more dubious way than through phraseology like this. To confuse a possible critical analysis of one's own theological assertions with the "cross of Christ" is as questionable as the use made of the Holocaust. To mention this by way of the phrase "the shock of the Holocaust," which hardly allows the message to be uttered at all, banishes the question about the interaction between a theology and its consequences to the realm of psychological disturbance. The author mentions the Holocaust simply and solely as an alibi so that he can pursue the same old, well-worn paths of Christian anti-Judaism. Like Goppelt, he describes "Jewish worship"*per se* as a misuse of the temple and the law that aims at "protection from God," and he uses Goppelt's words to emphasize once more that "Jesus really abolishes Judaism *from its roots*, replacing it by something new."[35] Rost does not, either, escape the anti-Judaism that makes itself evident here, simply because, a little later, he adopts the scheme of thought that sees the Jews as representatives of the world in general, stressing that "the Jewish misunderstanding of God and his righteousness" (i.e., "securing one's position towards God through contract, as it were") is "not at all specifically Jewish" but is characteristic of the "natural man."[36] This statement could certainly be salutary if we read it in Paul's sense, contrary to its own real intention—if, that is, the equating of Jews and "natural man" were exposed as *proton pseudos*. But this is not what Rost means. On the contrary, what he says is intended to level out all the differences between Jews and Gentiles where revelation is concerned.

Nor is the author prepared to differentiate in the matter of responsibility for the death of Jesus. Again, it is "the Jews" who "deliver up Jesus, the Son and the revealer of God, to the cross."[37] Using a comparison that simply will not hold water, Rost brings his argument down to the present day, comparing the Jewish community that does not acknowledge, or rejects, Jesus with a—putative—bride who ignores the arrival of her bridegroom, contenting herself instead with his love letters, so that her waiting is *gegendstandslos*, that is, "superfluous and pointless [sic]." Because this would be a "fatal mistake," "the duty of love laid upon the Christian church is still to testify to the Jews, convincingly and lovingly, that in Jesus the Messiah has come and that now the *only* way of *true* worship that *really* reaches God is bound up with the person of Christ. Problematical though it may be after the Holocaust, it would be *the worst form of anti-Semitism* to deny the Jews this testimony."[38]

In view of what the *truly* worst form of anti-Semitism did in our own century, this last sentence, which applies theological thumbscrews to the preacher, unmasks the whole uncharitable and implausible thoughtlessness of the writer. Moreover, his description of the Christian duty of love shows where an interpretation of the gospel under the auspices of the exclusiveness of salvation in Christ ends up: in the sweeping denial that the worship of the Jewish people can be true worship that really reaches God.[39]

Baumann is not the author of the contribution we have just discussed, nor could he ever conceivably have written a meditation of this kind. But all the same, as editor he must be held partly responsible for it. It would therefore seem fundamentally doubtful (in view of the exegetical and homiletical way of dealing with the "exclusive" claim that this writing represents) whether the "mistake" in dealing with the question of an absolutist claim really does lie in the development from an "absolute confession of faith in Jesus Christ as the Messiah" to the "absolutist claim of Christianity." It would rather seem that the game with the concept of the absolute itself or with the motif of exclusiveness already sets the argument off on the wrong track. It proclaims in formal terms what would actually require substantiation in every given case. But if this substantiation were really arrived at—and through dialogue—its salutary relativity would emerge all by itself. People who talk about "salvation" as if the word were a slogan all too often believe that everything necessary has then been said, because the word itself is so positivist; and yet what is really meant still has to be explained. Consequently the effect of the word used in this way is to obscure rather than to illuminate. If anyone has really found "salvation" in and through Jesus Christ, there is every reason for rejoicing. But has it to be safeguarded by the use of absolute or exclusive terms? The whole thing reminds one of children who are not content to enjoy their own game but who are happy only if they can accompany it by saying that it is nicer than the game the other children are playing—or indeed the nicest game ever. This way of treating one's own faith is theologically dubious—just how much so, Lothar Steiger pointed out precisely, when he remarked that a church that sets up an absolute claim over against Israel loses "its partitive relationship to the whole, and thus to reality and to her own truth."[40] So on the basis of what has been said, and especially the destructive implications involved, neither the concept "first the Jews" nor even the existence of Jewish Christians can be used as ground for insisting on the absolute character of the confession of faith in the Messiah or on the "exclusiveness of salvation in Christ."

However, before this excursus we touched on points that are just as important as those just discussed: the alteration that has taken place in the understanding of mission in general, and also practically, in the relationship between Jews and Christians. Even Jewish Christians can hardly disregard these facts today. If we remember the highly depressing relationship between the church and its Jewish Christian members that we mentioned earlier and, on the other hand, the new encounter between the church and the Jewish people, it is possible to pick out a few essential aspects of the Jewish Christian testimony.

The church of the Gentiles would be greatly benefited by the testimony of the Jewish Christians, and their verbal testimony especially, for it is this that can make the church as a whole aware of the roots from which it springs. The more it listens to this testimony, which also means the testimony of Jewish Christian groups that are not incorporated in any one of the major recognized church communities,[41] the stronger its ties will be not merely with the Bible (both the Old Testament and the New) but also with "all Israel," and the more the church's own testimony among the Gentiles will thereby profit. The recognition that the church's ecumenical creeds were formulated in the patristic period, without Jewish Christian congregations or their representatives, could give the church a salutary detachment toward these creeds, for the sake of fellowship with these Jewish Christians and in attentive awareness of their understanding of Jesus Christ.[42] This could also make the European churches more flexible in their encounter with the young churches. These churches drank in neither Plato nor Moses with their mother's milk, but they will surely find themselves, in case of doubt, not in Greek philosophy but in the Jewish Bible and in Jewish Christianity.[43] I may again remind readers of other aspects, for example, that the testimony of Jewish Christians—which means the testimony of "Israel in the church"—will be a reminder to that church of "all Israel."

The Jewish Christian witness to Israel will probably find especially appropriate expression if it allows itself to be guided by the form rabbinic tradition and the New Testament suggest to be specifically Jewish and also —in its conformity with Jewish understanding—specifically Christian. For example, the *Mekhilta*, the early rabbinic commentary on the Book of Exodus, contains the following passage, the context being a discussion about the Sabbath (on Exod. 31:14):

> "Because it [i.e., the Sabbath] is holy for you": that is, the Sabbath imposes holiness on Israel [as may be seen from the following examples]. Why is X's business closed? Because he keeps the Sabbath. Why has X laid down his work? Because he keeps the Sabbath. Thus he bears witness to the One who spake, and the world was; He who created the world in six days and rested on the seventh. For thus it is written: "Therefore ye are my witnesses, saith the Lord, that I am God" (Isa. 43:12).

It is entirely in agreement with this when, at a central point in the Sermon on the Mount, Jesus follows up his description of his people as the "light of the world" and his sayings about the city set on a hill and the light set on a stand, by saying, "Let your light so shine before men, that they may see your good works and praise your Father in heaven" (Matt. 5:14–16).[44] In this sense, the function of the Jewish Christians in relation to all Israel can be interpreted as a lived testimony that, *as* Christians, they are also Jews, children of Israel, sons and daughters of Abraham, Isaac, and Jacob; and that they are differentiated from the rest of Israel only by their acknowledgment of Jesus as the Messiah and, as a result of this acknowledgment, by their fellowship, ecclesiologically, with "the Gentiles." For, at least according to the New Testament, the coming of Jesus Christ means that not the difference but the wall of partition between Israel and the nations has been broken down. Again, through this fellowship with the Gentiles, Jewish Christians testify that they see themselves as "lost sheep of the house of Israel" who have experienced the mercy of Israel's God through Jesus Christ and who proclaim that now, *together with* the Gentiles, they are living from the grace of God and in hope for that grace. And if this lived testimony should then evoke the inquisitive question, Why has so-and-so joined the church of Jesus? the Jewish Christian, like the Jew in a similar situation, is challenged to obey the admonition in 1 Pet. 3:15: "Always be prepared to make a defense to any one who calls you to account for the hope that is in you."

PARTICIPATION IN ISRAEL'S UNDERSTANDING OF ITSELF AS STATE

If one refuses to see the relation to the Jewish people of gentile Christians (and Jewish Christians too) in a traditional missionary context, one's reasons will be hard to dismiss, on other grounds as well. The founding of the state of Israel in our own century can be traced back to a whole series of factors. But its presupposition, at all events, is the faithfulness of the Jewish people to its way of life with the Torah during the past two thousand years, and it is inconceivable without the ties with the land of Israel that have been maintained in the context of that faithfulness. So if today Jewish Christians exist in Israel and if, like a great part of the Jewish people, they have found there a place of refuge and the opportunity to pursue their lives as Jewish Christians in a more authentic way than in the Diaspora of the gentile churches, they are to a large degree indebted for this to the Jewish people as a whole. In this fundamental sense they have therefore always implicitly recognized for themselves the positive significance of "all Israel."

This significance is not merely political. It has a theological connotation as well, at least for some of the Jewish Christians. For example, the creed of a small group of Jewish Christians calling themselves the Messianic Church of Israel says in its third article, "We believe in the Holy Spirit; we believe in the Hebrew Bible as God's Word; we believe in the rebirth of Zion, as a state and in spirit, in accordance with the firm promise of the Lord."[45] The final assertions refer, on the one hand, to the state of Israel as a political reality, which is thereby interpreted in the light of the scriptural promises. On the other hand, they are formulated in so open-ended a way that this reality, interpreted in the light of the Hebrew Bible, is not understood statically. On the contrary, "the rebirth of Zion . . . in accordance with the firm promise of the Lord" is also the object of trusting hope. But in the framework of this dynamic understanding, the new foundation by the Jewish people of the community of Israel as state in the land of the fathers is seen as an expression of God's faithfulness to his word and—to the extent that this saying has a bearing on Israel—to his people as a whole. This means that the saying is understood theologically.

If, therefore, the synodal resolution "On the Renewal of the Relationship between Christians and Jews" of the church of the Rhineland sees the state of Israel as a token of God's faithfulness, this is the acknowledgment of an assurance that, at long last, links gentile Christians both with Jewish Christians and with "all Israel." This goes beyond the bonds of the traditional patterns of assurance that are merely restrictive in function.[46] It is with this proclamation of a specific, concrete assurance of God's faithfulness to his people that a church has been able to testify to the message laid upon it through Paul's gospel: that Israel experiences God's mercy not just sometime or other but "now" (Rom. 11:31).

Although the phrase "sign of God's faithfulness" is restrained enough, it has been greeted with the most violent opposition.[47] Its opponents have appealed to Paul's gospel, among other things, and to its Lutheran adoption and interpretation in the form of the doctrine about the justification of the sinner "through grace alone." But this is to overlook the fact that it is this very doctrine which permits the interpretation that its supporters dispute (although it cannot be used to legitimate questionable government decisions in Israel). According to the proclamation of justification, Christian existence is authentically described in the formulas *peccator in re, iustus in spe*, "a sinner in fact, righteous in hope," and *simul iustus et peccator*, "a sinner and at the same time righteous." These phrases are expressions of the certainty that God turns to the sinner, a certainty that remains—under the presupposition of human trust in the God who so commits himself—

even if, to the end of his life, the human being never loses the status of sinner but continually fails to behave as he should toward God and the community in which he lives.

The question whether in his proclamation Paul is essentially interested in the individual or not cannot be discussed here.[48] Whatever the answer to that question may be, in Romans 9—11 (esp. chap. 11), the apostle certainly talks about Israel not as a collection of individuals but, in the true biblical way, as a people or nation. He affirms that God has not rejected his people (Rom. 11:1–2), and he discloses the salvation of "all Israel" as a mystery (Rom. 11:26). Just because of this revelation, the interpretation *peccator in re, iustus in spe* can be genuinely applied to "all Israel" in the light of what Paul says. And the same may be said of the apparently more radical interpretation *simul iustus et peccator*, in view of what the apostle says about God's faithfulness to Israel—which applies to Israel now—and because of the interdependence of the two formulas.

Seen in this light, the interpretation of Israel's existence as a sign of the faithfulness of God is surely both corroborated and safeguarded against misuse. Our consideration of this interpretation started with the affirmed participation in the state of Israel by Jewish Christians living there, and with the way Israel as state understands itself. We saw how from this standpoint—and especially since the synodal resolution of the Protestant church of the Rhineland—a connection with the church of the Gentiles does exist. Perhaps this example will therefore make it especially clear who the Jewish Christians are, in the light of what Paul says and according to their own view: they are Israel's presence in the church and at the same time the church's presence in Israel.[49]

But of course another aspect also began to emerge quite clearly in this connection, and this aspect is just as important. Neither the existence of the church in general nor the existence of Jewish Christians in particular means a denial of the permanent importance of the Israel that does not believe in the gospel. This importance, for the church or for the Gentiles particularly, is something we must look at more closely in the chapter that follows. In the framework of the points we have considered in this chapter, we asked first about the importance of Jewish Christians (Israel in the church) *for the church*, and only then about the relevance of these people for Israel. In the next chapter, accordingly, after considering the meaning of the phrase "all Israel" for the church, we shall look again at the reverse point: What service could the church as a whole possibly render the Jewish people?[50]

— 5

Israel and the Church
Existence in Partnership

ISRAEL'S IMPORTANCE FOR THE CHURCH

Israel owes its origin to the word of promise given to Abraham. The present time of God's people is marked by the unswerving and infrangible validity of its election (Rom. 9:1–5; 11:29). Its future is determined by the unshakable assurance that "all Israel will be saved" (Rom. 11:26). All this remains true although, and even if, most of the Jewish people reject the gospel as medium of participation in the redemption of the end time. This is the viewpoint recorded in Romans 9—11. And that means that this is the angle of approach taken by a testimony belonging to the gospel of the early period that is now part of the canon. From this testimony the right to existence and the permanent endowment of God's people of Israel can be deduced so unequivocally and with such cogent theological justification that all glib theological talk about the "end of Israel" etc. is, according to Paul's gospel, the purest heresy, whether the proponents of this view term themselves Lutheran, Protestant, Catholic, Orthodox, or Christian.

It was with Augustine, at latest, that this viewpoint acquired its determining form. For this father of the church, and ever since, Israel's raison d'être was simply and solely to be a witness for the church.[1] This allegedly constituted its right to existence, a right dictated by the stronger party and pressed into the service of that party's own ideological aggrandizement. The examples of the picture of the synagogue given above, in chapter 1, are pieces of medieval evidence we encounter in many variations. And even today it still represents the viewpoint of extensive Christian groups.

This kind of theological thinking is dominated by the desire for absoluteness and by fears for Christian identity. It is only in recent times that a new attitude has come into being side by side with this. This new attitude is marked by a readiness to listen to the "voice of Jacob" and is willing to hear more in that voice's written and spoken testimony than an echo of its own traditional view, which is in any case familiar. Where this new attitude is found, the Jewish people are no longer listened to as a witness to the truth of the church. Their testimony is heard more, much more, as a witness to the church, of the truth of God. I mentioned some exemplary American work of this kind at the beginning. In Germany, Friedrich-Wilhelm Marquardt is deserving of special mention, and particularly, among his contributions on this subject, his pioneer essay "Feinde um unsretwillen: Das jüdische Nein und die christliche Theologie" ("Enemies for Our Sake: The Jewish No and Christian Theology").[2] The only thing that can surmount Christian anti-Judaism is a positive interpretation of the Jewish no to the gospel,[3] and the struggle for just such an interpretation leads Marquardt to a profound insight, which he arrives at by way of Rom. 11:28 (". . . for our sake"):

> The testimony of the Jewish no [is rooted] in the judgment and will of God himself . . . , for he has "not yet" permitted the consummation of all things and has thereby (according to the Protestant view) "still" reserved for himself everything decisive, last, ultimate, and the final realization of reality, withholding it from us Christians and Jews. Israel witnesses in world history to this "not yet" of the divine will. With its no Israel represents the eschatological proviso of God himself. It resists the impassioned Christian claim to the final era and to ultimate truth and opinions. It exists as a ferment, to break down false finalities and perfections. With its acknowledgment of the transcendence of God *in spite of* Christ, it witnesses not to an idolatrously abstract "God above God" or to any "hidden God" but to the eschatological proviso in God himself, which even the mission of Jesus Christ does not revoke and which Paul proclaimed in the concept of the eschatological subjection of Jesus Christ "that God may be all in all" (1 Cor. 15:28, AV). And Israel's no is a witness, too, to God's freedom toward himself and the proviso he has hitherto still maintained toward himself and his purposes.[4]

The subject of Israel's services for the church has many facets,[5] and it would therefore seem to be the obvious course to pick up the theme of the understanding of God that Marquardt chooses, considering this further from a complementary perspective. What is meant is Israel's acknowledgment of the one God, which is the scarlet thread that binds together Jewish existence: "Hear, O Israel: The Lord our God is one Lord; and you shall love the Lord your God with all your heart, and with all your soul, and with all your might [capacity]" (Deut. 6:4–5). This confession of faith not only leads into the center of Jewish life, it also points into the depths of Jewish history. In order to indicate more clearly the meaning that the life of the Jewish people with this creed has for the church, and in order to include the theme of a possible mutual service between Judaism and Christianity, it may be helpful to outline something of what the biblical history has to tell about the meaning and context of this bond between the people of Israel and its God as the one, sole God.

Excursus: Israel's Acknowledgment of the One God

For considerable periods of its history, Israel's idea of God was initially henotheistic in character. We find the classic expression of this understanding in the prophet Micah: "All the peoples walk each in the name of its god, but we will walk in the name of Yahweh, our God, for ever and ever" (Mic. 4:5). The existence of the gods of other nations, and their importance for the national groups concerned is not disputed. It is recognized. But this is not seen as affecting Israel's own religious world. The basis of this religious coexistence is the concept of native soil.[6] As long as the integrity of the soil is guaranteed, there can be coexistence of the kind described in Mic. 4:5. It is only if the nation's own living space is threatened that conflict flares up. But when it does, it is then of course a conflict on both levels, the earthly and the heavenly, because of the unity between a nation and its gods. In the land of Israel this conflict cropped up relatively regularly throughout history. But the reason was not Israel's contentiousness. One cause was rather her political situation, caught as she was between the millstones of the great powers in the northeast and the southwest, and another was her determination not to be like her neighbors but to remain Israel—even if this determination was often expressed by isolated individuals such as the prophets.

This concept of Israel's relationship to the gentile nations runs right through the history of the first centuries in the promised land. But for all that, it will hardly reflect the whole truth. It seems to have been overlaid by other, wider vistas. We may think here of the promise to Abraham in Gen. 12:1–3, for example, the promise that in him (which means through Israel's God) all the families of the earth would be blessed; or the psalms belonging to the Jerusalem cult, which in anticipation acknowledge the God of Israel as the Lord of all the earth (Psalms 93; 96—99).

Two fundamental events determine the later form of the relations between God's people and the surrounding nations—which also means the relationship between Israel's God and the gods of the other peoples. In 722 B.C. the Northern Kingdom, Israel, was conquered by the Assyrians. The upper classes were carried off to the east, their place being taken by new, foreign rulers. Rather more than a century later, the Southern Kingdom of Judah, with its capital, Jerusalem, suffered a similar fate when it was conquered by the Babylonian Nebuchadnezzar. In 597 its aristocracy were deported to Babylon, and eleven years later a large section of the people were carried off as well. Finally the temple, the place of God's presence, was also destroyed. These two events more than any other happening (and especially the destruction of city and temple) are reflected in the testimonies of Scripture.

Contrary to every expectation, the God of Israel is not silenced by the double defeat of his people nor even by the loss of the land. He rises more mightily than ever in Israel's testimony. In Albrecht Alt's view, the oldest part of Deuteronomy reflects the struggle to arrive at a planned concept of a new way of life among the groups of people in the Northern Kingdom which had been spared deportation.[7] Deutero-Isaiah witnesses to the new understanding of the God of the fathers to which the people from the Southern Kingdom won through, after they had been carried off to Babylonian exile. In Israel as in Babylon, one theme took on central importance: the uniqueness of Israel's God. It is this confession of Israel's faith we hear among the people who passed on the deuteronomic traditions: "Hear, O Israel: The Lord our God is one Lord" (Deut. 6:4). In Deuteronomy this acknowledgment of the one, sole God is matched by the demand for a single cultic site and by the call to destroy all the altars in the land belonging to the gods of other peoples (Deuteronomy 12). It is coupled too with the far-reaching interpretation that, with her election, God has handed over to Israel the earlier inhabitants of the land so that they might be destroyed (Deut. 7:1ff.; 9:1ff.). So the heightened acknowledgment that there was only one God led in Deuteronomy to an intensified relationship of hostility between Israel and the gentile nations.

The group that passed on the Deuteronomic traditions were evidently still living in the land of Israel, even if under conditions of oppression. Here, because of this unbroken tie with the land of their fathers, the borderline between henotheism and monotheism is still fluid. Matters were different in the exilic community in Babylon. In their separation from the land of Israel, exposed to the superior numbers of their oppressors and those oppressors' gods, these people learned to know Israel's God as the one before whose uniqueness all the gods of the Gentiles become "as naught," nothing more than his obedient servants or, where they are still worshiped, dumb masters, mere firewood. Existence as a minority in a hostile environment led to a polemical, aggressive development of their own religious tradition, in its relationship to the Gentiles. And yet at the same time, as the reverse side of the same phenomenon, it also meant that the Israelites developed a sense of a missionary charge in relation to the goyim. Although the Gentiles (in this case Babylon) have conquered God's people, we are told on the one hand that they are nevertheless "like a drop from a bucket," "as the dust on the scales," null and without being; no more than a breath is needed to topple their princes and kings. For the Holy One of Israel is identical with the Creator of heaven and earth and is hence Lord over the other nations, not merely over his people, whom he has chosen since time immemorial (Isa. 40:12ff.). Yet, on the other hand, the community in Babylon sees the Servant of God—itself—as commissioned to bring God's precepts to the Gentiles (Isa. 42:1–4) and, in line with this, has a vision of the nations pilgriming on the road to Zion at the end time (Isa. 45:14ff.; 49:22ff.).

Life in the Diaspora resulted in another phenomenon as well. In earlier centuries, when the Israelites had to come to terms with the Canaanites, who were the previous inhabitants of the country, they had taken over elements from their religious traditions, making them their own, and now in the new situation of the exile, there is also a give-and-take, dissociation going hand in hand with the acceptance of what the religions of the other nations had to say—an acceptance hesitant at first, more marked in the period that followed.

We encounter both these sides of Israel's relationship to the Gentiles in Deutero-Isaiah, and in the succeeding centuries both were maintained even though the form shifted. Israel struggled for its special path, the way marked out for it as God's people, to witness to the uniqueness of its God and hence to reject with the utmost rigor all idolatry in its own midst and among others. And yet it courted the Gentiles, approximating to some of their views in the process. In the third century, and even more in the second, when, after the peaceful era of Persian rule, Israel came under the suzerainty of, first, the Hellenistic rulers of Egypt and, then, Syria, the Jerusalem aristocracy's assimilation to the culture of the Hellenistic world assumed such forms that Israel's identity as God's people was acutely endangered. When obedience to the Torah was forbidden and the temple was desecrated, the people who had kept the faith with the God of Israel in the traditional way rebelled (167 B.C.).

I have already given a brief sketch of Israel's history in the two centuries that followed,[8] so here it may suffice to consider the importance of the happenings of those years, up to the reconsecration of the temple, and especially the faithfulness to its God that Israel preserved in these events.

The resistance at the beginning of the Maccabean wars was motivated by faithfulness to the temple and the Torah and by opposition to the total Hellenization of the Jewish people in the land of Israel, with the assimilation to the surrounding culture that would have followed. This resistance is therefore quite correctly seen as one of the most decisive events in the history of ancient Judaism, if not the most important event of all. For it meant the preservation of Israel's ties **with** its own One God. Elias Bicker-mann has expressed in a few apt sentences the whole dimension of this victory of faithfulness to the Torah over Israel's own Hellenized, and ruthlessly Hellenizing, groups:

> If they [the Maccabees] had been defeated, the light of monotheism would have gone out too. No external oppression could have led to its annihilation, for there was always a fraction of the scattered people that would have kept the true faith. But things would have been different if the people themselves had fallen victim to polytheism, if the pilgrims to Zion had been met by hierodules in the precincts of the temple, and if they had led the strangers to the altar of an Allat or a Dusares [i.e., gods worshiped among Israel's neigh-bors]. The martyrs through their blood, and the holy warriors through their swords, saved Judaism's watchword: "Hear, O Israel, the Lord is our God, the Lord alone."[9]

It is not the Jewish people only who today still live from this resistance and the insight it safeguarded. The church lives from it also. For without that struggle, Jesus' life, teaching, and ministry, with the proclamation of the imminent dawn of the rule of God which sustained it, would have been quite inconceivable; the same may be said of the rise of Christianity, which, right down to the present day, has lived—in however enfeebled a form—from the certainty that the Father of Jesus Christ is identical with the God of Abraham, Isaac, and Jacob (Mark 12:26–27), the God of Israel.[10]

This perspective has been kept more actively alive in the Roman Cath-olic church than in the Protestant ones. On August 1, Catholics honor the memory of the "holy Maccabees" about whom we read in the seventh chapter of 2 Maccabees—the mother with the seven sons who died martyrs' deaths in the religious persecutions under Antiochus IV. Compared with the tendency (especially popular today) to see and stress particularly the close links between the Hellenistic Judaism of the Diaspora and the early church, this recollection of the Maccabees is a wholesome corrective. We are indebted to Bertold Klappert for showing from the Epistle to the He-brews how important this phase of authentic Jewish witness in the land of Israel was for the New Testament and—in the light of the Jewish people's history of persecution and suffering in our century—for the Christian church. This history of suffering has made it unmistakably plain that, as was already shown in exemplary fashion in the days of the Maccabees, "the particular vocation of the people of Israel and the synagogue . . . [is] the sanctification of the divine name," the *kiddush ha-shem*, which finds expression in the recitation of the "Hear, O Israel" and in the life that conforms to that acknowledgment.[11] To the degree to which the attack on the Jewish people in the period of persecution and murder was also an attack on the Christian church, Israel was ratified in this time of suffering as "martyr of faith for the Christian church too."[12] To be together "wit-nesses of active hope" is therefore the charge to Christians and Jews that, according to Klappert, results similarly from the testimony of the Epistle to the Hebrews and from Israel's representative sufferings in our own century.[13] All this means that the Jewish people have demonstrated bodily to the church, down to our own time—and in our own time especially—who they are and who they have to be in God's sight: a community in suffering for God, which is to say, a "community of the cross."[14]

MUTUAL LIMITATION AS A BENEFICIAL MUTUAL SERVICE

There is no need to modify anything that has already been said, but, in addition to presenting Bickermann's interpretation of religious and political resistance in the Maccabean period that I have just summarized, it is worth offering a second comment, one that to some extent accords with Bickermann's viewpoint and to some extent deviates from it. Just because this second interpretation is somewhat different in form, it may help us to grasp another dimension of Israel's deeply rooted bond with the one God, and along with it, a further dimension of the service Israel performs for the church. And since this further dimension can ultimately only be discussed together with the question about the church's service for Israel, it also carries over into that domain.

Morton Smith also sees the Maccabean victory over the votaries of assimilation to Hellenistic standards as an event of momentous importance, and in this he agrees in principle with Bickermann. But his summary assessment differs considerably in substance, when he writes,

> The success of Judas [Maccabaeus] saved the monolatrous Yahweh cult and thereby preserved for the Western world the tradition of religious intolerance: either Yahweh or the other gods; either "the true" religion or "the false"—a tradition which, by way of Christianity, rabbinic Judaism, and Islam, remained one of the main factors in intellectual and political history.[15]

Now, nothing could be more inappropriate than to play off Bickermann's interpretation against Smith's. It would seem to be more in line with the facts if we saw the two as complementary. But of course this does not exclude critical questions. For example, in view of the completely different social and political circumstances, it appears exceedingly problematical in this particular context to mention movements such as rabbinic Judaism and Christianity in the same breath and without any differentiation. For instance, in the last thirty years of the first century, rabbinic Judaism, which was in its beginnings, had unquestionably more pull than the group of Jewish Christians. And, as can be shown, it used this pull to extend the *birkhat ha-minim* (the cursing of heretics) to the Jewish Christians.[16] In the centuries that followed, however, the balance gradually shifted. In the second and third centuries the life of the synagogue and the church were in many respects analogous, for both were minorities in the Roman Empire. But in the course of the fourth century the picture changed, feature by feature, as Christianity progressively acquired the constitution of a state religion.

Since that time and down to our own century, the Jewish communities have always been in a minority in a more or less hostile (Christian) environment—tolerated, oppressed, or persecuted to death. With the exception of some dissident groups, the Christian churches either were largely on the side of the rulers or were actually the rulers themselves. So in the history of rabbinic Judaism, "the tradition of religious intolerance" that Smith talks about developed in an essentially ideological sense, whereas in the history of Christianity ever since the fourth century, its development has been to a varying degree heavily political, with all the irksome, often terrible consequences which that involved for the people concerned. Unless this serious difference is taken into account, to present rabbinic Judaism and Christianity as parallels gives a quite distorted picture, for the parallelism between the two is in this sense restricted from the outset.[17]

Having taken note of this difference, which made itself felt over more than fifteen hundred years, we can look more closely at the theological dimension of the political and social problem of religious intolerance to which Smith refers and which theoretically applies to Judaism and Christainty in a similar way.

Smith's phrase "either Yahweh or the other gods" is a reminder that religious intolerance, whether ideological or practical, is a result of the acknowledgment of a single God—a result, that is to say, of the "monotheism" that Judaism, Christianity, and also Islam share.[18] The catchword "monotheism" indicates that the fundamental theological theme in both Judaism and Christianity is the sovereignty of (a single) God over a world that belongs to him alone. Monotheism therefore contains imperial, "total" features, seen formally and on the level of God himself, so to speak. Even if creation in the present is not yet subject to the rule of God, in both Judaism and Christianity the end of all the paths that run through time and history is "that God may be all in all" (1 Cor. 15:28). Of course the substantially unique character of this "total rule" must immediately be particularized. It aims at "peace and blessing, glory and joy and length of days" (1 QM, I,9), at a new creation in harmony that will make an end of all injustice on earth, and is thus profoundly different from any totalitarian domination by human beings. And yet the problem remains. The one God is witnessed to by certain groups who carry on that faith, who serve him— *and whom he serves.*[19] The faithfulness of the groups who uphold God's cause as his servants finds its correspondence in their expectation that they will have a part in his kingdom. Thus, according to Dan. 7:27, when the new world comes, God will give the rule over all the world "to the people of the saints of the Most High"—that is to say, Israel.[20] In a similar way, Paul expects that the church of Jesus Christ will reign through him in life (i.e., in the life of the coming world; Rom. 5:17) and that it will even sit in judgment on the angels (1 Cor. 6:2–3).[21]

It is precisely this association of ideas that shows the strength and weakness of this belief. Its strength is that it sets a wholesome limit to all human rule, in the form of the specific expectation of the rule of God. Its weakness is that, the moment political conditions permit, the expected and total heavenly kingdom, testified to in suffering, is in danger of being set up here not through divine power but through the might of men. The old cry "Compel them to come in!"—that is, into the church, because outside the church there was no salvation—is not by any means the mere beginnings of this misuse of the expected rule of God to which the church testified; it already represents its advanced stage. For the beginning is the verbal misuse, which can take many forms, the most violent being the execration of opponents or people of different beliefs. We already come across a considerable volume of this verbal misuse of personal assurance and expectation in the New Testament.[22] And it is certainly to be found as well in a number of different forms in ancient Judaism, whether it be anti-Egyptian polemic in "Joseph and Aseneth" (a writing coming from the Diaspora), or the horrified rejection and execration of the "children of darkness" by the Qumran community as "children of light," or contemptuous rabbinic sayings about the Gentiles.[23] We should not extenuate any of this, on either side. What we should do is follow up the traditions in which assurance and expectation are developed beneficially and healingly, not destructively. And we can find these traditions in both Judaism and Christianity.[24]

It is true that in individual cases a differentiation must be made with regard to the polemic and distortions of the other side. For example, the polemic of the Qumran community and the attacks made by the early Jewish Christian groups on the rest of Israel can still quite well be viewed as family quarrels, whereas the same contentions take on a completely different coloring and weight the moment they are taken over by the growing gentile church and turned against the Jewish people from outside. Or to take another instance, it is easier to conjure up sympathy for the polemic of minorities against the environment with which they are at loggerheads than for the actions and reactions of any given majority. Thus the New Testament testimonies, rather like the Qumran documents, came into being in a period in which not merely Jewish Christianity but the Christian congregations as a whole were in a minority in the land of Israel and in the Diaspora, compared with the Jewish people. This constellation is reflected in the New Testament writings, where anti-Jewish polemic goes hand in hand with the development of the Christian message—in the Gospel of John especially. This certainly does not justify the damning of opponents such as we quite literally find in John 8:44, for example. That is all the less excusable since the Fourth Gospel appeals to Jesus of Nazareth, whose life, on the evidence of the Gospels, was characterized by powerlessness *and* love of his enemies. But in spite of that, the situation of groups that were an afflicted minority (like those behind the Fourth Gospel) makes something of the embitterment explicable and moves us to a certain sympathy for the, after all, very human people who passed this polemic on.

But the matter is very different when what is at issue is the exegesis and interpretation of these documents in theology and the church today— that is, in the context of our time, when these writings are understood as canonical testimonies. First, when the New Testament era was past, it was only a relatively short period (compared with the two thousand years that have elapsed meanwhile) before the course of church history brought with it the change we have already mentioned, reversing the situation and making the Jews a minority in a hostile world. And second, that history offers a wealth of examples to show that the New Testament writings, in apparent ignorance of the changed situation, were turned into legitimating texts for endless hostility toward the Jews, and even persecution.[25] Theologians and other interpreters of Scripture who in their hermeneutics ignore the use that has been made of these texts, with its sad, indeed fatal, results, and who attempt in every possible way to palliate the New Testament's anti-Jewish polemic by clothing it in the garb of timeless truths are not only acting irresponsibly, theologically speaking; in their deliberate ignoring of history they are not even acting as what they generally purport to be—critical historians.[26]

The extremist structures of community and doctrine in Qumran and among the group of people behind the Gospel of John make even more evident what was already, on the basis of some individual Old Testament testimonies, indicated in the excursus: the more a community turns its acknowledgment of the one God into an absolute claim—through whatever medium this acknowledgment may be arrived at—and the more it sees itself, in concurrence with that acknowledgment, as a unit of its own, cut off from others, the more dualistically it defines its relationship to its environment; and in this case dualistically means destructively.[27] For example, when in Qumran the community and its life is described as a unity, a oneness (*yachad*), this corresponds on the other hand to its dualistic interpretation of its relationship to the world. The same is true of the Gospel of John with its marked stress on unity christologically (John 10:30) and ecclesiologically (John 10:16; 17:11) and its also dualistic relationship to the world. This rigid absolutism rests on the view that God has revealed himself to his community in full authenticity—completely and utterly, so to speak. It is not difficult to recognize this view as the attempt to cover up the empirically essential distinction between the present hidden (i.e., partial) rule of God and his coming manifest (i.e., complete) sovereignty, by an appeal to an unreserved and ultimate revelation, and to bolster the identity that is under attack through a dualizing self-interpretation.

It is in line with this that in these communities there should be an exceedingly strong trend toward a "presentative" or "realized" eschatology which, however, just as necessarily exhausts itself in the mere gift of knowledge.[28] The theology of Rudolf Bultmann, which takes its bearings throughout from the Gospel of John, is a striking example of the connection I have suggested between revelation absolutism, dualism, and a realized eschatology that consists in the fact of knowledge alone.[29] And logically enough, for Bultmann's pupils particularly, and for other votaries of Christian absolutism, the postulate that any part of this claim to the possession of absolute truth might be renounced is ground enough for hectic, and hence all the less convincing, reactions.[30]

In view of what we can observe here on the ideological level, it is anything but desirable for the kingdom of God ever to be set up on earth by Christians (or Jews or Moslems either). Attempts in this direction made in the course of history teach that the result would probably always be no more than a community in the form of a totalitarian state. The establishment of the perfect rule of God as a beneficial event is therefore only conceivable as a work brought about by God himself (or by all his creatures *together*). Wherever this proviso is set aside, in whatever way, monotheism becomes an unparalleled danger. So it is this latent danger or proviso (both being only two sides of the same thing) that invite us to see the Jewish people and the Christian church as there to help each other, in their particular ties with the one God. Perception of the danger, or the proviso, leads us to see that if Jewish communities mean a limitation for the church and if, conversely, the existence of Christian communities means a limitation for the synagogue, this limitation is not a danger; on the contrary, it is salutary. One may also very well ask how much one's own certainty is worth if it can be so quickly and severely damaged by a limitation of this kind instead of being strengthened by an understanding of the other point of view, so that both can be viewed in terms of mutual enrichment.

All these reflections may be hard to reconcile with a Christian devotional pattern such as we find in the Gospel of John. But—apart from problematical structures in the epistles too[31]—what we have said accords all the more with the Pauline view of Christian existence, in its tension between "now" and "then." For example, in his great hymn on love, in which he develops the criterion of criteria for theology and the church, the apostle says about the question of knowledge, "Now we see as if through a [cloudy] mirror, in hints, but then directly, face to face. Now I know in part, but then I shall know fully, even as I am known" (1 Cor. 13:12). And this statement about the limits of our present knowledge is not merely a theological extravaganza. That is evidenced by the apostle's earlier statement in Phil. 3:12–13 that I mentioned earlier and that is similar in structure: "Not as though I had already obtained this . . . but I press on to make it my own, because Christ Jesus has made me his own."

In the face of the latent dangers of monotheism that I have shown, Jews and Christians can offer each other help through their salutary mutual limitation. To understand what this could mean as matters stand at the present day, we must once again recollect the imbalance that is the mark of Christian-Jewish history. For most of that history, the Jewish people have been in a minority position, whereas the church has been on the side of the majority. In view of the church's hostility towards the Jews, practiced for centuries, a history of the misuse of the bond with the one God would therefore here too largely be a history of Christendom, hardly of Judaism, which has been characterized by what Geis calls the "immeasurable mercy of powerlessness."[32] In view of history as it has actually been, it is probably true to say that it is Christian theologians above all who are challenged to listen to the Jewish testimony along the lines marked out by Marquardt and Klappert. It is they who should think further about the question, What does Israel's acknowledgment of the one God mean for the Christian church? And what is the significance for the church of the preservation of this bond in the Jewish people's history of suffering, with its protest "against all paganism . . . whether it takes the form of the idolization of nature or of power or of religion"?[33]

This, surely, would be the greatest service of all that Christians could perform for Israel, if the church were thereby led to permit Israel, "delivered from the hand of its [Christian] enemies, to serve God in holiness and righteousness" (Luke 1:74–75) *and* if the church were also moved to take Israel seriously on this, its own specific path as God's witness.

CONSEQUENCES FOR CHRISTOLOGY

All this applies all the more if we go beyond what has been said and once more include the sphere of Christology. It already became clear at an earlier point that the history of early Christology is characterized by a development that, though it may perhaps be understandable enough,[34] can hardly be justified. The experience of the prolongation of the times was not interpreted as being perhaps an indication of the difficulty of Jesus Christ's struggle with the powers hostile to God and hence as a sign of the helplessness that belongs to love. Rather, in the creed of the church the *kyrios* was invested, step by step, with an incomparable fullness of power. So it is in the field of Christology too that we can see the process I have indicated—the gradual softening of the clear difference between the present partial rule of God and his future all-embracing sovereignty. "*All* power in heaven and on earth *has been* given to me" (Matt. 28:18); "The Father loves the Son and *has given all things* into his hand" (John 3:35)—these statements and others like them are the milestones marking this development, even in the New Testament. It is true that the underlying theme is still the transfer of power from the Father to the Son, so that the unique character of the Father is not infringed. But even as early as the New Testament we can already detect the beginnings of a trend to lend Jesus' relationship to God a deifying impress—a trend that was to have momentous consequences. It is in this context that we have to put the confession of the Johannine Jesus "I and the Father are One" (John 10:30); or the address of "doubting Thomas" to the risen Jesus, 'My Lord and my God' (John 20:28); or the description of the Logos as *theos* in the prologue to John's Gospel (John 1:1). Hans Conzelmann commented on this last passage: "The Logos is with God and he is God. Is this di-theism? The Jewish 'Wisdom' [i.e., as comparable figure] is the first of created beings, and is hence dissociated from God. But the Johannine Logos is not created. Here we really can glimpse the underlying concept of two Gods."[35]

This indicates the sphere in which the Jewish acknowledgment of the one God is again of special importance for Christian theology. It is true that the Jewish theologian Philo of Alexandria also provides evidence for the idea touched on here, when he talks about the Logos, the mediator of creation, as "second God."[36] But quite apart from the merely peripheral importance of this title and the functional interpretation of the Logos in Philo,[37] the character of Philo's philosophy remains significantly exceptional in the history of Judaism, and at this point particularly so, whereas the Gospel of John is positively symptomatic of the development Christology underwent in the centuries that followed.

The details of this development do not belong to our present concern, and we certainly cannot arrive at a general judgment on the basis of the points that have been considered here. But so much may nonetheless be said: Israel's testimony to the one God is for the church an enduringly important challenge to the integrity of its own confession of faith, which is the same where the oneness of God is concerned. It therefore represents the crisis of every Christology that is not unequivocally subordinationist in its bearings—every Christology, that is, which is not developed on the premise of the clear subordination of the Son of God to God himself, and which is not therefore also functionally oriented.[38]

The importance of this question to the Christian church is shown not least by the fact that it has the full support of the New Testament testimonies, which—with the possible exception of the Gospel of John—all maintain a subordinationist Christology. The assertion that the teaching and ministry of Jesus Christ in word and deed are only expressible and valid if we assume that he himself is to be understood as God "for the salvation of every one who has faith" (Rom. 1:16) is supported by at most one witness in the New Testament, not the two or three the Bible requires.

It could of course be that the Old Testament part of the Bible, together with rabbinic tradition, has preserved a tradition that it would be worth thinking about further. In Exod. 7:1, Moses is told by God, "See, I make you God for Pharaoh." According to rabbinic tradition, this act has no bearing on the first commandment, because Moses' divinity is restricted to his relationship to Pharaoh;[39] on the contrary, the appointment has the precise purpose of safeguarding God's uniqueness: Pharaoh, who has made himself God, is to be cast down from the throne he has bestowed on himself. So it could be that among the Gentiles, with their striving for self-deification, the uniqueness of God can only be established in an analogous christological sense: appointed to be God for the Gentiles—God for the Gentiles *only*—just as Moses was once for Pharaoh only, not for Israel.[40]

JEWISH AND CHRISTIAN LIFE UNDER
THE INSIGNIA OF THE SOVEREIGN RULE OF GOD

The bond of Jews and Christians with the one God means a bond with the God of Abraham, Isaac, and Jacob as the only God; and it also means a lived acknowledgment of God's rule, though that rule has to be differentiated according to whether it is past, present, or future. When we are thinking on the theological and christological levels in the narrower sense, we have also to think in terms of synagogue and church, if we are to arrive at an approach, at least, to a more comprehensive understanding of the rule of God in both places.

When the Jew recites the "Hear, O Israel," remembering what God has done for him with and since the exodus from Egypt, he takes upon himself the "yoke of the heavenly rule." This phrase describes both the recitation of the Shema Israel itself and, it may be, the martyrdom suffered in faithfulness to this confession of faith and its implications. All that this confession of faith includes can be summed up in general terms in the phrase "Jewish observance," which means the shaping of life according to the norms of the halakhah. By taking upon himself the yoke of the heavenly rule, that is, by acknowledging Israel's God as the only God, and therefore as Lord, the Jew simultaneously takes upon himself the "yoke of the commandments." The two are directly related to each other. The lordship of God is given space, a terrain, in the form of obedience to the commandments, as this obedience is defined by the halakhah. One example among many is the way the "Hear, O Israel" goes on after the opening sentences quoted above (Deut. 6:4–5): "And these words which I command you this day shall be upon your heart; and you shall teach them diligently to your children, and shall talk of them when you sit in your house, and when you walk by the way, and when you lie down, and when you rise. And you shall bind them as a sign upon your hand, and they shall be as frontlets between your eyes. And you shall write them on the doorposts of your house and on your gates" (Deut. 6:6–9). Down to the present day, by obedience to these precepts in the form they have assumed in Jewish tradition, every Jewish family that is faithful to the Torah in the traditional sense, witnesses to the oneness of the God of Israel and to his sovereignty over his people. The example quoted is only one facet, even if it is one that touches on the essentials. It teaches above all that it is senseless to talk about the "sovereignty of God" if this is not testified to in each individual existence through a life in accordance with the precepts of the Torah, and hence quite specifically. And that means both cultically and ethically, through a life of partnership and concord, determined by compassion.

The "Hear, O Israel" can be compared with an early confession of faith from the Christian tradition that is also exemplary. Paul has passed this down to us in 1 Cor. 8:6: "For us there is one God, the Father, from whom are all things and for whom we exist, and one Lord, Jesus Christ, through whom are all things and through whom we exist." The extension of the acknowledgment of the one God by the acknowledgment of Jesus Christ as Lord brings out what has just been said: that for the Christian church the lordship of God is revealed christologically, through Jesus Christ as representative. Just as for the Jewish people the acknowledgment of Israel's God includes acceptance of the yoke of God's commandments, it may correspondingly be said about the Christian church that its acknowledgment of the *kyrios* Jesus implies acceptance of "his yoke" (Matt. 11:30), that is, the yoke of his commandments, which establish and confirm the Torah (Matthew 5—7) or are *his* Torah (Gal. 6:2). And just as his "rule" in the form of his "existence *for* . . ." is the opposite of rule in the human sense, because it is service, so the testimony to his rule that the church offers through the way it lives takes the form of the service for one another in which "the whole Torah is fulfilled" (Gal. 5:13–14).

The confession of faith in 1 Corinthians 8:6 that I have quoted refers to a concept that only assumed any considerable importance after Paul: the mediating function of Jesus Christ in creation. The corresponding view in Judaism is the mediating function of the Torah in creation. In both ideas, what is initially an experience in the present is thought back into the primal period. The essential medium of God's rule among the Jewish people is the Torah, whereas in the Christian church it is Jesus Christ. It must be said that this parallelism, or rather contrast, is only a seeming one from the Christian perspective at least (though not from the Jewish side). For since both Matthew and Paul tell us that Jesus Christ is the fulfillment of the Torah[41]—or the beginning of its fulfillment—the Torah and Jesus Christ are closely related to each other.

Whether we consider the one or the other, the Torah or Jesus Christ, what is at the center in either case is the lordship of (the one) God. Christians cannot then comprehend Jesus Christ as the medium of this rule without the Torah. So in this respect too, Jewish witness to the Torah is of eminent importance for theology and the church. To take one example, it is surely the halakhah especially from which we can learn anew that the lordship of God is a lordship that goes into detail—detail that is hardly grasped under the general commandment of love by itself. But on the other hand, when Christians make the commandment of love the lodestone that gives the Torah its direction, this can be a help in distinguishing between what is important and what is less important in the law (Matt. 23:23).[42] The supreme and all-comprehensive standing attributed to the Torah by Jews and to Jesus Christ by Christians (which finds expression, for example, in the theme of mediation in creation) is the reason we can find other analogous statements too in the rabbinic and the New Testament traditions. For instance, we are told about the Torah, "Turn it here and turn it there, for everything is to be found in it" (*Avot* 5.25). Similarly, the Epistle to the Colossians acknowledges that "in him [Christ] are hid all the treasures of wisdom and knowledge" (2:3). In this certainty on both sides, Jews and Christians see themselves commissioned to be a light to the Gentiles, as God's witnesses.

These considerations may offer a sufficient reason not to see the fact of the other's certainty (whether Jewish or Christian) as negation of one's own. It should rather be regarded as both a wholesome limitation and a constructive challenge so to learn from each other that we may live more authentically the service laid upon us, for ourselves and for the kingdom of God. In this sense the fundamental situation of the Christian-Jewish relationship might be described as follows, echoing the words of Mic. 4:5: Jews and Christians alike walk in the name of the one God, Jews by listening to the word of the Torah, Christians in their bond with Jesus Christ. But if we take up a rabbinic tradition about the quarrel between the Hillel and Shammai schools, we could supplement this by saying that "these and those are words of the living God" (*j. Berakhot* 1.7.3b). So in this context too the perspective we perceived earlier still applies. Once the children of Israel have been able to discover and experience over a long period of time that it is really the God of Abraham, Isaac, and Jacob, the God of Israel, who speaks to the Gentiles through the gospel, then perhaps they too will, tacitly or even joyfully, understand the acts of Jesus Christ or his church for the Gentiles as acts performed vicariously for Israel, though this does not mean that they will become Christians, thus forfeiting their own particular calling.[43]

THE PHENOMENON OF CHRISTIAN
ISRAEL PROSELYTES

At the present time, however, we have to note a trend that rather runs counter to this. Christians are becoming Jews in hitherto unknown numbers, occasionally in Germany, in Israel too, and above all in the United States.[44] In the previous chapter we explored the question about the importance of the confession of faith in Jesus Christ when this is made by Jews; so at the end of this section we ought at least to touch on this crossing over by Christians to the Jewish people. More than a bare mention of the fact will not be possible, however, if only because the most important preliminary to an adequate discussion would be an attempt to interpret the phenomenon from the Jewish side. Are these proselytes in the traditional sense? Or is it particularly important that these people come to Judaism as Christians and that they already bring with them an acknowledgment of the one God and the bond with the Bible of the Old Testament? Do these facts mean that this group must be interpreted in a different way from other proselytes? And does this therefore lead to a special theological or religious evaluation that puts these people in a position comparable with that of Jewish Christians in the church? Once all these open questions have been answered from the Jewish side, it will be easier to consider them from the viewpoint of Christian theology. Initially we may weigh up the whole complex on the basis of two examples.

A few years ago, Georg Fohrer, who was earlier professor for Old Testament in Erlangen, was converted to Judaism, together with his family, and then emigrated to Israel. Some time after his conversion, Fohrer published a little book with the title *Glaube und Leben im Judentum* ("Faith and Life in Judaism"),[45] his intention being to do something to mitigate what he calls the "unfathomable ignorance about Judaism." Rudolf Pfister paid an apt tribute to this book when he wrote that here "we are provided with a way of access to Judaism that is both factual and affectionate."[46] So it would seem that, because of his knowledge of Christian traditions about Judaism and of Christian attitudes to the Jewish people, a Christian who has become a Jew is positively predestined to describe Judaism to Christians in an especially sympathetic way, and that someone like this can contribute more durably than other people to a correction of inaccurate and mistaken notions about the Jewish people.

It also occasionally happens that in Germany too Christians join one of the small Jewish congregations that have sprung up again. It could well be that decisions of this kind should not merely be treated with the respect they in any case and in principle deserve. It could even be that these conversions, *once they have actually taken place* out of a totally serious decision, can be in one sense a matter for rejoicing, since they mean a strengthening of the congregations that in our country have been maimed and are often hardly viable, because they are so small. Though of course reinforcement of this kind can never be in itself a reason for conversion.[47]

However we may judge the one case or the other, the fact that there was once a Bodo on the Jewish side and a Pfefferkorn among the Christians should not stand in the way of an open-minded receptivity to new dimensions of understanding.[48]

— 6 —————————————————

The Church in Its Relation to
Israel and to Creation

ANALOGIES

Neither the Jewish people nor the Christian church exists by itself and for its own sake. Nor are they there simply for the sake of the service they can render each other. Each in its own way is called to be a "light to the Gentiles," the one taking its bearings from the Torah and the prophets, the other from Jesus Christ.[1] And so the charge they are given together with their existence reaches out beyond themselves and into the world of the nations. To discuss in any detail this dimension of Jewish and Christian existence for the world would go beyond the scope of our present investigation.[2] But one aspect touches our present subject particularly closely, for it is an aspect we perceive because of observations we can make about the relationship of the church to Israel, on the one hand, and to "the nations" or to creation as a whole, on the other.

Marcion,[3] who in the second century was excommunicated by the church in Rome, offers a glaring example. In his gnostic system he replaced Scripture—that is, the Jewish Bible—by a canon of his own consisting of Luke's Gospel and ten Pauline epistles, which he had previously consistently purged as far as possible of all Jewish biblical references. For in his view the Bible was not the document of the history with his people of the God who was also the Father of Jesus Christ. Rather, according to Marcion, Jesus revealed the good God who had been unknown previously and who stands in blatant contrast to the feeble God of Israel. For Marcion, Israel's God is the God of cold justice and righteousness who enslaves humanity, who had initiated his own unsuccessful creation and reigned over Israel as the "worst nation of all."[4] Accordingly, salvation is to be found in a rejection of all three—Israel's Bible, Israel's God, and the creation brought about by that God—and hence, once again, of the people of Israel.

Although this view was already branded as heretical in the patristic church, it still lives on today in Christian circles, in the vulgar Christian error about the God of the Old Testament as the "God of revenge" and the God of the New Testament as the "God of love." Moreover, in a theologically more subtle and modified form, we meet it down to most recent times in the publications of well-known theologians, in which statements are made about the relationship between the Old and the New Testament and about the understanding of God to which the two testaments witness. Hans Conzelmann, for example, sees the unity of Scripture in "the identity between the God of the law and the Father of Jesus Christ, who is the end of the law."[5] In saying this, Conzelmann—whether intentionally or not—cuts the ground from under the feet of the "God of the law." He tries to retrieve what he can by going on to say that, in spite of that, the gospel does not make the law invalid, it merely allows it to be "that which it really is, the historical ordinance of the Creator but not a means of salvation in the hand of man."[6] But in saying this he simply manifests the inappositeness of talk about the "end of the law," for he makes it evident that what he means is in fact a particular *relationship* to the law.[7] Another point shows how misleading it is to put the law in the place of a criticized relation to that law, and how dangerous if the rejection of the law is carried over to God himself by entitling him the God of the law. Conzelmann's intention is to bring out the force and authority of Paul's theology; but for Paul, the God of Israel is from the very beginning the God *of promise and* of the law, and this is especially evident in the context of Galatians 3—4 and Romans 9—11, the relevant passages to which Conzelmann refers.[8]

As this example shows, when Conzelmann claims for his investigation that it aims at objectivity, "being drawn directly from the sources,"[9] this claim must be received with at least a certain degree of vigilance. Conzelmann's own theology has at the very least acted as a very vigorous sponsor. This is shown in, among other things, the inadequate and much too brief sections on the New Testament and on the question about the possible anti-Judaism of its writings.[10] It must be said that this reserve is the less surprising, since Conzelmann himself, in commenting on the "inhumane anti-Semitism [in] the West" says merely that it has had a religious *component.*[11]
  Other deficiencies can be seen in the fact that, except for the welcome appeal to end the "unendurable, theologically impossible altercations about responsibility for the death of Jesus,"[12] the range of problems involved in the Christian-Jewish relationship is dealt with above all in the form of a few powerful polemical blows, inspired by the fear that if the definition of the relationship between Christians and Jews is changed, one would "simply have to shut up shop"[13] on the Christian side. Quite apart from this somewhat remarkable understanding of the church, Conzelmann is not convincing with his plea not to water down the claim to exclusive "salvation" in the bond with Jesus Christ by way of a "historical relativization of the Pauline doctrine of the law" because, in Conzelmann's view, any such attempts would only make the "conversation" between Jews and Christians "unfruitful" and "unpleasant on a human level."[14] Here he starts from an erroneous assumption—as if those long periods in which Christians allowed their relationship to the Jews to be determined by the Pauline doctrine of the law (taken in an absolute sense) had been characterized by "fruitful conversations" and by "pleasant encounters on a

human level." One may also ask oneself how a "fruitful conversation" is to be conceivable in the future if the directive is, "It is not possible for Christians to recognize Israel as a holy people, or to recognize its law, though an understanding on the human—not the religious—level is possible; for Christians in the world are subject to the commandment of love, the end of the law."[15] But it is of course only possible to maintain this thesis in this form if one consistently refuses to listen to Paul (Rom. 9:4 on the law; Rom. 11:1–2 on the people), and Conzelmann accordingly attests that Romans 9—11 is a "vain" and "self-contradictory" attempt.[16]

Having explained without any further commentary in the text in what sense "the Jews are the children of the devil" (John 8:44), Conzelmann remarks in a footnote that the important thing is "not only what the evangelist means, but how he is read after one hundred or one thousand or two thousand years."[17] It is a pity that Conzelmann himself shows no recognizable signs of having himself taken this essential hermeneutical insight into account.

The connection I have just touched on between the relationship to Israel and the relationship to creation is brought out in especially marked form in Marcion's theology. But there are already testimonies in the New Testament itself that offer evidence for this correspondence, although these testimonies certainly differ widely in content both among themselves and compared with Marcion.

For example, in the first sentences of its prologue, the Gospel of John testifies to a distinct theology—or Christology—of creation. But the Gospel as a whole (and the prologue in germ) makes it plain that the statements about creation are of interest to the writer merely as the necessary presupposition for the legitimacy of the claim of the incarnate Logos to the world of men and women. Otherwise the creation appears as a cosmos that is subject to the devil, as its "ruler." That is why the dualistic alternative that confronts the human being in his encounter with Jesus (and that runs right through the Gospel) is God or world.[18] If one decides in favor of God, by accepting the claim of the revealer, one is certainly manifested as a created being who is the property of the Logos—one of "his own." But this acquisition of creatureliness in the form of rebirth through Word, Spirit, and faith does not bring with it any new incorporation into creation. Unlike the individual person, creation remains what it has been: cosmos, the place of "fear" (John 16:33) where the believer experiences the promise that Jesus has already overcome the world and that he will draw out of the world to himself all those who belong to him. A future for creation as a whole is something of which John knows nothing.

In the Fourth Gospel the relationship of Jesus and his church to the Jewish people corresponds to this flawed relationship to the world. Where Jews accept Jesus as the Son, who reveals the Father, they show themselves to be true Israelites. Where they reject him as authentic revealer, they show themselves as belonging to the cosmos and hence as children of darkness, indeed as children of the devil (John 8:44), in accordance with the rule of the "prince of this world" over the cosmos. The lack of any hopeful perspective for either the world or the Jews unless they believe the Gospel agrees with the parallel derogation of both. John sees no place in the future activity of Jesus or God for creation as a whole, and he sees no place for the Jews either. From the evangelist's own starting point this is quite consistent, though the starting point itself is dubious. Genuine statements about the future are merely a surface gloss painted onto his work like a thin coat of varnish. On the contrary, what is determining is the assertion that the expected second coming of Jesus has already taken place. But then of course there really is nothing more to wait for. No future world event will bring anything new, and all the apocalyptic images of the future are empty dreams: this is the way in which Rudolf Bultmann summed up his own pessimism, and in tendency it is an apt summary of the pessimism of John also.[19]

In all this the Gospel of John is closer to Marcion than to the apostle to the Gentiles, to whom the Gnostics appeal, though unjustifiably. The very subject we are considering here makes this indisputably clear. It is true that in a passage of heated polemic, Paul can for a moment take up a position close to that of the evangelist and the heretic. In 2 Cor. 4:3 he moves into a theologically dualistic orbit when he describes as lost the Christians who follow another gospel than his, adding that the "god of this world" has blinded them; the context suggests that it is at least possible that Israel is also meant here (2 Cor. 2:14—3:18). But as has been sufficiently demonstrated, the apostle in spite of this—unlike Marcion and unlike the Gospel of John—has in Romans 9—11 left us an explicit and unequivocal testimony of his steadfast and unswerving hope for all Israel. And it is in accordance with this that, although Paul's letters do not pass down any fully developed doctrine of creation, they do transmit the equally unambiguous expectation that the whole groaning creation, which is in bondage because of its transience, will be freed for that liberty from transience which is bound up with the eschatological gift of the lost divine doxa (Rom. 8:19-22). And again, it is in harmony with this assurance (which includes nonhuman creation as a whole) when in Rom. 11:26, in the context of what he has to say about the hope for Israel, Paul proclaims his expectation that it is not just this or the other blessed individual who will enter the kingdom of God, but the "full number of the Gentiles." This different relation of the apostle's to reality is reflected in a whole series of other contexts. It comes out, among other ways, in his attitude to the reality of death and also to the Torah, that is to say, to Scripture. But it is impossible to give this more than a brief mention here.[20]

These examples from the New Testament may suffice. Nor can we go beyond Marcion and enter into the course of history and the history of the church. Instead, let me take two more general, modern examples to show that the correspondence between a given attitude to Israel and the attitude to creation is still very much alive in all its virulence.

The title of Günter Altner's book *Schöpfung am Abgrund* describes his diagnosis of the present state of the world: "creation on the brink of the abyss." Following Jean Améry, Altner attributes this condition to a "long history of Christian disobedience that thought that it could prolong to eternity its paramount claim" to dominate creation.[21] It is difficult to believe that it is no more than chance when, in the same century, the greatest crime against the Jewish people was committed at the very heart of the Christian west while the whole creation at the disposal of man is also taken to the brink of chaos by the methods of that same west. So Altner's second thesis can be analogously transferred to the persecution and murder of the Jews during the period of Nazi rule: without almost two thousand years of Christian disobedience, with its merciless results and its exaggerated claim, the murderous pogrom of the years from 1933 to 1945 is inconceivable.

In the framework of this pogrom, the correspondence between a given relationship to the Jewish people and a relationship to the world in general can be seen once more, this time in political form. The inhumane behavior of the Nazis towards the Jews began in 1933 with the "Aryan paragraphs." It became manifest at latest with the Nuremberg edicts, in which the human dignity of Jewish citizens in Germany was annulled by law. As the political behavior of the Nazi regime at home and abroad proved in the years that followed, the attitude to Germany's Jewish citizens that these edicts reveal was symptomatic of the Nazi attitude to men and women in general. The human being meant nothing unless he was a "coordinated" Aryan—which meant that he was robbed of his human rights in a different way. So as long as the Aryan paragraphs and the Nuremberg edicts are not viewed as being in themselves already the expression of the criminal way in which the Nazis dealt with Jews who were their fellow citizens, even events after the beginning of their rule of violence will be insufferably minimized.[22]

TASKS AHEAD OF US

Elie Wiesel, who is one of the surviving victims of Auschwitz, has interpreted the far-reaching dimensions that are involved in the remembrance of the Jewish persecution and murder during these years. He writes:

> If I could try to understand—though I shall never succeed—why my people became the victim, other people will have to understand, or try to understand, why the murderers were Christians—bad Christians certainly but Christians all the same. Someone will have to explain why so many of the murderers were intellectuals—people with university degrees, professors, lawyers, engineers, doctors, theologians. The action units who gave orders for the killings were led by intellectuals. They showed that knowledge without morality destroys, that science and scholarship without an ethical foundation can be perfected to an instrument of inhumanity.[23]

It is in America particularly, though not only there, that theologians as well as scholars and scientists belonging to other faculties took this recognition seriously, long before "the Holocaust" was a familiar term in Germany. They have worked to see to it that, with the absorption of the Holocaust into the curricula of schools and universities, the wider questions about ethical issues involved for teaching and research were asked and discussed, so that responsibility in the general sense could be trained and practiced.[24] At the present time this is perhaps the most important way in which the indissoluble connection between the relationship to the Jewish people and the relationship to the world—to creation in general—is brought out. And it may be added that reflection on our coresponsibility for creation is the sphere in which cooperation between Jews and Christians has to cross the fewest hurdles, since here those diverging theological viewpoints which are traditionally hardest to bridge recede somewhat into the background.

The fact that, as I have shown, the relationship to Israel and the relationship to creation or to the world correspond with striking regularity leads to the conclusion that an altered relationship to the Jewish people means a change too in the relationship to the rest of creation. The American movement "theology after the Holocaust" can serve as an example in the present day. But here I shall not pursue this line further but shall attempt once more to trace back the relationship to the New Testament. This seems all the more urgent since even Paul—though differing widely from John in so many ways, and though certainly including creation, or the nations of the world, in the hope of the gospel—did not develop the relationship of the church to any non-Christian groups or communities with the exception of Israel, the reason being his confidence that the form of this world was going to pass away in the imminent future. However, in spite of this, he does at a central point offer an approach for further reflections.

Anyone who believes in the gospel and hence in Jesus Christ is a "new creature" according to the apostle. The power of the new creation is the Spirit of God, which is conferred through gospel, faith, and baptism. The gift of the Spirit is manifested specifically in the individual gifts or charismata that belong to the various members of the church and that are lived out in mutual service (1 Corinthians 12). Since this is a way of describing "new creation" or "new creatures," it may seem to have little to do with the old creation. But the picture changes if we look more closely at the charismata that Paul lists. These are largely capabilities that depend on "natural" gifts or gifts acquired through training, for example, prophecy, teaching, healing, administration, helping (1 Cor. 12:28). They are hardly what can be considered in a numinous way as gifts from heaven. These gifts were already potentially or actually present *before* the new creation. What turns them into charismata in the Pauline sense is the fact that the people who possess them put them at the service of the community of Jesus Christ, living them there under the insignia of the mutual love of the "brethren." Even if they are only called charismata when they are consciously lived as such (i.e., in the bond with Jesus Christ and in the church), these gifts all the same belong to the old creation hardly less than to the new. And only the person who, guided by the proud confidence that "outside the church there is no salvation," would seek to draw the line for the divine Spirit (although that Spirit blows where he lists) can deny that even outside the church of Jesus Christ gifts are lived in the context of service, under the sign of selfless love, however impossible this may be from a human point of view.

Israel's charismata (Rom. 11:29) are well known, and Paul reminds us of them in Rom. 9:4–5. The charismata of creation or "the nations" are unknown and therefore have to be discovered. Christians have forgotten the gifts of the Jewish people and have for all too long failed to seek for those of "the nations." In both cases they have been sure that they were solely the givers, spiritually speaking, and they have been all too often equally confident that they could take materially in return. This past attitude means that the church is confronted with a task and a promise toward both the Jewish people and the nations. Though taking their own specific form in each case, this task and promise correspond. The task is to discover what is "true, honorable, just, pure, lovely, and gracious" among the others (Phil. 4:8), and what they have to offer in this respect. This is another reason that dialogue is the means of communication on which weight is increasingly and rightly laid in the church's relationship both to Israel and to the nations.[25]

— 7

On Dealings with Scripture

All the paths that lead to a Jewish-Christian encounter start from Scripture and lead back to Scripture again. Any relationship to the Jewish people that is not in essence based on a negation involves a new, different relationship to the Bible that Jews and Christians share, the Tanach of the Jews, the Old Testament of Christians. Anyone who, following Paul, rejects the dogmatic, destructive theory about the "end of Israel" and who takes Jews down the ages seriously as discussion partners cannot ignore one fact: that it was only after Israel had allegedly become a thing of the past theologically that Jewish research into the (Hebrew) Bible developed in all its richness. What Helmut Gollwitzer once said about the importance of discussion with Jews for scriptural interpretation is equally true of this whole tradition of interpretation: "If it is impossible to understand the New Testament without the Old, then it is impossible to understand the Bible as a whole without a discussion with the Jews. What arrogance for Christians to believe that they have nothing to say to us!"[1]

Admittedly, there are almost insurmountable barriers on the way to this receptive approach. These barriers have been built up and defended not indeed by all Christian Old and New Testament scholars but by a considerable number of them, although the work of Hans-Joachim Kraus, Walther Zimmerli, and Rolf Rendtorff especially—some of it pursued over decades—shows that there are exceptions.[2] It is often especially scholars who pride themselves particularly on their historical research who without scruple apply theological categories in their scriptural interpretation that are historically completely inappropriate. We may think here of the application of the Lutheran antithesis between law and gospel to Pauline theology, or talk about the Old Testament instead of Scripture and "the law and the prophets" in Paul, to mention two particularly serious and common examples in the field of New Testament exegesis. A corresponding and frequent practice among Old Testament interpreters is to legitimate the Christian understanding of the Hebrew Bible from the very outset as the only authentic interpretation, by means of ideas drawn from fundamental theology. Or investigations into the Old Testament—that is, work on the Jewish Bible—are indirectly Christianized by attempts to show that what is being examined has been superseded or fulfilled or that it is developed further in the New Testament.

Here it is all too easy for theological dogmatics to wield the pen, while the historical and philological research that is otherwise so much lauded and defended is set aside in the interests of theological dogma. One example may serve to illustrate this. It is an important passage from a recent book written by A. H. J. Gunneweg and is of central significance for the theme of our present investigation. The work is entitled "Understanding the Old Testament" (*Vom Verstehen des Alten Testaments*), and it was published in 1977 in the series *Grundrisse zum Alten Testament*.

In chapter 2, in which the subject is the Old Testament as heritage, the author devotes one of the nine sections to the "breach with the Jewish past." He places this breach in the wide span of time between Jesus himself and gentile Christianity after the destruction of Jerusalem:

> The differences compared with Judaism and (where the Jewish Christians were concerned) the distance from their own religious origins found symptomatic expression in liberty towards the law, with all the serious practical consequences which that entailed. This was *already so with Jesus, then* in the theology and proclamation of *Paul* especially, and *finally in gentile Christianity* in general, which, especially after the destruction of Jerusalem (70 A.D.), came far to outstrip Jewish Christianity. A breach developed between fathers and sons, between the heritage and those who administer it—or who, indeed, claim it exclusively for themselves.[3]

One is struck by the vagueness and cloudiness of these remarks. They seem to tend toward anchoring the breach in gentile Christianity but at the same time see its foundation "already . . . in Jesus," so that the title of the chapter is here interpreted as meaning that Jesus himself broke "with the Jewish past." This is about as sensible as to assert that Luther's turning point meant a rejection of the "Christian past."[4] But admittedly the wooliness of Gunneweg's remarks seems to be deliberate. It therefore seems best to let him first of all speak for himself in a more extensive passage in which he defines what he means by this "breach" more closely, with reference to the self-understanding of the Christian church:

> As is generally known, the Christian church saw itself as being the true Israel of God (Gal. 6:16), in contrast to the empirical people, which is merely Israel after the flesh (1 Cor. 10:18, AV), and as the true sons of Abraham (Rom. 4:12–15; 9:6–8; Gal. 4:22–28). If the church of Jewish and gentile believers in Christ is, according to its own view, the true Israel of the end time, then the heritage of the patriarchs is in truth Christianity's very own possession, and all the promises and assurances contained in it—but also its warnings and admonitions—apply to the church of the end time. This hermeneutical act of

possession affirms and accepts the heritage, but the hermeneutical problem is not yet solved. This applies both to the church of the patristic period and to the present theological warrant for the Christian retention of the Old Testament. Here it is not enough to point to the heritage as such and to the title of the new, true Israel. For the new or true Israel was and is *not the historical continuation* of the old Israel. Nor was it, or is it, a sect within the Israelite-Jewish religious association, which is what it might seem to be initially, at a superficial view. No historical development leads from Israel to Judaism *and from there* in a continuous line to Christianity, even though much, historically speaking, may bind together Israel and Judaism on the one hand and Christianity on the other—so much that an adequate understanding of Christianity is impossible without these historical links. But here we are not concerned merely with a historical understanding. We want to grasp and define the essentials. The confession of faith in the crucified and risen Jesus as the Messiah or Christ and as Lord does not merely assume that the Messiah has already come (in contrast to Judaism, which is still waiting for him). The difference does not lie initially in the dating of the Messiah, so to speak, important though that undoubtedly is. But in acknowledging the crucified and risen Jesus Christ, faith at the same time acknowledges the eschatological—that is, end-time and final—act of God, which sets an end to everything that has existed hitherto, in an absolute qualitative sense; lets it be a thing of the past (2 Cor. 5:17); leads from death to life (Rom. 5:12–21; 6:3–11; Gal. 2:20; 1 Cor. 15:21–22; 2 Cor. 4:10; 13:4; Col. 3:3–4); and constitutes the new Israel as being in the absolute qualitative sense the new community of the end time—a community that now already participates in faith in the salvation of that end time.

But if the new Israel is distinguished and divided from the old Israel through God's eschatological act in Jesus Christ—if indeed it is actually "called forth" from Israel and all the world—then the question would have to be, Has this new Israel still anything more in common with the old Israel than the mere name? The Old Testament is addressed to the old, historical Israel and presupposes the existence of Israel as an association of tribes, a national people, and finally the ethnically linked community of a cult and a law. How can this *Old* Testament still be important for the new Israel, which God in Christ has eschatologically "called forth"? For after all, the Christian faith, in spite of all its inherited belief in Scripture, is not faith in Scripture first of all. Nor does it grow out of Scripture, not even out of Scripture newly interpreted in a Christian sense. It is faith in Christ, who in the witness of the Christian proclamation proclaims himself.

This shows that the problem of the law is no more than part of a question. It was bound to emerge first of all, for obvious historical reasons, but the real problem was not solved by freedom from the law. It was and is not merely a *hermeneutical* problem—how the heritage that has been passed down as a historical and historically contingent heritage can be made comprehensible over the centuries in spite of the passage of time, that is, how it can be interpreted and understood. That question arises for all literature and for all the manifestations of human life in general. The problem that presents itself here—here only, and not also in connection with the New Testament writings—is also and preeminently a strictly *theological* one: how the heritage that is in the qualitative sense old can be valid for the Christian church, as an end-time and, in the strict sense, new Israel. This question was not yet asked with this precision and rigor in the early church, or even in the strongly reflective theology of Paul, for example. But the question existed, as we can see from the actual way the heritage of tradition was dealt with—and not merely the law.[5]

If we keep to the passages of Scripture that Gunneweg adduces—which are taken exclusively from the Pauline epistles—we are bound to get the impression that his remarks about the Christian church as the allegedly "true Israel" are, if not a lecture on Paul, at least supported and given credence by Paul's interpretation of the church in general and by the passages cited in particular. But if we examine what he says in the light of these two criteria, we do not merely find imprecisions here and there. We frequently discover the exact opposite of what Gunneweg thinks he is able to maintain with the apostle's support. This is true of the very first sentence, which is in a sense typical of the whole. When Gunneweg begins, "As is generally known, the Christian church saw itself as being the true Israel of God (Gal. 6:16)," he suggests that this understanding of Gal. 6:16 is a generally accepted interpretation. But in actual fact it is, first, uncertain even today whether the phrase in question in Gal. 6:16[6] applies to the Christian church or to the section of Israel that does not believe in the gospel.[7] And second, in Gal. 6:16 the phrase is "the Israel of God" and not "the true Israel of God." Paul has no particular interest in this adjective, but it is evidently of immense importance for Gunneweg, according to the evidence of the whole context.

The facts as we find them in the Pauline epistles are quickly summed up. Once and once only, the apostle calls the Israel that rejects Jesus Christ "Israel after the flesh" (1 Cor. 10:18, AV), but he does not use the phrase in a polemical sense. Nor does he, for example, call the church of Jesus Christ in contrast "Israel after the spirit."[8] The term "Israel" itself is therefore still applied to the Jewish people in this connection. And the only passages where Paul really goes into this subject make the matter abundantly clear: in Romans 9—11 the Jews who reject the gospel are called Israelites (without any additional predicate; Rom. 9:4), or "his [God's] people" (Rom. 11:1), or even—together with the Jewish Christians—"all Israel" (Rom. 11:26). The whole context, especially Romans 11, therefore shows that for Paul the term "Israel" is, in the first place, only transferable to the Christian church to the extent to which it embraces Jewish Christians, and second, that applying the term in this sense does not mean that it is wrested from, or taken away from, the rest of the Jewish people. On the contrary, they still remain Israel in the full sense of the word, that is, God's people.[9]

In the passage I have quoted from Gunneweg's investigation, however, the relevant passages in Romans 9—11 are of course completely ignored, so he can go on unwaveringly calling the church—with the ostensible support of Gal. 6:16—"the true Israel of the end time," "the new, true Israel," "the new or [sic] true Israel," "the new Israel as being, in the absolute, qualitative sense, the new community of the end time," and see it as so deeply "distinguished and divided from the old Israel" that "the question

. . . must be, Has this new Israel still anything more in common with the old Israel than the mere name?" It is certainly true that if one has built up a house of cards like this, and if one sets aside the clear exposition of the gospel in Romans 9—11, then one probably "must" ask this question, because this is what one really wishes to do. It is undoubtedly correct that, according to Paul, the church of Jesus Christ has been given an eschatological impress through the gift of the Spirit, and that this marks it as standing apart from the people of Israel too. But this antithesis is precisely not absolute, insofar as the Jewish people *at the same time*—in accordance with God's promise—belongs permanently on the side of those who are loved by God (Rom. 11:28). Gunneweg represses this second aspect. That already became plain through his dubious use of the term "Israel" to which I have already drawn attention. So he "must" ask his question in the sense described. But even if this question were not worked out by means of a highly arbitrary method, and even if it were not false from the very outset —since Paul does not talk about a "new, true Israel" and would never have applied the name of Israel at all to a purely gentile Christian church— even then Gunneweg's question would still undoubtedly have to be answered in the negative, in the face of Romans 9—11.[10]

For Gunneweg, the deep cleft between the allegedly old and the allegedly new Israel is the reason for the further question which is for him of central importance: how the heritage which is in the qualitative sense old can be valid for the Christian church as an end-time and, in the strict sense, new Israel. The question, he says, already existed in the early church, but neither there nor in the strongly reflective theology of Paul was it asked "with this precision and rigor." After the criticism that has been leveled against Gunneweg's dealings with Paul, the question about the precision may be passed over in silence. But though the rigor no doubt applies to "ancient Israel" (or rather—since, according to Gunneweg, it is the church that is the "true Israel"—to what he later describes as "the community that calls itself Israel")[11], it does not, at least, touch the Old Testament. For, in accordance with the writer's own field of studies and the title of his book, the whole investigation after all aims to show how important in the positive sense the Old Testament is for the church, and Gunneweg pursues this purpose precisely in the form of a doctrine about the way in which the Old Testament is to be understood. But it must be said that what he has really "accomplished" in the passage I have quoted is much more than to elucidate the question asked, with its "precision and rigor." By transferring the spurious title "new and/or true Israel" to the church he already creates the theological and terminological presuppositions for allowing "the Old Testament" to find in the church its authentic addressee and upholder. The transference of the title is an example that is characteristic of Gunneweg's whole Old Testament hermeneutics, and of like conceptions.[12] In line with the title of the second chapter, it ministers to the attempt to legitimate theologically the traditional thesis about the disinheriting of the Jewish people as addressee and conveyer of the Scriptures. It is therefore consistent enough when, at the end of the study, the Old Testament is also termed an "irrelinquishable Christian possession."[13] What is dubious here is not the linking of gospel, church, and theology to Old Testament Scripture; what is so questionable is the exclusiveness with which this "possession" is reclaimed for the church as the allegedly "true Israel."[14]

It is in the very sections of his book in which he would like to appropriate Old Testament Scripture for the church that Gunneweg involuntarily reveals the questionability of the Christian claim to possession that he asserts. Here he at times strikes a completely new note, if not with respect to Israel, at least where Scripture is concerned. In the passage I have quoted and discussed, he writes (in order to present as unbridgeable a cleft as possible between the Jewish people and the church) that one has to ask whether the allegedly new Israel has still [sic] anything more in common with the old than the mere name—that is (or so the trend of the sentence, with its "still anything more" suggests), whether what the two have in common is more than a mere formality. A little later, where the subject is the "unity between old and new" (i.e., old and new Scripture), Gunneweg surprisingly affirms the inseparability of word and content, the term and the thing named: "But word and language are certainly more than a mere garment or empty vessel, more than a neutral and exchangeable description of any given content, and in the same way, the connection between the Old and the New Testament was certainly . . . from the beginning a connection in substance. . . ."[15] He writes very similarly in his final chapter: "If the Christ event is in essence a *proclaimed* event and an event *that has continually to be proclaimed* anew . . . , and if language is something different, and something more, than a mere verbal shell and a freely interchangeable form for certain things that have to be communicated, then the essential and substantial connection between the message of the New Testament and the language of the Old becomes intelligible."[16] Here "connection" seems much too feeble a term. One would really have to talk about identity if one were to follow Gunneweg's unexpected inference: "This language [i.e., the language of the Old Testament] brings to expression an understanding of existence and the world that, in spite of all dependences, cross-links, and analogies with the culture and religion of the nations round about, is unmistakably different. But this understanding of existence is the same as that of the New Testament, the same as the Christian view of existence compared with the Greek, humanist, or idealist concept."[17] And after Gunneweg has defined what this is, by means of a quotation from Bultmann, he goes on to supplement and explain what he has said, by pointing out that "the idea of God [corresponds to] this attitude on the part of the human being."[18]

If this is really all true—if, that is, the understanding of existence, the world, and God that we find in the Old Testament is the same as that which we find in the New—what meaning can we attach to the rhetorical question, Do the biblical people of God and the church "still have anything more in common than the mere name [Israel]?" The only significance

we can really find in the question is the attempt to rob the Jewish people
of Old Testament Scripture (though it is this people whom the church has
to thank for its participation in Scripture at all) and hence to assert that
the Old Testament in the interpretation it has been given is a permanent
Christian possession.[19] For to say that Israel has conformed to this understanding of the world more, or less, or not at all could really only be
offered as argument by a Christian theologian if the church could say of
itself that *it*, as the supposedly true heir, and unlike Israel, has shown that
it is obedient to this understanding.

So one can certainly agree with Gunneweg when he says, "*But this is the
question*, whether Israel, like Abraham, continually goes out anew 'as the
Lord had told him' (Gen. 12:1ff.), leaving country, people and clan, prepared to abandon all his possessions and all his security and to press forward so that he might receive salvation from God's hand, prepared to
sacrifice Isaac in order then, after all, and in this way, first of all, to get
Isaac back again, and together with Isaac all salvation in the present and
the future, as a pure gift (Genesis 22)."[20] But if this is really to be the touch-
stone of two thousand years of history, the history of the Jewish people
and the history of the Christian church, surely nothing but human arrogance would venture to assert that this is a criterion the church can meet
but not the Jewish people.

However, Gunneweg's Bultmann-oriented theology is not open to historical perspectives of this kind. What counts is the dogmatic presentation
of the "eschatological Christ event" and the "end-time community," quite
irrespective of whether—tested against the language of the Old and New
Testaments—the description "end-time" can still usefully be applied in the
same unbroken sense, in view of two thousand years of history and also in
the face of actual ecclesiastical forms of existence today. It may be asked
whether if the term is simply applied in this way as a kind of slogan, it
is not bound to lead to distortion from the very outset. What is discernible,
essentially speaking, is merely the ideological function of the description
in the framework of the present theological argumentation. Like Gunneweg's way of using the term "Israel" ("old," "new," "end-time"), it serves
essentially to legitimate in a biblicistic way the absolutist claim of the
Christian faith.

"Without the language of the Old Testament, the church would run out
of language altogether."[21] As his own comments show, this fine sentence of
Gunneweg's implies an—involuntary—affirmation of the Jewish people.
But that is not the only reason the sentence has another implication too:
that without the Jewish people there can be no church. For the "language
of the Old Testament" does not exist simply in the form of the testimonies of the canon that have been passed down to us in written form.
Down to the present day, it is a language still spoken among the Jewish
people, both literally and in a transferred sense. It is in this way that,
down to the present day, not only has the letter of Old Testament Scripture been preserved. More, the community of people who were and are its

original vehicle has been preserved also. This is true even if this group has gone through many transformations in the past two thousand years. For this can be said of the church similarly or, if anything, in a more striking sense, and yet the church sees itself in the succession of the apostles of the early period. It is therefore the church above all that ought to have a particularly sensitive feeling for the continuity of the Jewish people as the biblical people of God through the changes and chances of the times.

THE OUTLINES OF AN ALTERED VIEWPOINT

If, then, we understand Israel as no more fundamentally terminated, superseded, or replaced by the church than the Old Testament is replaced by the New, we can consider the question, What perspectives emerge from what has been said for the interpretation of Old Testament Scripture? And what bearing, especially, does the theologically justified parallelism and partnership between the Jewish people and the Christian church have on that interpretation? Because this is above all a matter of showing the conclusions to be drawn from what has already been said, an indication of a few essential points of approach may suffice.

The Christological Approach

Just as the relationship of the church to the Jewish people is disclosed and determined by Jesus Christ, the same may correspondingly be said about its relationship to the Jewish Bible, Old Testament Scripture. This christological "opening up" of the Torah, the Prophets, and the Hagiographa (the third part of the Hebrew Scriptures) is already the characteristic mark that runs right through the testimonies gathered together in the New Testament. The relationship of both Jesus Christ and the church to Scripture is therefore a reciprocal one. Jesus Christ opens up access to Scripture for the church, and he himself becomes transparent through the word of Scripture, because this offers both the historical framework and also—as Gunneweg, for example, aptly stresses—the language in which Christ is to be interpreted. It is true that the boundaries of this language can be transcended, but even then it remains efficacious as a corrective that has to be listened to and, if necessary, brought to bear. Since this was already demonstrated earlier from the childhood stories in Luke, this bare indication may be sufficient here.[22]

No single aspect exhausts the whole wealth of the subject, but perhaps the most important way in which the church benefits from the access to Scripture opened up by Jesus Christ is in the clear historical "placing" it offers. Through the Messiah as he is interpreted in the light of Scripture, the church is given a historical past, because it is gathered into God's history of promise with his people. And in the same way and at the same time it is also given a future. The acquisition of a historical past means participation in Israel's history in the form in which this is testified to in

Scripture. This participation can find various forms of verbal expression and is often no more than hinted at. So when Jesus Christ is proclaimed in the Gospels (Mark 14:22–25; Matt. 26:26–29) and in Paul (1 Cor. 5:7–8) as the Passover Lamb, the community of his people is in this way led to participate in the recollection of the exodus from Egypt as an event that, from now on, is part of their past too and links them with the people of Israel.[23] Or when, on the basis of what God has done through Jesus Christ, the New Testament calls Abraham "our father" or "the father of many nations" (Rom. 4:1, 17–18; cf. Galatians 3), this shows that the primal history of Christians living in central Europe, for example, does not take us to the forests of *Germania* but leads far back to the land and history of Israel. But the participation in the future or hope that is founded on God's word of reconciliation nowhere finds a clearer testimony than in Romans 9—11. Where both past and future are concerned, the concept of participation helps to avoid that error which we find in unvarnished form in the second century in the *Epistle of Barnabas*. Its author—reminding his readers that Moses broke the first tables of the law on Sinai—maintains the thesis that there never was an efficacious covenant between God and his people (*Barnabas* 14). The *Epistle of Barnabas* therefore eliminates Israel as vehicle of God's history with his people, to which Scripture testifies, before that history has so much as properly begun.

In extensive sections of the New Testament, the opening up of Scripture through Jesus Christ follows the pattern of promise and fulfillment (a fulfillment that has already taken place, as well as a fulfillment still to come). The strength of this pattern is first of all that it brings out a central aspect of God's relationship to the history of his people and of the Gentiles. He promises, and effects what he has promised. This dimension is of particular importance in the context we are considering. It points to the fact that the church of Jesus Christ participates in the history of Israel to which the Bible testifies, by acquiring a share in the promise heard in that history. The identity of the Jewish people as vehicle of this history remains thereby uninfringed. Israel remains irreplaceable as regards past, present, and future. But in the sphere of the past, its irreplaceability finds particularly vivid expression in the context of the theme "promise and fulfillment." It is by no means the case that the two terms can be separated, in the sense that the promise would be identical with the word of Old Testament Scripture and the fulfillment would be identical with the word of the New. Rather, both promise *and* fulfillment are the marks of Israel's history from its very beginnings. Thus Abraham finds that the unexpected promise of an heir is fulfilled, and Moses discovers the truth of the promise given to the patriarch that his descendants would be as numerous as the stars (Gen. 15:5; Deut. 1:10).[24]

Through Jesus Christ, therefore, the Christian church is drawn into a history into which the traces of the promising and fulfilling acts of God were etched long before the church existed. To look at the constitution of the church, which sees itself in the light partly of the fulfillment, partly of the affirmation of the promises through Jesus Christ, makes it possible to advance yet another step in the differentiation already made in the relationship of the church to Scripture.

Ecclesiological Differentiation

In this ecclesiological context, the distinction that Paul makes in Romans 9—11 between the character of the different groups is important. It prevents us from defining the Jewish people and the Christian church as the "old" and the "new" Israel. The apostle shows that there are, in all, three groups—in a certain sense, even four. The first group is the church of Jesus Christ (I), and this is the start of all his reflections; it is made up of (a) Jewish Christians and (b) gentile Christians. The Jewish Christians are for him the "remnant" of Israel and are as such also the beginning of "all Israel" (II). The group that corresponds on the gentile side to the Jewish Christians (the "remnant" of Israel) and "all Israel" are the gentile Christians and the "full number of the Gentiles" (III).[25] The background is therefore the traditional antithesis between Israel and the Gentiles, which in the Christian church, through the partnership of Jews and Gentiles, becomes in anticipation the unity of those who are different, so that the antithesis is overcome.

The attempt to start from this distinction in arriving at a Christian understanding of Old Testament Scripture means that biblical statements that apply to the people of Israel are not interpreted as applying wholesale to the Gentiles (the church). They apply rather to Israel in the form of the "remnant" and to "all Israel," though precisely *how* they apply has to be specified in each given case. The statements about the Gentiles have correspondingly to apply analogously to the gentile Christians and to the "full number of the Gentiles," again in a way that has to be specified. The proof that statements about the one also apply to the others is then the new task given to theological reflection. The testimonies of the New Testament themselves always proceed in this way when they relate scriptural statements or promises about the Gentiles to the Gentiles living at the time of the early church as well—as Paul does in Rom. 15:9–12, 21, for example. For after all, conversely, the distinction between the "primeval history of mankind" in Genesis 1—11, the history of the patriarchs that leads on to Israel, and the history of Israel itself is also traditionally preserved in scriptural interpretation, and it would hardly occur to anyone to interchange the groups who are the subjects of these different complexes.

Chronological and Ethical Orientation

As well as the christological and ecclesiological starting points we have mentioned, a chronological and ethical one may be considered of special importance. In accord with their acknowledgment of Jesus as the Messiah or Christ, the early Christian congregations saw themselves as end-time community. This was certainly not regarded in any completed, consummated sense, but it was thought to represent a beginning. For these people, the imminence of the Parousia and the end of the world was, largely speaking, not in doubt. It was only step by step that the congregations had to learn the historicity and temporality of their existence, in the sense of its unpredictable temporal prolongation, and it was a lesson that they were also for the most part doubtless forced to learn sorely against their will, constrained by the facts of a still-existing world. The Jewish Bible, with its firm relation to the world, its profound historical dimension, and its ethic, was an incalculable support in helping the church in its first decades—if not in its first centuries—to preserve its biblically founded identity.[26]

The messianic character of the initial period, on the one hand, and, on the other, the church's totally unmessianic existence in the history that followed are the two poles whose joint existence has represented a fundamental tension in Christian life ever since that early period. But if both these poles are valid, the church can neither take over the Scriptures without remembering its own original messianic impress nor stress its eschatological character without considering the question of how this has stood the test of history. In *this* respect the church's relationship to Old Testament Scripture can very well be formulated along the lines of an entirely beneficial "surpassing" or "outdoing"—that is to say, expressed in rhetorical terms, through a conclusion *a minore ad maius* (*qal-wachomer*, from the lesser to the greater). To take only one example, if even in the period before the coming of the Messiah, love of the stranger is a valid precept (Lev. 19:33–34), how much more does this apply in the era after his coming. . . . I can only indicate the general lines of this way of access to Old Testament Scripture. It is an approach that is not so easily exhausted. An examination of Old Testament Scripture along these theological lines is not merely in accord with the intention of the Sermon on the Mount (Matt. 5:20), it also corresponds to the Christology developed in the present study. In this way, if Old Testament Scripture is christologically and ecclesiologically thrown open, and if it is taken seriously, with its specific precepts for practical living, it can help to avoid a "spiritualization" of the messianic heritage; it can help that heritage stand the test of history, so that it may become a shalom for this world.

Joy in the Law[27]

What has just been said touches on a point to which Rolf Rendtorff has recently drawn attention. It affects the eclectic treatment of the material and epochs of the Jewish Bible in Old Testament scholarship:

> If one looks at the contemporary discussion about the Christian interpretation of the Old Testament, it emerges that the question of the law simply does not enter into it at all. . . .
> This links up with a second observation. In the recent theologies of the Old Testament by Zimmerli (1972) and Westermann (1978), the heading "Judaism" is missing altogether in the index. For both these writers—and they are without any doubt representative of the trends that dominate Old Testament

scholarship today—the Old Testament leads on to the New, but Judaism is not mentioned in the process. The same may be said about the various outlines of a "biblical theology". . . .

But what is really happening here only becomes fully clear through a third observation. In the theologies, the postexilic Judaism of the Old Testament is also almost entirely missing. Postexilic prophecy and apocalyptic are certainly discussed, but the name of Ezra does not occur at all. Here the road that began with De Wette's distinction between Hebraism and Judaism is consistently followed through to the end. Only Hebraism is now discussed. Old Testament Judaism is ignored, passed over in silence, or even deliberately pushed into the background. The Old Testament is tailored to Christian needs by robbing it of its Jewish character. It is de-Judaized. The result is a Christian Old Testament, a Bible without the Torah.[28]

This fact is even more serious than would appear at first glance, and for three reasons. First, Old Testament Scripture as a whole (though not all of its individual testimonies) is the work—and hence the gift—of that postexilic Judaism which apparently, like Schiller's Moor, can go once it has done its duty. Second, not only has the identity of the Jews as God's people been continually preserved through its life with the Torah, but—as we saw from the example of the Maccabees—through this life with the Torah it contributed essentially to the circumstances that allowed the Christian church to come into being two centuries later. And third, Old Testament scholarship down to the present day draws willingly and gladly on the work of Jewish scholars belonging to the centuries that are actually much later than the period of postexilic biblical Judaism, for they take as the basis of their research the text of the Bible with the vocalization given to it by the Masoretes. So even if theological interests block access to postexilic and postbiblical Judaism, historical curiosity should at least prompt the question, What kind of group could it be that, in a period when it was supposed to be already dead or fossilized, was still able to confer gifts as welcome to Christians as these?

The theological interests I have touched on, which hinder an appropriate relationship to postexilic and postbiblical Judaism, are not hard to detect. It is true that Old Testament scholars in Germany have begun to free themselves from vulgar errors and distinctions on the Christian side, so that some of them are not prepared to go along with the simple equation, Old Testament = the law; New Testament = the gospel.[29] But the aversion of Christian theology to the law seems to remain and, as Rendtorff has shown, is nowadays expressed in such a way that the period in Israel's history in which the Torah began to develop into the very center of life is largely pushed into the realm of the unimportant. This is unfortunate for two reasons especially. First, the verdict on the Jewish understanding of the Torah is still that it has to be the same as the understanding of the law in the Pauline or Lutheran view. And second, the elucidation of the New Testament gospel itself is very much more hindered than helped by a dogmatic, extremely prejudiced, and hard-and-fast interpretation of the law. An approach to the Torah by Old Testament scholars that would really make an effort to understand it would therefore be of considerable benefit where both Testaments are concerned, historically and theologically. The first beginnings of an approach of this kind, presented by Hans-Joachim Kraus especially, strongly supports this view.[30]

The value of a different approach to the Torah for Christians extends as far as the sector where the "Jewish law" holds most terrors for Christians—casuistry. The ministry of Jesus is still often described by saying that he wanted to free his contemporaries from the casuistic sophistry of the scribes, and indeed there is much to be said for the view that Jesus really did not concern himself with the minutiae of the law.[31] But although Christian theology appeals to this fact in its attack on casuistic thinking, its polemic has in fact very little to do with the attitude of Jesus; it belongs within a quite different context. For the churches, unlike the group of Jesus' disciples, possess whole volumes of casuistic legal tenets that have—at least theoretically—binding force for the church's life. This points to a completely different organizational form in the two groups, but it means also that the plea of Christian theology for a pure situation ethic passes the real point at issue by. An ethic of this kind has its authentic *Sitz im Leben* "on the move," in the wandering life,[32] in the exodus from conventional society. This was one of the marks of Jesus and the group of his disciples and it no doubt characterized parts of the early Christian congregations too. But the moment these congregations make themselves at home in this world as church, in the form of a macro-organization and for a prolonged period of time, the one-sided call for a situation ethic conjures up at least three dangers:

— Ethics become the private affair of the individual since it is the individual in making particular decisions who, if anyone, is so spontaneously free as to meet the standards of situation ethics.

— People are defenseless in concrete individual cases if these have not been studied by way of the joint reflections of teachers and pupils so that ethical thinking is in this way trained and practiced.

— Actual church casuistry is displaced, so that there is no longer any guarantee that it will be thought through "day and night," critically, progressively, and in accordance with the actual situation.[33]

It is not least the New Testament itself that encourages reserve where the usual hasty polemic against casuistry is concerned. Paul is often brought forward as principal witness against casuistic thinking. But he is as impressive a master of casuistry as was Matthew later on. First Corinthians 7[34] and Matthew 18 are evidence enough where both writers are concerned.

The Benefit of Jewish Interpretation of Scripture

Theological prejudices against the Torah as law and, as a result, lack of comprehension of the positive aspects of casuistic thinking mean that not only are certain parts of Scripture disregarded in Christian theology but postbiblical, rabbinic Judaism is also largely a closed book for Christian understanding, which views it as irrelevant. We should therefore again recollect the connection between the Jewish Bible, the Christian Old Testament, and the Jewish people—a connection that endures down to the present day. "What arrogance, for Christians to believe that they have nothing to say to us!": Gollwitzer's dictum applies to Jewish interpreters of Scripture in the present day. These themselves are part and parcel of an oral tradition that is a thousand years old and grew up over centuries. This oral tradition has been passed down in written form preeminently in the testimonies of postbiblical, rabbinic Judaism, in Mishnah and Talmudim, as well as in the commentaries on Scripture, the Midrashim. Their traditions as a whole count also as being the Torah from Sinai, but the oral Torah as distinct from the written Torah of the Bible. We already drew on examples from these compilations in chapter 2, where their importance for an understanding of the Jewish people was at least touched on. For Christian theology the benefit offered by these Jewish voices belonging to the postbiblical period can perhaps be made particularly clear from complexes that, on the one hand, reach far back into history, and on the other hand, extend into the present and can be checked in and against that present, so to speak.

I am referring here to the so-called medieval religious discussions, which were disputations forced on the Jews by the church, especially in later centuries.[35] The Jews who took part in these disputations had their spiritual home in the world of postbiblical Judaism that is manifested in the compilations I have referred to. The center of these disputes was of course scriptural interpretation. The subjects were relatively constant, many arguments on the Jewish side being already familiar from ancient times. What gave rise to controversy were, for example, the well-known passages of Scripture Isa. 7:14 and Gen. 1:26. Christian interpreters saw the announcement in Isa. 7:14 that *ha-almah* would bear a son as being the promise of Jesus' birth from the Virgin, and they appealed for their interpretation to the Latin or Greek translation of the Hebrew Bible. Their Jewish opponents countered with the original Hebrew text, which talks about a young woman but not about a virgin. Again, in the invitation "Let us make man . . ." in Gen. 1:26, Christian interpreters saw a biblical testimony to the church's doctrine of the Trinity, interpreting the sentence as addressed by the Father to the Son. Jewish scribes, on the other hand, interpreted the words as an instruction given to the angels who surrounded God. Now that Old Testament scholarship has freed itself from the norms of Christian dogmatics, it interprets both passages in the way that Jewish scholars have done for centuries.[36]

Bernhard Blumenkranz (whom scholarship has to thank for penetrating investigations into the relations between Christians and Jews in the Middle Ages) has drawn attention to another phenomenon as well. Among the new elements in Jewish polemic against Christianity in the Middle Ages are above all scripturally based attacks on the veneration of the saints, iconolatry, and celibacy. In connection with the disputes about the two passages of Scripture I have referred to, Blumenkranz points out the closeness between Jewish and heretical Christian interpretations, and he is then able to sum up as follows: "The agreement between Jewish arguments and those of Christian heretics emerges with increasing frequency. Quite apart from the ancient heresies, which have in part been forgotten, who does not recognize in the Jewish attacks on the veneration of the saints, on iconolatry, and on celibacy, the forerunners of these more recent 'heresies'?"[37] In these last cases, a broader indirect Christian assent to both Jewish and heretical arguments of yore[38] was arrived at much earlier than in the case of the interpretation of the two biblical passages I have mentioned. The "more recent 'heresies'" at which Blumenkranz hints were, as we know, supported by none other than Luther and the other Reformers.

So much for this illustrative example. When we see how here positions on the Jewish, or on the Jewish and heretical side, have become matter-of-course elements of Protestant Christian theology and the Protestant churches—whether through the Reformation, whether through later scholarly work on the Scriptures—then the synagogue of the Middle Ages (like the group of heretics) can hardly have been as blind as the statues of the period suggest when they represent the synagogue with bandaged eyes. It is true that what seems to be a positively insurmountable theological tradition stands in the way of a new and different interpretation of the Jewish people and its life with the Torah, a tradition that seems to be carefully cultivated by some people, as if it were a matter of faith to do so. But the experience of our own theology and church history, at least, shows that centuries later, Jewish insights and knowledge have been affirmed on the Christian side. This experience should at least be a reason for us to think more deeply and should impel us to watch with eager curiosity as the Jewish scribe, like the one in Matthew "brings out of his treasure what is new and what is old" (Matt. 13:52).[39]

— 8

Israel and Christian Identity
Summary and Conclusion

Every summing up of an inquiry is open to the danger that the reading of it may serve as a substitute for the reading of the book—or even that this may be the actual purpose of the summary. But the relationship between Christians and Jews is the last place where we can subsist on catchwords and synopses. So although this final chapter certainly indicates the main lines of the book as a whole, it is not intended to be a slavish repetition of the individual lines of argument. My purpose here is to fill in the outline of the fundamental theme through one or the other additional aspect that is deserving of note, and to take up a few questions that have been raised in response to the German version of the book. This chapter is also more than a pure summary in that it includes the important question of the bearing of the Christian-Jewish dialogue on Christian identity.[1]

1. In a recently published book of sermons, Yehoshua Amir, of Jerusalem, includes an address he gave to Christian listeners on Abraham's intended sacrifice of Isaac (as recorded in Genesis 22). He closes this address with the following words: "Your community of faith also acknowledges the God of Abraham, Isaac, and Jacob. For two thousand years the paths of our two religions have been paths of separation and opposition. God grant that in the far-off future, when the historian has recorded all the appalling facts about which we have had to speak today [the Holocaust], he will be able to close his account with the words used here of Abraham and Isaac: 'And they arose and went together.' "[2]

These few sentences of Amir's offer us no more than key words, but they have something essential to say about the background and function of theology in the Christian-Jewish dialogue. We should hardly be asking about this theology at all if it were not for the history of horror and terror during the years 1933–45, and if Christians had not undeniably been an intrinsic part of that history and everything that made it possible. We should not be concerning ourselves with a new definition of the relationship between Christians and Jews if we had not learned from the experience of that history that no blessing rests on the conflict and separation between

159

Christians and Jews. We should not be beginning to *reread* considerable sections of the biblical traditions if it were not, ultimately, for the hope that a different relationship may yet be possible—a common way such as Yehoshua Amir has suggested. This, in brief, is the initial historical and hermeneutical context for every theological work that tries to define the relationship between Christians and Jews.

A companionship on our common path such as is envisaged here aims on the one hand to overcome our traditional antagonism. But it also excludes a vague and cloudy intermixture, or a coexistence devoid of any profound concern. What it has in mind is the community of a shared way, on which the two groups remain themselves but on which they are nevertheless not unrelated to each other. So the shared path for which we hope accepts the fact that Jews and Christians will preserve their own identity, but accepts too that part of this identity will be a link with the other, in the sense of a constructive relationship.

This by definition excludes any description of one's own identity—and life lived in that identity—that would conduce to contempt instead of respect, to enmity instead of friendly commitment, to condemnation instead of encouragement. This consequence emerges from Jules Isaac's analysis of the church's relationship to Israel, which is still valid today: on the Christian side, the gravest sin in the relationship to the Jewish people has been the teaching of contempt for the Jews. This has been pursued right through the centuries, in many different ways, conscious and unconscious. In building a new relationship between Christians and Jews, this is one of the greatest hindrances, for throughout the ages this has been an actual component in Christian identity and is often enough still so, even today, in a subtle and sophisticated way. If the shared path of Christians and Jews means preservation of the identity of both, it therefore means that the association should not be viewed as something static; we should see it as a dynamic process. It means, among other things, that the definition of one's own identity, and life in that identity, will change when the common path is affirmed and will become free from the destructive features of the kind we have described.

With this as a starting point, the task of theology in the context of the Christian-Jewish relationship can be defined as follows:

First, on the Christian side we have to identify individual factors that serve to cement the traditional antagonism and estrangement and that obstruct efforts to find a shared path. Second, we must discover perspectives in our own tradition and history that are capable of promoting the possibility of a new relationship, in the sense of this shared path.

It is not difficult to see that two points in particular are at issue here: on the one hand, we have to find a new way of access to Israel's understanding of the Torah, and on the other, we must discover a new approach to the question of the meaning Jesus Christ has for the relationship between Christians and Jews. For Israel's understanding of its identity circles with the same intensity around the Torah as does Christian self-under-

standing around Jesus Christ. The task I have indicated is the more necessary and the more difficult because, on the Christian side, the traditionally
derogatory view of the Torah and Israel's dealings with the Torah is
extremely closely connected with certain ways of interpreting Jesus Christ.
That is to say, certain forms of Christology are the source of anti-Jewish
assertions. Consequently it will be a central task for a theology in the
context of the Christian-Jewish relationship to work out a christology that
is not per se anti-Jewish but that will instead help to overcome anti-
Judaism in Christian theology.

All in all, therefore, what is at issue is a comprehensive rereading of
the Jewish and Christian traditions, directed by an understanding based on
new assumptions. Christians can no longer be content to hear, believe, or
understand the *gospel* in such a way that they are in the first instance
understanding *themselves*. It is rather time that they instead begin to listen
to the other person too, and to listen with the same attention and warmth
that they pay to their own tradition. The complex of "faith and understanding"[3] must therefore be expanded by "listening and understanding."
This is the only way of preventing the position of the other person from
being seen only in the light of one's own preconceptions, so that that
position is always and from the outset determined by one's own valuation.
Without a listening of this kind, every conversation would be doomed to
failure from the very beginning, because the other person would not really
come into view at all.

These ideas suggest two clear conclusions. First, Christian statements
about the Jewish people can no longer be based solely on what the Christian traditions have to say about the Jews. Instead, what we have to discern, with sympathetic understanding, is what Israel says about itself, what
it says about its relationship to God, and what it says about its interpretation and practical application of the Torah in both the past and the
present. Second, it is not merely Jewish tradition we have to listen to in a
new way. We have to look anew at the Christian tradition as well and
to seek new foundations capable of sustaining a new, different understanding of Israel from the Christian perspective. The question about these
foundations is of course directed first of all to the Bible, and especially
to the New Testament, as what Martin Kähler calls the "charter for the
implementation of the preaching on which the church is founded."[4]

2. Yet in our efforts to find new beginnings for a relationship between
Christians and Jews, the New Testament, the second part of the canon, is
particularly stony ground. As we know, the New Testament testimonies
grew up at a time when the early Christian congregations were in the process of detaching themselves from Judaism. They therefore, page by page,
reflect the structure of this conflict. To take an analogy, we might say
that the New Testament as a whole is characterized by the same "person-
ality structure" we often meet in a convert. The convert's way to what is
"authentic" or "true" is frequently marked by anti attitudes and anti
assertions about things as they were before his conversion. We may think

of Paul or Luther, or we may take as an example some contemporary of our own who has gone through the process of abandoning a Christian or prochurch position in favor of an anti-Christian or antichurch attitude. Because of this, we do not often find a series of connected statements in the New Testament in which the Jewish people are included that is not "anti" but "co"—a structure in which Jews and Christians are seen in an enduring partnership, side by side.

It is part of the greatness and profundity of Paul, "the convert," that he does not confine himself to a purely "anti" position. Rather, in Romans 9—11 he carries the Jewish people forward with him into present and future, in a positive sense, even where Israel says no to the gospel.

These chapters have time and again been forgotten in the course of church history. And if Romans 9—11 was drawn upon at all, it was often no longer Israel that was considered. Let us assume that we were to base our information about these chapters on Martin Luther's fine and concentrated preface to the Epistle to the Romans, written in 1522: it would never occur to the reader of this preface that in these three chapters Paul has anything to say about the relationship to Israel. What the reader would expect to find would be a treatise on predestination.[5] It is impossible to overestimate the loss if Romans 9—11 is suppressed, abbreviated, or watered down, for these chapters are the only sustained passage in the New Testament where the relationship between the church and Israel is really made the subject of discussion. To take an analogy: Romans 9—11 has the same constitutive function for the question about the relationship of Christians and Jews as the words of institution have for the interpretation of the Lord's Supper. These chapters are therefore *the* source providing New Testament guidelines for a theology in Christian-Jewish dialogue.

The positive foundational statements in Romans 9—11 can be quickly summed up. At the beginning of the chapter, Paul insists that in spite of the Jewish people's no to the gospel, things are by no means at an end for Israel. The Jewish people are still what God chose them to be: the children of Israel, God's chosen people, furnished by God with a whole wealth of gifts (Rom. 9:1–5). And the end of the passage corresponds to this beginning: because God's gifts and his calling are irrevocable, the people's future before God is not judgment, but salvation in judgment (Rom. 11:25–32). The remarkable thing about this conclusion is still that Paul does not mention—as many Christians expect and therefore read into the text—any previous confession of faith on the part of Israel as a whole as a condition of this salvation. The only precondition he talks about is the gathering in of the "full number of the Gentiles"—that is, those who are not Israel—under the rule of God. We shall come back to this later.

As gifts given to Israel as people of God, the apostle lists (Rom. 9:4–5) the sonship, the glory, the covenants, the Torah, worship, and the promises, as well as the patriarchs and the Messiah "according to the flesh," that is, as far as his earthly origin is concerned. According to Paul, these gifts are irrevocable, and it is part of the profundity of Romans 9—11 that, on the basis of this list and what Jews have to say about themselves, it is possible to give a comprehensive answer to the question, Who is Israel the people of God? It is not my intention to trace again here the contours of this answer in any detail (see chap. 2). It is only the central theological aspect, founded on the gospel, that I should like to recall: Israel is and remains the chosen people of God. It is true that her no means a crisis (Rom. 11:11–24), but in spite of this no, her future is a future of salvation through and through (Rom. 11:25–26, 31–32). The judgment that "Paul does not regard the revelation at Mt. Sinai as being an election which is effective for salvation"[6] would certainly seem to be correct on the basis of Galatians 3, for example. But it is confuted by Romans 9—11, which is determined by the dialectic I have described.

What Paul has to say with such expectant confidence about Israel in Romans 9—11 is based on the foundation of his gospel of justification through God's grace alone. So, on the basis of Romans 9—11, only one conclusion can be drawn *for* a church and *about* a church which still claims to stand on the ground of that "by grace alone": the assurance that God adheres to his election of Israel and to his commitment to his people, even if it says no to Jesus Christ, is not merely biblical and not merely Jewish, it is part of the Christian faith itself. This truth is as simple as it is profound, but if it were to be truly grasped and appropriately lived, the healing process in the relationship of Christians to the Jewish people would be well under way.

3. The question, Who is Israel? is balanced by the other question, Who is Jesus Christ, and who is his church, in its relationship to Israel especially? How is Jesus Christ to be understood, and how is that understanding to be developed in the framework of a Christology that affirms Israel as people of God and aims to overcome anti-Judaism? In the fundamental christological elements I have developed in the present book, I have tried to touch on the whole wealth of the New Testament's christological aspects: the ministry and proclamation of the earthly Jesus, his death on the cross, the proclamation of him as the risen One, and the expectation that he is the One who will come. I have no intention of recapitulating all this here. But besides summing up the central points, I should like to mention some aspects that, though they are implicit in the study itself, have not been particularly stressed. These again touch on Romans 9—11.

In Rom. 10:9–10, Paul summed up in tersest form the essence of his gospel, and in doing so he was probably drawing on a tradition that had already taken form. He writes, "If you confess with your lips that Jesus is Lord and believe in your heart that God raised him from the dead, you will be saved [in the final judgment]. For man believes with his heart and so is justified, and he confesses with his lips and so is saved." These sentences imply the following consequences. The faith Paul describes in the Epistle to the Romans as being the proper attitude to God is the confidence that God has raised Jesus from the dead. The public acknowledgment of Jesus Christ as Lord corresponds to this faith. Just as faith is the foundation for the confession of faith, so the resurrection is the foundation for Jesus' position as *kyrios* or, according to other texts (e.g., Rom. 1:3–4), as Son of God. The Christian faith is therefore, at heart, faith in God as the One who has raised Jesus from the dead; it is hence at the same time faith in the raised Jesus, who is one with the earthly suffering Jesus of Nazareth who died. The specific characteristic of Paul's talk about faith is its essential reference to this—believed—reality.

Except when he is talking about Abraham (Galatians 3; Romans 4), Paul uses the concept of faith exclusively in the sense of faith in the God who raised Jesus from the dead. This has two consequences, consequences that belong together in the closest possible way. From this center Paul is no longer able to conceive, or even to concede, that the Jewish people has faith in the one God and trusts in him irrespective of its attitude toward Jesus Christ. And that means that in a sense he is compelled to pursue the track of the statements about Israel and her dealings with the Torah that we find in his letter (even in chaps. 9—11). This means that God has acted eschatologically. He has raised Jesus Christ from the dead. In faith we find access to this reality. Why does Israel not accept it? To this question Paul replies with his thesis: Israel wished to be justified not through faith but through the "works of the law." The apostle's polemical statements about Israel and the Torah, or the law, are therefore his attempt *to interpret* Israel's no to the message of the raising of Jesus Christ. If this is not understood and if the statements are presented as if they were meant to record empirical or objective facts, the result is inevitably a distorted picture of the Jewish people and its dealings with the Torah. Of course the problem is not to be found solely in the way Paul's statements have been interpreted. It extends to what he actually says in his letters. The interpretation that Israel wishes to be justified on the basis of "works of the law" is a view that takes no account of Israel's own confession of faith. If we draw on Israel's own understanding of what it is according to the Bible, the realities that correspond to each other are by no means the realities the Pauline statements suggest—righteousness through faith, on the one hand; righteousness through works, on the other. It is true that, according to Paul, the basis of Christian existence is the justification of the sinner through faith, but this foundation does not correspond to justification through works on the Jewish side. What it really corresponds to is the election of the people, which has its primal foundation in God's promise to Abraham and which becomes reality in the events of the exodus and Sinai. In this framework the performance of works has its place, but as an upholding of God's faithful covenant, *not* its foundation. If we wish to develop an appropriate comparison, we have to take, on the Jewish side, the link between "election and sanctification," and on the Christian side, the connection between "justification and sanctification." It is understandable that Paul in his own time, with his own experiences of Christianity in its earliest form and in view of the circumstances of his own life, interpreted

Israel's no to the gospel—or to the message of the resurrection of Jesus Christ—as he did. But *we*, at least, cannot in this respect behave as if we were still living at the time of the apostle.

This applies all the more cogently since Israel has quite other and specific reasons for denying that message. The fundamental experience from which the Jewish people still lives is the event of exodus and Sinai. Because of their own traditions, many Christians expect the Jewish people to allow this fundamental experience to recede into second place and to give precedence to the experience of Jesus. But we could surely expect this only if the Jewish people had ever really learned, or could have learned, to know Jesus Christ as the Lord of life. The history of the church teaches that in proclaiming the raised Jesus, Christians have all too often witnessed to him as the Lord of death, or as the deadly Lord, where the Jewish people is concerned, not as the Lord of life at all. The question about Israel's no is therefore a boomerang and turns into a question to the churches and Christian congregations, a question to the testimony of their lives and their attitude to the Jewish people. So if Christians think that in talking to Israel or about Israel today, they are bound to reiterate Paul's polemic against alleged Jewish dealings with the law, they are simply diverting attention from the true scene of action.

The statements in Romans 10:9–10 that we have just looked at are in their wider context linked with an assurance we also find in many other passages in Paul, as well as in the whole of the New Testament: the assurance that the appearance, ministry, acts, words, suffering, death, and resurrection of Jesus Christ are an event that has a meaning "for us," "for you," indeed "for all." It was this assurance that lent the early Christian mission its élan and was the reason its preachers turned to Jews and non-Jews alike. Even if the old forms of polemical witness are no longer tenable today, the question still remains, Has Jesus Christ a meaning for Jews, and how can this meaning be expressed?

This question inescapably presents itself for at least two reasons. First, it imposes itself on us through the very form of the New Testament gospel as I have indicated it; and second, the question has fundamental importance, for without it we could very well end up with coexistence between Christians and Jews without any real relationship between the two, instead of a "hand in hand" rich in mutual reference. The first thing we have to ask is, What is concealed behind those phrases, "for you," "for us," "for all"? Paul develops the content implicit in this promise, drawing especially, in his epistles, on the concepts of reconciliation and, even more, justification. According to what the apostle says, the self-surrender of Jesus Christ on the cross, his resurrection, and the trusting bond between him and men and women are a transforming act on God's part. They turn the human being who was God's enemy into someone who lives with God in a relationship of reconciliation and peace, and correspondingly, they turn the sinner into someone who is made righteous before God, someone whose relationship to God is determined by righteousness and integrity. The essential point is that the previous enmity was not on God's side; it came from human beings. It is men and women who have to be reconciled with God. To be reconciled with God, to live in a relationship of integrity with him—that is, as someone justified—means living in accord with God's will and recognizing that it is his will that is binding, not one's own. In Romans 9—11, Paul now shows what God's will is for his people of Israel: at the beginning his will is their election, which is steadfast and irrevocable; and correspondingly, at the end his will is the salvation of all Israel. To be reconciled with God through Jesus Christ—through Jesus Christ to live in a relationship of integrity with God—therefore inevitably includes the yes to God's will in Israel's election. According to the standards of Paul's gospel, a Christian church that refuses this yes simply testifies that it *itself* is living in a relationship of enmity to God and is unreconciled. But if it is the case that Jesus Christ reconciles non-Jews to God's irrevocable commitment to his people, this indicates a possible fundamental meaning of Jesus Christ for the Jewish people: Jesus' position as conferrer of peace not merely between human beings and God but also between the Gentiles and Israel. And this is in fact what the aging Zechariah, the father of John the Baptist, already celebrates: with the birth of Jesus Christ God's oath to Abraham finds its fulfillment—the promise that Israel, saved from the hand of its enemies, should serve God fearlessly in holiness and righteousness (Luke 1:73–74).

For the Christian church this gives rise to the following decisive question: What does it mean, to live in relationship to the Jewish people in the church of Jesus Christ, as people who have been reconciled and justified? In our time, the most important aspects of this life are probably witnessing to this reconciliation instead of pursing mission to the Jews; intervening in behalf of the state of Israel's right to existence as a matter of course (which permits the questioning of specific political acts on the part of Israel's government); and admitting instead of suppressing Christian guilt toward the Jewish people. All this leads to a comprehensive new orientation in Christian theology, upbringing, and instruction.

The last text we mentioned (Luke 1:73–74), like the whole of the New Testament, lives from the assurance that Jesus is the Messiah, and therefore Israel's messiah as well. It is true that Christian voices are sometimes heard that plead that this title for Jesus should be dropped.[7] But any such surrender would probably have a destructive effect on the relations between Christians and Jews, not a liberating one. It is indubitable that no Christian has the right to sit in judgment on Israel's rejection of Jesus as Messiah. But Christians have equally little right to decide the question in Israel's stead, so to speak. However, the decisive point in our context is probably that Christian faith in Jesus and the Christian acknowledgment of his messianic title at heart binds the church to Israel much more closely than it divides the church from it. We need only remember that it is the conviction that Jesus is the Messiah that establishes the common bond with the God of Abraham, Isaac, and Jacob. The faith and expectation that Israel will greet its messiah as such when he comes—whether it be "on the clouds of heaven," or on the ass of Zech. 9:9, as the bringer of peace—is a tribute to the Jewish people rather than an infringement of its rights and dignity. And in the same way, the specifically Christian expectation that the One who will come is, in continuity and discontinuity, identical with the One who has come, cannot *fundamentally* be viewed from the Jewish side as an illegitimate appropriation, or as something that has to be suppressed in the Christian-Jewish relationship, because of the very structure of the understanding of God that is alive among the Jewish people themselves. For if Jewish faith includes the expectation that one day all the nations will fall down in worship before the God of Abraham, Isaac, and Jacob, what is meant is the same: that people who at the present time do not share the expectation we have described are nonetheless included in that expectation—and certainly often enough against their will. What is decisive is therefore how the expectation is lived in each case.

The basic christological guidelines laid down in this book are based on a particular christological maxim. This was formulated by Melanchthon and aptly characterizes the whole of the New Testament. "To know Christ," writes Melanchthon, "means to know his benefits."[8] In the relationship between Christians and Jews, this christological and soteriological principle must be supplemented by an ecclesiological aspect: it is through his church and through no one else that Israel will discover whether or not Jesus Christ is a "benefit" for Israel. It is through the church that the Jewish people discovers whether Jesus Christ is, for Israel, a reason for joy or a reason for fear, that is to say, whether Jesus Christ increases Israel's enemies or her friends. This is true even though Jesus himself is not identical with his church, and even though Christians have all too often distorted the vision of Jesus more than they have unveiled it.

4. What we have just said is based on the fact that the Christian churches today consist almost entirely of gentile Christians—that is, that the church's structure has fundamentally changed compared with the early Christian churches. But in spite of this, there are even at the present day individual Jewish Christians, and in the country of Israel there are also Jewish Christian congregations. (The reverse is of course also true: there are Christian proselytes, conversions to Judaism being as a whole very much more numerous.) Although, psychologically speaking, these Jewish Christians are for Jews a thorn in the flesh, Jews should in fact mistrust us if, in the Christian-Jewish encounter, we forget the Jewish members of the Christian church. Many of them, in their bond with Jesus Christ, wish to continue to be Jews. If we really take these people seriously as Jews (which is what they understand themselves to be), our relationship to Jews and to Jewish Christians can only be one and the same. Theologically, the presence of Jewish Christians in the church should above all be understood as a sign of the divinely willed common path of Israel and the Gentiles in this era. The presence of Jewish Christians in the church represents a ministry, and this ministry consists in, among other things, the fact that in the church the

Jewish Christians are links in the chain. That is to say, they make it possible to build an important bridge between the church's past (the Old Testament and the Jewish Christian witnesses of the early period) and its future (the shared path of Israel and the Gentiles). And in this way these Jewish Christians can testify both to the identity between the God of Israel and the Father of Jesus Christ and to the identity between the past and the present of the Christian church. Conversely, the gentile churches have the task of helping these little Christian groups that stand between Israel and the Gentiles to shape their own identity. But in spite of this, the fact remains that there are highly problematical forms of Jewish Christian existence, for example, in the movement Jews for Jesus.

5. A new understanding of the Jewish people logically includes new reflections about the relationship between the church and Israel, and especially about the meaning Israel has for the church. Ever since ancient times, the Jewish people has been viewed theologically solely as a witness to the truth of the church. But once it is perceived and listened to for itself, it emerges once again in the form that accords with its biblical definition. Israel then appears among the Gentiles as God's witness, and thereby—to take up traditional terminology—as witness to the truth of God, for the churches also. The central aspect of this testimony is the acknowledgment of the *one* God, expressed in the "Hear, O Israel" and in the benedictions that surround it. This embodies a rejection, to the point of martyrdom, of all other so-called gods. As a result, the history of the Jewish people has been a history of continual martyrdom, and thus over long periods a testimony to the one God and an expression of faithfulness to him. The church has regularly interpreted this history of suffering as a sign of divine judgment. In so doing it has blocked off an essential biblical dimension: the understanding of suffering not as punishment but as sign of the elect and a consequence of faithfulness to the charge given. Yet the Old Testament and the way of Jesus might have taught the church differently. For the beginning of Jesus' path of suffering is marked by the saying "You are my beloved Son; today I have chosen you." And this path of election leads to the Passion, which is characterized by the prayer that the cup of suffering might pass—yet that the will of the Father might be done.

This Gethsemane prayer has in essence been prayed innumerable times in the life of the Jewish people when faithfulness to their election meant a threat to life itself. So there is a passion history of the Jewish people in which Israel and Jesus Christ draw incomparably close to each other, and in which they have often been nearer to each other than Jesus and those who confessed him verbally. For in the history of Israel's passion, Christians have too often been not merely among the sleeping disciples but also in the company of the pursuing mob who went out with swords and staves. Thus the suffering of the Jewish people in their faithfulness to the one God appears over long stretches of history as a radical challenge to the century-long path of the churches, in its liaison between religion and power. It testifies to the direction the church ought rather to have taken, in the bond with the one God and in the discipleship of Jesus.

The actual way taken by the churches shows that the biblical proclamation of the one God—and life in the bond with him—requires what R. R. Geis calls the "grace of powerlessness" if it is to remain beneficial. When the power of the dominating group increases, there is a growing danger that the rule of God will be disastrously allied with the rule of men. The "total" or absolute aspects that are part of the biblical proclamation all too easily become totalitarian on human lips and in human hands. With their biblical roots, both Israel and the church are in principle faced with this problem. Of course, it is a question the Jewish people—unlike the churches—have actually had to cope with only on the theoretical level for the most part, because of the grace of powerlessness conferred on them in their history. The situation of the churches has certainly changed where political power is concerned. But in the struggle about absolute claims—that is, the claim to absolute and final truth—the old problem is still virulent on both the Jewish and the Christian side, even though in varying form.

In this situation, which is based on the clash between the rule of God and the *condition humaine*, the testimony to the rule of God by both Jews *and* Christians—Jews in their ties with the Torah, Christians in the bond with Jesus Christ—must be seen as a mutually salutary limitation. And the main question determining their relationship should be how far they can help each other and the world with their witness to the one God.

We might again name a number of different aspects here, but one above all must be stressed. The Jewish testimony to the one God is a continuing question to the biblicity of the Christian faith. Is this faith really faith in the God of Abraham, Isaac, and Jacob? Does it really lead to acknowledgment of *the one* God? Jewish testimony therefore means calling in question every Christology that does not proceed from a clear distinction between God the Father and Jesus Christ as the Son of God, and that is not functionally oriented—any Christology, that is, which asks not about the efficacy of the Son as "God the Son" but about his essential being.

In a recent sensitive review, Hans Hermann Henrix raises two main questions in response to this viewpoint.[9] He asks, first, if I have not unjustly neglected the incarnation Christology initiated in the Johannine writings, and second, whether my "criticism of the development of the statement about the unity of substance of the Son and the Father" does not ultimately stand "in strange tension" with my other and different interest in postbiblical Jewish interpretation of Scripture—whether, that is, greater theological importance should not be attached to postbiblical development in the church. I should like to emphasize the justice and importance of these questions, and I believe I have meanwhile taken both into account in an inquiry into the meaning of central postbiblical traditions in the church, such as the Apostles' Creed.[10] To this extent there is *in prin-*

ciple unanimity about this point. But *in actual fact* it is still a question how far the specific development of the church's Christology can be adopted in wholesale form. Let me here make one point clear at the very outset: the plea for a subordinationist Christology means no limitation to the authenticity of the revelation of God in Jesus Christ. That is to say, subordinationist Christology in the sense used here does not mean that the revelation of God in Jesus Christ is a revelation "at second hand." Insofar as the phrase "unity of substance" is an expression of this authenticity, it would therefore seem to be entirely commensurable with the biblical testimonies, and fully appropriate. It is at any rate much more adequate than the alternative phrase "similarity of substance." If Johannine Christology is then freed from its anti-Jewish dualism, the statement in John 1:14 can similarly be understood as authentic, as a statement about the presence of God in Jesus Christ in the form of the *Word* of God. Beyond this, I have tried to show in what sense it is possible to talk about Jesus Christ as God in the gentile Christian context—with the support of Exod. 7:1 and picking up rabbinical tradition.

Yet in spite of this the exegete hesitates to follow a linguistic usage on the part of the church that purports to be biblical but whose biblicity—if only in the sense of its intention—must first of all be proved. Thus what is in John quite clearly the incarnation of the divine *Word* (in distinction from God) becomes in the church's theology the "incarnation of *God*," as if this were to be found in the Fourth Gospel. In the framework of Old Testament interpretation, these deifying christological statements all too easily result in the christologizing of theological traditions, so that, for example, the God of the Old Testament is identified with Jesus of Nazareth. What is thereby lost is the New Testament testimony that Jesus Christ is the revelation of God eschatologically and *in history*.

But the formulation of the essential questions here is a task for the systematic theologians rather than for the exegetes, and this is particularly true in the context of Christian-Jewish dialogue. Dietrich Wiederkehr, for example, has picked up a number of insights into the limits of traditional (i.e., patristic) Christology and Trinitarian doctrine. These insights have been acquired independently of the relationship between Christians and Jews, but Wiederkehr considers them in their bearing on that relationship.[11] He shows that the history of theology and dogma is determined by an unwarranted parallelism between Christology and Trinitarian doctrine that is based on the fact that both of them have been detached, as it were, from historical revelation. "The Trinity is in itself fully constituted even before God reveals himself as Father in his Son, even before as Spirit he draws human beings into the same relationship."[12] This detachment of Trinitarian doctrine from the context of salvation history and the history of revelation is true also of Christology. The character of the Logos as the *Son* of God, and hence his relationality to the Father, is leveled out. The concentration on the relationship of the two natures that constitute the one godhead means that the Trinitarian relationship to some extent becomes a separate intrachristological one. The reality of the divine relationship is "no longer the Father, as the origin of the Logos and Son; it is now only the divine nature of the Logos himself: to him—that is, to himself as God—Jesus the human being prayed and called, in him he trusted, and him he obeyed."[13] What becomes clear from this, in Wiederkehr's view, is the necessity of regaining the continuity between the Christian and the Jewish faiths. The way this has to happen, he believes, is by beginning with Jesus of Nazareth's proclamation of God and his relation to God, including the dramatic story of his life and faith—from the remoteness from God of the crucifixion to the divine closeness in the resurrection. This is the outline that has in fact been attempted in more recent studies. The specific character of Jesus' relationship to God should thereby be embedded "in an overriding continuity of faith in God." That means, in brief, that "in distinction from Judaism, the Christian faith confesses Jesus as the historical and eternal Son of God; together with Judaism, the Christian faith confesses the one living God: the discontinuity is embedded, and must be embedded, in the wider continuity."[14]

In fact the movement we see particularly in Romans 9—11—the text that forms the basis for this study—could not be more aptly described. In Romans 5—8, Paul closes section after section, or chapter after chapter, with the full liturgical phrase: "through Jesus Christ our Lord." In Romans 9—11, however, where the subject is Israel's beginning (her election) and her end (her salvation) in the context of her particular bond with God, any such phrase is missing; it gives way to a wholly theocentric close (Rom. 11:33–36).

6. The church's relationship to Israel cannot be compared to its relationship with any other community. For with no one else does the church share the Old Testament as canon, and of no other community can it be said, as it can of Israel, that it has been chosen as a people. Whenever, for example, any other nation has believed that it could put itself on a level with Israel and proclaim its own election, the very attempt has been a revolt against the God of the Bible. And another point can be noticed at the same time. Astonishingly often, when the relationship of the church to Israel is given a destructive definition, or has even been lived in a destructive way, the relationship to creation as a whole has been affected as well. The Gospel of John witnesses to this in the New Testament period, as does Marcion in the era of the early church; in our own century the circumstance that creation has been brought to the edge of the abyss in the same cultural sphere in which anti-Semitism and anti-Judaism have raged is a fact that leaps to the eye. This is symptomatic, for in the relationship to God's people the relationship to his creation is always at stake too. A positive New Testament example of the link between the two is offered by none other than the apostle Paul. It would seem to be by no means chance that in the Epistle to the Romans, the passage in which he expresses the hope for creation (chap. 8) is followed directly by a section on the hope for Israel (chaps. 9—11).

This inward connection between the relationship to Israel and the relationship to creation as a whole is represented today, for example, when people ask how the Holocaust can be taught—what conclusions emerge from it for ethics in the widest sense and how we can train and practice a comprehensive responsibility for the world. We have begun to ask what special charismata have been given to Israel—gifts that are helpful for us too. In the same way, creation in all its variety must be encountered not as object but as a subject or partner, a partner to whom a wealth of valuable and beneficial questions, insights, and ways of behavior have been given.

7. What Jews and Christians most obviously share is a book—in Jewish terminology, the Tanach; in Christian parlance, the Old Testament. Consequently the relationship between Christians and Jews throughout the ages has been to a particular degree a continuing dispute about the interpretation of this book. In the medieval religious disputations, as they were called, it was a dispute that was forcibly imposed. At other times the dispute has exhausted itself in a polemic that denied wholesale that the other partner could claim an authentic interpretation of the common Scripture at all. It is true that, besides this, there has been an awareness in the Christian church ever since the patristic period that the Bible could not be interpreted without the help of Jews, in at least one respect: it was only through them that access could be gained to the Hebrew Bible, the source of the translations used in the church. So the Jews counted as guardians of what was called the *veritas Hebraica*—the verbal sense of the Old Testament. Of course the Jews were not viewed as anything more than living philological lexicons. Interest did not extend to them as a living biblically-founded religious community, nor did people go so far as to ask what significance could be derived from the fact that it was the Jewish people who had preserved and kept alive the *veritas Hebraica*. The question about a *veritas Judaica* in dealing with Scripture remained outside the horizon of the Christian mind.

This attitude has very largely remained current coin, even—or especially —in theological circles. The theological legitimation is constituted by a view of the Christian church as the "true Israel," which has entered into the heritage of the Jewish people and which therefore also possesses the sole key to the authentic disclosure and exposition of Scripture. This claim has been supported by an appeal to the New Testament. Yet not merely is the concept of the "true Israel" foreign to that Testament, the Christian church was able to call itself the Israel (of God) at all only because of its Jewish Christian groups. On the basis of the New Testament, therefore, the use of the name Israel for the church at times when the churches were exclusively gentile can only be seen as a pseudo theological use of language and an illegitimate attempt to disinherit Israel.

This means that today the Christian church is faced with the question whether it is prepared to understand the Tanach, or the Old Testament, as a heritage it shares with the Jewish people. Without such preparedness to share the inheritance, to accept the other as a legitimate interpreter of Scripture, and to learn from its rich treasure of interpretation, a Jewish-Christian conversation deserving of the name seems inconceivable.

This change of attitude does not mean a departure from the fundamental conviction of the New Testament that for the Christian church Jesus Christ and Scripture interpret each other, and that it is through Jesus that his church acquires its place in the divine history of promise. But it does certainly involve the introduction of a whole series of differentiations in the theological interpretation of the Old Testament—differentiations that prevent the history of God with his people Israel from turning into a crypto-history of Christ or a crypto-history of the church. To take only one example, the worldwide churches are prefigured not in biblical Israel, but in the gentile nations who will one day, according to the promise, "flow" to join God's people of Israel (Mic. 4:1). This single example may suffice; it would go too far if we were to repeat all the individual differentiations here. The different attitude to Scripture I have indicated has another implication also, which is of related importance: a curiosity about Jewish interpretation of Scripture in the framework of narrative (haggadah) and binding interpretation (halakhah), and above all, a curiosity about Jewish dealings with the law. This is bound up with the question about the usefulness for Christians of this scriptural interpretation.[15] As I have already pointed out, Christians have from earliest times listened to Jewish interpretation of Scripture to some degree. The scholarly biblical exegesis of the last two hundred years has at many points tacitly conceded the correctness of Jewish interpretation rather than the traditional Christian one. This, not least, should encourage us to heed the insights that emerge in the framework of Jewish interpretation of the Bible.

8. This brings us back to the beginning of this chapter, and to the notion of Christian identity that I touched on there. The response to a view of the relationship between Christians and Jews such as I have developed here can often be summed up in the question, But then what is left? What is left if the church renounces its missionary attitude toward Israel and tries to give its relationship to the Jewish people, theologically and practically, the form of the bond between brothers and sisters? The question about what will in this case be left can easily be seen as the symptom of an identity crisis. And indeed without a crisis of this kind no new relationship to Israel can be had. But because the question, What is left? nonetheless requires an answer, we shall here in summing up try to enter a little way into the question of our identity: Who then are we?

As the church of Jesus Christ we are inextricably bound up with the Jewish people. We share with them their Bible, the Tanach or Old Testament. We share with them their faith in God the Father, even if we express this faith in different ways. We share with them the hope for God's kingdom of peace over Israel and the nations at the end of time. Like Israel, we know that we have been chosen and called by God the Father—in our case, by Jesus Christ. And like Israel, we live not from what we are able to achieve but from the faithfulness of God, in which we are still permitted to hope in spite of all our many noes. Thus our experience before God depends on God's commitment to us. And that being so, we begin to comprehend that we are able to rely on God's faithfulness only to the degree we believe that his faithfulness towards Israel is unbroken and unbreakable. We have begun to perceive that irrespective of its attitude to the gospel, the Jewish people has been enduringly chosen by God, and that it has been called and commissioned to be in his presence. And we have begun to perceive that this certainty is actually part of the Christian faith. In this sense our Christian identity has been profitably and beneficially transformed where the relationship to the Jews is concerned. For the foundation of our relationship has now again become what it was for Paul: God's enduring yes to his people, not Israel's no to the gospel. On this basis we have come to recognize the enduring gifts Israel has received, and have become aware that we can learn from the history of its life and from the treasures of its tradition.

Israel and the church will be saved in the divine future by virtue of God's commitment and mercy. Of course, in this promise the New Testament presupposes trust in this divine mercy as the appropriate behavior on the part of human beings. But who—after even a fleeting glance into the Jewish prayerbook—would maintain that Jews do not put their trust in God's mercy? The difference is rather a difference in time, so to speak: the ties of the Christian church with Jesus Christ include the confidence that the church *now*, in the present, *already* experiences something of the eschatological mercy of God in the final judgment, whereas the Jewish people hope for proof of this eschatological mercy *then*. But this future hope is by no means what we call pure hope. It is hope in the God who, on the evidence of Jewish testimonies, is already constantly present to Israel as its God and the God of its fathers.

The person who has begun to see the Jewish people like this by no means becomes blind to the flawed behavior of individual Jews, or politically uncritical toward Israel's government in any given case, or any less dubious about the possible limits of particular religious assertions or ways of behavior. On the contrary, the proclamation of the gospel shows that we ourselves are sinners and gives us the strength to see other people and ourselves as we really are—and that includes our history too. And in the same light we shall be led into a similar relationship to Israel. It is surely only on the basis of this yes that we have even the possibility of questioning in a positive and beneficial way or have the chance to enter into a conversation that is helpful and hopeful for both sides. So the injustice done to the Jewish people in the years 1933–45, and in the centuries before, has unquestionably triggered a severe identity crisis for the Christian faith. But on the basis of the gospel and, not least, with the help of many encouragements from the Jewish side, this crisis holds within itself the chance of a new beginning. And so the new definition of the relationship between Christians and Jews that I have put forward does not mean that the identity crisis will end in a loss of identity. On the contrary, it means regaining an identity long since lost.

"He told this parable to some who trusted in themselves that they were pleasing to God and who despised the others: Two men went up into the temple to pray, one a Christian, the other a Jew. The Christian went forward and prayed to himself, 'God, I thank thee that I am not like the Jews, who seek salvation in works of the law, but that I put my trust in Christ, in whose name alone is salvation.' But the Jew stood far off, lifted up his eyes and said, 'Our God and God of our fathers, have mercy on us.' I tell you *this* man went down to his house justified rather than the other."

If we can bear to read this version of the story side by side with the version so familiar to us (Luke 18:9–14), then we have already begun to live out the question of Israel and Christian identity in a new way.

Notes

For full bibliographical details of books cited only under short title, see Bibliography.

CHAPTER 1

1. C. Thoma, *Theology*; F. Mussner, *Tractate*.
2. On the origin of the term, see Thoma, *Theology*, 23.
3. D. Flusser, "Reflections," 4–5, 9–10, 18.
4. Ibid., 9.
5. Ibid.
6. Ibid., 9–10.
7. Thoma, *Theology*, 176.
8. Mussner, *Tractate*, 16.
9. On the relationship between the two poles "return to the land" and "exile and dispersion," see S. Talmon, "'Exil' und 'Rückkehr' in der Ideenwelt des Alten Testaments," in *Exil*, ed. R. Mosis, 54: "The periphery is conscious of being profoundly bound up with the center, with the land, and that it must strive toward that center." Cf. A. Altmann, "'Exil' und 'Rückkehr' in heutiger jüdischer Sicht," in *Exil*, ed. Mosis, 95–110.
10. Cf. F.-W. Marquardt, "Feinde," 331, 334ff.; Mussner, *Tractate*, 45ff.; H.-J. Kraus, *Reich*, 75–76.
11. The adjective is an attempt to describe in abbreviated form what Flusser describes precisely ("Reflections," 9) when he says, "Even Jews who wandered away from their religion and know little about it are part of Israel."
12. Cf. pp. 72–76 below.
13. Cf., e.g., the title of another of C. Thoma's contributions to the subject: "Jüdische und christliche Exilserfahrungen und Exilstheologien: Deutung des nachbiblischen Judentums aus christlich-theologischer Sicht" ("Jewish and Christian Exile Experiences and Exile Theologies: An Interpretation of Postbiblical Judaism from the Standpoint of Christian Theology"), in *Exil*, ed. Mosis, 81–94.
14. The gain becomes all the more evident the more one considers the work of other interpreters in recent years. For an example, see pp. 136–37 below. Nonetheless, P. Lenhardt's study *Auftrag* goes deeper theologically in many respects than the work of Thoma and Mussner. A detailed discussion of Lenhardt's contribution (which also comes from the Catholic side) would go beyond the scope of our present investigation, but we shall be considering his work from time to time as the context requires. Among Protestant authors writing in German, F.-W. Marquardt deserves special mention. We shall be examining his contributions to special themes also.
15. Cf., e.g., his note on 1 Thess. 2:15b: If Paul was the author (of this seriously anti-Jewish statement addressed to the Gentiles), then "one of those [anti-Semitic] expressions common among non-Jews *crept into his writing automatically* and *involuntarily*" (Thoma, *Theology*, 157; my italics).

16. Ibid., 158.

17. Cf. pp. 51–56 below.

18. Cf. his excuses for the anti-Jewish fathers of the church (p. 160) as well as, in the same sense, the cloudy, vague statements such as that "most" of the church's representatives in the pre-Nazi era "*could not predict fully* the evil consequences of their anti-Jewish sermons" (p. 160; my italics). Does this mean that some of them could? And what does "not fully" mean with regard to the "most"?

19. Mussner, *Tractate*, 161–62.

20. Ibid., 158 (ET altered).

21. Ibid., 144.

22. Cf. P. von der Osten-Sacken, "Verständnis." Also Mussner, *Tractate*, 137–38. R. R. Ruether, in *Faith*, has inquired most deeply into the connection between the New Testament and anti-Judaism. The New Testament section of her study is certainly in need of discussion, but her thesis, which aims not at intentions but at concurrent factors, hits the center when she maintains that religious anti-Judaism is Christology's left hand. Cf. G. Baum's preface (pp. 9ff.) to the German edition of Ruether's book (*Nächstenliebe und Brudermord: Die Theologischen Wurzeln des Antisemitismus* [Munich, 1978]), as well as my epilogue (pp. 244ff.).

23. Mussner has a number of other dubious theses. Here we may mention his reference to Jesus' "un-Jewishness." The word is borrowed from J. Klausner and is supposed to describe Jesus' special position (*Tractate*, 216ff.).

24. Thoma, *Theology*, 159; Mussner, *Tractate*, 44.

25. Mussner, *Tractate*, 44–45.

26. Ibid., 254.

27. E. L. Fackenheim, *Presence*, 40. Cf. Fackenheim's criticism of christological associations (p. 75).

28. Ibid., 40.

29. Y. Amir, "Positionen," 453.

30. J. B. Metz, "Ökumene," 138; Metz put this passage in italics.

31. J. C. Rylaarsdam, "Common Ground and Difference," *Journal of Religion* 43 (1963): 264.

32. J. Greenberg, "Cloud," 13.

33. Ibid., 36.

34. For guidance on more recent literature, see H. H. Henrix, "In der Entdeckung von Zeitgenossenschaft: Ein Literaturbericht zum christlich-jüdischen Gespräch der letzten Jahre," *ThJb* 22 (1980): 177–92; and A. R. Eckardt, "Recent Literature on Christian-Jewish Relations," *Journal of the American Academy of Religion* 49 (1981): 99–111.

35. A. R. Eckardt, *Brothers*, 160 (quoted from the 1973 reprint).

36. Z. Kolitz, "Rackower," 21, 25.

37. Greenberg, "Cloud," 40.

38. E. Berkovits, *Faith*, 99, 131. On other statements about the Holocaust, see Alice and A. R. Eckardt, "Christentum und Judentum: Die theologische und moralische Problematik der Vernichtung des europäischen Judentums," *EvTh* 36 (1976): 406–26; Greenberg, "Cloud," passim; Amir, "Positionen"; Edna Brocke, "Der Holocaust als Wendepunkt?" in *Umkehr*, ed. Klappert and Starck, 101–10; M. Brocke and H. Jochum, eds., *Wolkensäule und Feuerschein: Jüdische Theologie des Holocaust* (Munich, 1982).

39. A. R. Eckardt, "Christians and Jews: Along a Theological Frontier," *Encounter* 40 (1979): 116.

40. Ibid., 127.

41. F. H. Littell, *Crucifixion*, 15ff. Cf. Greenberg, "Cloud," 36ff.

42. Littell, *Crucifixion*, 1.

43. Ibid., 79–80.

44. Ibid., 96.

45. P. van Buren, *Way*, 116.

46. Ibid., 117.

47. Ibid., 119.

48. Cf. U. Tal, "On the Study of the Holocaust and Genocide," *Yad Vashem Studies* 13 (1979): 7–52; Alice and A. R. Eckardt, "The Holocaust and the Enigma of Uniqueness:

A Philosophical Effort at Practical Clarification," *Annals of the American Academy of Political and Social Science* no. 450 (1980): 165–78.

49. A. J. Heschel, *God*, 68, 156, 196, 291. Cf. Amir, "Positionen," 454: "What does 'an answer to Auschwitz' mean? What act could provide any such answer? . . . I think . . . it could well be that God needs us for this, that God has destined us to make life again more possible for faith."

50. The term "Holocaust theology," which is used by Thoma (*Theology*, 152ff.) and others, is a distortion.

51. Cf. Eckardt, *Brothers*, 56 and frequently elsewhere.

52. For example in the framework of the religious dispute in the Middle Ages. Cf. also p. 135 below.

53. Van Buren (*Way*, 64–65) devotes a brief section to Jewish Christians, but the approach underlying his study does not permit any proper place for them since his theological reflections are always based on the assumption of a gentile church. This is shown, for example, by his tacit interpretation that the Pentecost event related in Acts 2 was the birthday of the gentile church (p. 72), his assertion that for Christians only *one* Jew is indispensable, Jesus himself (p. 155), and his thesis that the really new thing came about with the end of Jewish Christianity (p. 142).

54. Cf. J. Parkes, *Conflict*; J. Isaac, *Genèse de l'antisémitisme* (Paris, 1956); idem, *Jesus*; idem, "Antisemitismus"; L. Poliakov, *History of Antisemitism*, trans. R. Howard and N. Gerardi (New York: Schocken Books, 1974); Ruether, *Faith*; E. T. Davies, ed., *Antisemitism and the Foundations of Christianity* (New York and Toronto: Paulist Press, 1979); R. Gutteridge, *Mouth*, 1ff., 35ff.; S. Lehr, *Antisemitismus—religiöse Motive im sozialen Vorurteil: Aus der Frühgeschichte des Antisemitismus in Deutschland 1870–1914* (Munich, 1974); H. Küng, *On Being a Christian*, trans. E. Quinn (Garden City, N.Y.: Doubleday & Co., 1976); F. Hasselhoff, "Die geschichtliche Notwendigkeit der Erneuerung des Verhältnisses von Christen und Juden," in *Umkehr*, ed. Klappert and Starck, 215–29; "Anti-Semitism," in *Encyclopaedia Judaica Jerusalem*, 4th ed. (Jerusalem, 1978), 3:87–160 (bib., 160); "Antisemitismus," in *Theologische Realenzyklopädie* (Berlin and New York: Walter de Gruyter, 1978), 3:111–68 (bib., passim). The way the church prepared the ground for the anti-Semitism of modern times, with its destructive tendencies, is precisely defined by Isaac as "instruction in despising the Jews" and "the system of degrading the Jews" ("Antisemitismus," 345ff. and frequently elsewhere).

55. K. H. Miskotte, *Gods*.

56. U. Tal, *Christians*, 304. The readiness for obedience that had been ingrained for centuries, above all in Germany, was another reason that racist anti-Semitism was hardly resisted once it had become established by the state; cf. p. 292.

57. Ibid., 292–93.

58. *Bible moralisée*, Paris, Bibliothèque Nationale, cod. fr. 166, fol. 40v, Paris (ca. 1410) in *Katalog für die Ausstellung "Judentum im Mittelalter" im Schloss Halbturn*, ed. the cultural department of the Amt der Burgenländischen Landesregierung, Burgenland, 1978; illustration 26. Luther's comment on Gen. 35:16ff. (the story of the birth of Benjamin and the death of Rachel) reads like a commentary on this picture: "Once the gospel given through Christ and the apostles begins, Rachel lays herself down and dies: that is the synagogue or Judaism. The child comes forth, but the mother must die" (quoted in H. Schmid, *Auseinandersetzung*, 37).

59. And yet the formula is not even a correct translation, according to the passage to which it appeals (Rom. 10:4). See below, p. 32 with 182 n. 42. The whole problem complex can be illustrated by the use of the term "late Judaism." M. Guttmann (*Umwelt*, 128) already pointed out that this term interpreted ancient Judaism as an entity "that is already on its deathbed."

60. Cf. F. Ohly, "Synagoge und Ecclesia: Typologisches in mittelalterlicher Dichtung" (1966), in his *Schriften zur mittelalterlichen Bedeutungsforschung* (Darmstadt, 1977), 318–19.

61. E. Käsemann, *Commentary on Romans*, trans. G. W. Bromiley (Grand Rapids: Wm. B. Eerdmans, 1980); idem, "The Spirit and the Letter," in his *Perspectives*, 146–47, 151, 154. H. Hübner is similarly pertinacious in the use of the term "pervert": see *Das Gesetz bei Paulus* (Göttingen, 1978), 115, 124, 126, 128, and frequently elsewhere. Cf. the comment by P. von der Osten-Sacken in *Römer 8*, 219–20. On the tendencies resulting from the inter-

pretation of Jesus Christ as the "end of the law," see also M. Barth, "Das Volk Gottes: Juden und Christen in der Botschaft des Paulus," in his *Paulus*, 133; and Lenhardt, *Auftrag*, 41–42. The results are kept more or less in check where they are counteracted by something more positive than mere talk about the "end," as, e.g., in Mussner, *Tractate*, 138; J. Blank, "Paulus," 147ff.; and U. Luz, *Geschichtsverständnis*, passim. Nonetheless, the problem remains and makes itself felt when the occasion arises—e.g., when Blank interprets the earthly Jesus' criticism of the Torah in the light of Rom. 10:4 as being "in actual fact . . . the end of the law" and when he sees the law purely negatively as a "structure of absolute power" (*Jesus*, 6th ed. [Fribourg/Basel/Vienna, 1980], 115–16). His other stock phrases, such as "Old Testament Jewish piety of the law" (p. 53) and "the pious, with their zeal for the law" (p. 114), correspond to this. This is particularly regrettable because Blank's book on Jesus contains many fine and apposite passages. For the whole complex, cf. the criticisms below, as well as Kraus, *Reich*, 75.

62. This motivates Lenhardt's work (*Auftrag*). His thesis is linked closely with the doctrine of the incarnation but combines this with the demolition of numerous anti-Jewish patterns of thought.

63. Cf. the work of Parkes, Ruether, Lenhardt, and others. See also, above all on the exegetical literature, Charlotte Klein, *Theologie und Anti-Judaismus: Eine Studie zur deutschen theologischen Literatur der Gegenwart* (Munich, 1974); H. Gollwitzer, M. Palmer, and V. Schliski, "Der Jude Paulus und die neutestamentliche Wissenschaft," *EvTh* 34 (1974): 276–304; P. von der Osten-Sacken, *Anstösse*, 111ff.; and E. Stegemann, "Paulus," 122ff. On catechesis and its traditional pattern, see T. Filthaut, *Israel in der christlichen Unterweisung* (Munich, 1963); H. Jochum, "Jesusgestalt und Judentum in Lehrplänen, Rahmenrichtlinien und Büchern für den Religionsunterricht," in *Jude-Sein*, ed. W. P. Eckert and H. H. Henrix, 114–39, esp. 115–16 (115 n.2, for further analytical literature in this sector); J. Jochum and H. Kremers, eds., *Juden, Judentum und Staat Israel im christlichen Religionsunterricht in der Bundesrepublik Deutschland* (Paderborn, 1980); P. Fiedler, *Das Judentum im katholischen Religionsunterricht* (Düsseldorf, 1980); and M. Stöhr, ed., *Judentum im christlichen Religionsunterricht* (Frankfurt, 1983). On church publications, see H. Müntinga, "Das Bild vom Judentum im deutschen Protestantismus: Dargestellt an den Äusserungen der Allgemeinen Evangelisch-Lutherischen Kirchenzeitung (AELKZ) zwischen 1870–1880," in K. Kupisch et al., *Judenfeindschaft im 19. Jahrhundert: Ursachen, Formen und Folgen*, (Berlin, 1977), 21–49; H. Engelmann, *Kirche am Abgrund: Adolf Stoecker und seine antijüdische Bewegung* (Berlin, 1984), esp. 23ff., 51ff.

64. Cf. F.-W. Marquardt, "Hermeneutik," 145, with a significant reference to this subject.

65. This is the title of the book published by Klappert and Starck (see bib.).

66. On the difficulties involved in genuine dialogue in the framework of the Christian-Jewish relationship, see Lenhardt, *Auftrag* 16 ff. and passim.

67. What the encounter means for Jews, only they themselves can say. As to what the church can perhaps mean for Jews according to the Christian view, see pp. 119–24 below.

68. Cf. here K. Immer, ed., *Erneuerung*; Klappert and Starck, eds., *Umkehr*; and for an evaluation, F. H. Littell, "A Milestone in Post-Holocaust Church Thinking: Reflection on the Declaration by the Protestant Church of the Rhineland Regarding Christian-Jewish Relations," *CNI* 27 (1980): 113–16; and the "Beitrag von Mitgliedern der Theologischen Fakultät Heidelberg zur Diskussion über den Beschluss der rheinischen Synode zum Verhältnis von Christen und Juden" (printed on pp. 184–85 of the report cited in n. 69).

69. Cf. the report, "Christen und Juden: Eine Schwerpunkt-Tagung der Landessynode der Evangelischen Landeskirche in Baden. 10.–11. November 1980," in *Bad Herrenalb: Referate, Diskussionen, Bekenntnisse, Konsequenzen* (Karlsruhe, 1981); and the declaration of the Baden synod of May 1984 in *EvKomm* 17 (1984): 335; as well as the resolution *Orientierungspunkte zum Thema "Christen und Juden"* of the provincial synod of the Evangelical church in Berlin-Brandenburg (West Berlin) of May 20, 1984, in *Berliner Theologische Zeitschrift* 1 (1984): 370–72 (intro., 369–70). Another encouraging sign is the section "Kirche und Israel," in *Kirche als "Gemeinde von Brüdern" (Barmen III)*, vol. 2: *Votum des Theologischen Ausschusses der Evangelischen Kirche der Union*, ed. A. Burgsmüller (Gütersloh, 1981), 98–103.

70. K. L. Schmidt, *Die Judenfrage im Lichte der Kapitel 9—11 des Römerbriefes* (Zurich, 1943).

71. K. Barth, *Church Dogmatics* 2/2, sec. 34 trans. J. C. Campbell (Naperville, Ill.: Alec R. Allenson; Edinburgh: T. & T. Clark, 1957), On Barth, see F.-W. Marquardt, *Die*

Wiederentdeckung des Judentums für die christliche Theologie (Munich, 1967); B. Klappert, "Israel"; L. Steiger, "Die Theologie vor der 'Judenfrage': Karl Barth als Beispiel," in *Auschwitz*, ed. R. Rendtorff and E. Stegemann, 82–98.

72. Mussner, *Tractate*, 36.

73. Cf., e.g., A. Lindemann, *Paulus im ältesten Christenum* (Tübingen, 1979); E. Stegemann, "*Alt,*" esp. 528ff.; and P. von der Osten-Sacken, "Theologia," esp. 493ff.

74. Cf., e.g., H. Adler, *Vater . . . vergib! Gedichte aus dem Ghetto*, ed. K. Thieme (Berlin/Hamburg/Stuttgart, 1950).

75. Cf. J. Maier's conclusions in "Jesus," 112: "The Christian claim becomes unconvincing if its presentation is linked with a more or less extensive polemical distortion and defamation of Judaism, and hence with a self-corruption of the Christian ethos." On the hermeneutical importance of agape, cf. also the hints in Heschel, *God*, 254; Y. Aschkenasy, "Mensch," 193; H. Stroh, "Gibt es eine Verständigung zwischen Juden und Christen?" *ZThK* 71 (1974): 227–38, esp. 237.

CHAPTER 2

1. For the stress on the present tense, see Mussner, *Tractate*, 24.

2. Cf. Luz, *Geschichtsverständnis*, 274.

3. On the translation, cf. F. Rosenzweig, "'Der Ewige': Mendelssohn und der Gottesname," in *Die Schrift: Aufsätze, Übertragungen und Briefe*, ed. K. Thieme (Frankfurt, 1964), 37. On the theological significance of the "name of Israel's God," see Kraus, *Reich*, 101ff.

4. J. Roth, "Juden auf Wanderschaft," in his *Romane, Erzählungen, Aufsätze*, 2d ed. (Cologne and Berlin, 1964), 571.

5. Fackenheim, *Presence*, 73. Cf. Kolitz, "Rackower," 22; and Berkovits, *Faith*, 76ff.

6. Cf. Fackenheim, *Presence*, 87 and 73ff.; Kolitz, "Rackower," 19ff., esp. 28; A. H. Friedlander, "Jüdischer Glaube nach Auschwitz," in *Schweigen*, ed. F.-W. Marquardt and A. H. Friedlander, 37–52.

7. Fackenheim, *Presence*, 84. Fackenheim is here citing an earlier essay of his own, and the omission marks are his. On the whole subject, cf. the similar view adopted by Amir in "Positionen," 451ff.

8. On this point, see the remarks on pp. 69–72 below.

9. Cf. the examples given in Gutteridge, *Mouth*, 57ff.

10. This does not exclude criticism of individual Jews or of Israeli governments and their actions. But it does, e.g., make the mere consideration of whether a German government should supply arms to one of Israel's enemies totally impermissible (cf. P. von der Osten-Sacken, "Jesus," 25). The qualification "in a sense that has to be continually rediscovered and reinterpreted" takes into account Greenberg's warning against new absolutism ("Cloud," 26–27).

11. This phrase is borrowed from Miskotte (*Gods*), who uses it to describe what he considers to be of vital concern for Christians too.

12. We need only note, e.g., the corresponding endings in the two groups of three terms (*-ia, -a, -ai*). Cf. O. Michel, *Der Römerbrief*, 4th ed. (Göttingen, 1966), 227 n. 2. For the historical exegesis of the catalogue, see esp. M. Rese, "Die Vorzüge Israels in Röm 9.4f. und Eph 2,12: Exegetische Bemerkungen zum Thema Kirche und Israel," *ThZ* 31 (1975): 211–22.

13. The third section comprises Num. 15:37–41.

14. The translation is based on P. Fiebig's German rendering in *Gleichnisse*, 48. On the significance of the adoption of the "yoke of the heavenly rule," see esp. E. E. Urbach, *Sages*, 400ff. On the interpretation of the Shema Israel and its benedictions, and for the question of the relationship of this central liturgical statement to Christian faith as this is attested, e.g., in the Apostles' Creed, see P. von der Osten-Sacken, *Katechismus*, chap. 2.

15. Heschel, *God*, 66.

16. Cf., e.g., Phil. 1:6, and esp. the well-known paradoxical exhortation in Phil. 2:12: "Work out your own salvation with fear and trembling; for God is at work in you, both to will and to work for his good pleasure."

17. Cf. here Osten-Sacken, *Anstösse*, 53ff. On the meaning of conversion (*teshuvah*) in rabbinic Judaism, see S. Schechter, *Aspects*, 313ff.; and Urbach, *Sages*, 462ff.

18. Here cf. pp. 131–33 below.

19. Cf. W. Michaelis, "*prōtotokos,*" in *ThWBNT* 6 (1959): 875.

20. There is an obvious substantial closeness here between the exodus tradition and the interpretation of the cross. See *Exodus*, ed. H. H. Henrix and M. Stöhr.

21. On the relation between the rabbinic concept of the *shekhinah* and the biblical term *kavod*, cf. A. M. Goldberg's fundamental study *Schekhinah*, 32, 33–34, 44ff., 60ff., 125ff., 206–7, 265–66, 322–23, 328, 329–30, 468ff. For the interpretation of the *shekhinah* as expression of God's presence, cf. also Heschel, *God*, 81ff.; and Urbach, *Sages*, 37ff.

22. *Midrash Echa Rabbati* 1.32. Cf. P. Kuhn, *Gottes Selbsterniedrigung in der Theologie der Rabbinen* (Munich, 1968), 89.

23. Kuhn, *Gottes Selbsterniedrigung*, 82ff.

24. Ibid., 89; Kuhn's italics.

25. Ibid. Cf. Goldberg, *Schekhinah*, 494–95, 522ff.

26. Cf. E. Kutsch, "*bᵉrit,*" 347.

27. Ibid., 348. Cf. A. Jepsen, "Berith," 201.

28. H. Hegermann, "*diathēkē,*" 720.

29. Kutsch, "*bᵉrit,*" 350.

30. Ibid., 347, 350.

31. Ibid., 349.

32. Cf. Jepsen, "Berith," 202ff.

33. *Authorised Daily Prayer Book*, rev. ed., Hebrew text, ET with commentary and notes by J. H. Hertz (New York/London/Jerusalem: Soncino Press, 1948), 114–17. Cf. R. J. Z. Werblowsky, "Tora"; A. Wittstock, *Toraliebe im jüdischen Volk* (Berlin, 1981), 21ff.; and E. P. Sanders, *Paul*, esp. 84ff. On the understanding of the Torah in the preceding postexilic period (which had a basically similar orientation), see H.-J. Kraus, "Freude"; M. Limbeck, *Die Ordnung des Heils: Untersuchungen zum Gesetzesverständnis des Frühjudentums* (Düsseldorf, 1971). The understanding of the Torah referred to means that Israel is not capable of seeing a contrast between "the covenant of promise to Abraham and the covenant of obligation given on Sinai" (such as is worked out by Paul in Galatians 3—4; cf. Hegermann, "*diathēkē,*" 721) as a reflection of its own relationship to the Torah.

34. M. Buber, "Kirche," 569. On the interpretation as "a statement of faith and hope, not something that is a matter of course," see H. Gollwitzer, "Judentum," 169–70. The phrase quoted is on p. 169.

35. A. J. Heschel, "The Ecumenical Movement," in his *The Insecurity of Freedom* (New York: Farrar, Straus & Giroux, 1966; Noonday Press, 1972).

36. Cf. here P. von der Osten-Sacken, "Die Bücher der Tora als Hütte der Gemeinde: Amos 5,26f. in der Damaskusschrift," *ZAW* 91 (1979): 423–35. On the Torah as Israel's stronghold, see also N. P. Levinson, "'Wäre deine Weisung nicht meine Freude . . .': Bewahrung durch die Thora," in P. von der Osten-Sacken, *Treue*, 118–23; and Marquardt, "Hermeneutik," 147. On the openness of the Torah to the future, even after a repeated entry into or return to the land, see J. van Goudoever, "Tora und Galut," in *Jüdisches Volk–gelobtes Land: Die biblischen Landverheissungen als Problem des jüdischen Selbstverständnisses und der christlichen Theologie*, ed. W. Eckert, N. P. Levinson, and M. Stöhr (Munich, 1970), 197–202, esp. 202: "The Torah shows us the path from oasis to oasis, for the goal has not yet been reached."

37. Cf. here L. Ginsberg, *Eine unbekannte jüdische Sekte* (New York: author's own pub. house, 1922), 289–90.

38. Cf. Heschel, *God*, 336ff.; Lenhardt, *Auftrag*, 66ff.

39. Werblowsky, "Tora," 162.

40. Among many testimonies and accounts, cf. J. Glattstein, I. Knox, and S. Margoshes, eds., *Anthology of Holocaust Literature* (Philadelphia: Jewish Pub. Soc. of America, 1973); A. H. Friedlander, ed., *Out of the Whirlwind: A Reader of Holocaust Literature* (Garden City, N.Y.: Doubleday & Co., 1968; New York: Union of American Hebrew Congregations, 1976); H. J. Zimmels, *The Echo of the Nazi Holocaust in Rabbinic Literature* (New York: Ktav Pub. House, 1975); R. Bryks, *Kiddush Hashem* (New York: Behrman House, 1977); I. J. Rosenbaum, *The Holocaust and Halakhah* (New York: Ktav Pub. House, 1976).

41. Werblowsky, "Tora," 162.

42. For a detailed account and evaluation of the positive aspects of Paul's interpretation of the law as outlined here, cf. Osten-Sacken, *Römer 8*, 245ff., 250ff., 256ff.; idem, "Befreiung,"

353ff.; idem, *Anstösse*, 11ff. On the apostle's interpretation of the law, cf. also esp. Sanders, *Paul*, 431ff.; and J. C. Beker, *Paul*, esp. 235ff. These two studies represent different approaches, but it is refreshing to find that both go beyond the usual treatment of the subject of Paul and the law. Beker is right in stressing that Paul bases—and intentionally so—what he says about the law on the Jewish interpretation of it. I agree with Sanders, however, in doubting whether the apostle gave sufficient weight to this Jewish interpretation. For a positive evaluation of the Jewish attitude to the Torah, see also Lenhardt's further open question (*Auftrag*, 128) concerning what positive value for Christians Jewish observances (*observances juives*, French manuscript, p. 127) could have.

43. See here W. O. E. Oesterley, *The Jewish Background of the Christian Liturgy* (London: Oxford Univ. Press, 1925; Gloucester, Mass.: Peter Smith, 1965); C. W. Dugmore, *The Influence of the Synagogue Upon the Divine Office* (London: Oxford Univ. Press, 1944); E. Werner, *The Sacred Bridge: Liturgical Parallels in Synagogue and Early Church* (New York: Columbia Univ. Press, 1959; Schocken Books, 1970); H. H. Henrix, ed., *Jüdische Liturgie: Geschichte—Wesen—Struktur* (Freiburg, 1979); S. Ben-Chorin, *Betendes Judentum: Die Liturgie der Synagoge* (Tübingen, 1980); and Osten-Sacken, *Katechismus*.

44. E. Fromm, *To Have or to Be* (New York: Harper & Row, 1976), here quoted from Abacus ed. (London, 1979), 57–58. Cf. Heschel, *God*, 262; J. König, *Den Netzen entronnen* (Göttingen, 1967), 18ff., as well as the other testimonies in Annette Bygott, *Wege Israels* (Berlin, 1981), 19, 23.

45. Osten-Sacken, "Befreiung."

46. G. Scholem, "Zur Geschichte der messianischen Idee im Judentum," in his *Über einige Grundbegriffe des Judentums* (Frankfurt, 1970), 167.

47. See here F.-W. Marquardt, *Land*, 91ff.; G. Eichholz, "Der ökumenische und missionarische Horizont der Kirche," *EvTh* 21 (1961): 19; O. Cullmann, "Ökumenische Kollekte und Gütergemeinschaft im Urchristentum," in his *Vorträge und Aufsätze 1925–1962* (Tübingen and Zurich, 1966), 601–2. K. Berger's insights point in the same direction: see his "Almosen für Israel: Zum historischen Kontext der paulinischen Kollekte," *NTS* 23 (1977): 188–204.

48. Cf. "Israel—Volk, Land und Staat: Handreichung für eine theologische Besinnung der Niederlandischen Reformierten Kirche. Von ihrer Generalsynode angenommen am 16. Juni 1970," German trans. from Dutch in *FrRu* 23 (1971): 19–27; Osten-Sacken, *Anstösse* 111ff.; Klappert, *Israel* 66ff.; idem, "Zeichen der Treue Gottes," in *Umkehr*, ed. Klappert and Starck, 73–78; and Immer, *Erneuerung*, 9. On the subject of the land of Israel in general, see Marquardt, *Land*; R. Rendtorff, *Israel und sein Land* (Munich, 1975); W. D. Davies, *The Gospel and the Land: Early Christianity and Jewish Territorial Doctrine* (Berkeley and Los Angeles: Univ. of Calif. Press, 1974); the review by S. Talmon in *CNI* 25 (1975): 132–35; M. Stöhr, ed., *Zionismus: Beiträge zur Diskussion* (Munich, 1980); and W. Kickel, *Das gelobte Land: Die religiöse Bedeutung des Staates Israel in jüdischer und christlicher Sicht* (Munich, 1984).

49. Cf. P. Schäfer, *Die Vorstellung vom heiligen Geist in der rabbinischen Literatur* (Munich, 1972), 135ff.

50. Ibid., 148–49.

51. Ibid., 112ff.

52. Cf. Lenhardt, *Auftrag*, passim. For a discussion about the question of Jesus in Judaism, see Maier's description of the situation in "Jesus," 79: ". . . we should be clear about the fact that, since Jesus had no effect on Judaism itself, interest in him can never be as intensive among Jews as among Christians, but that in view of the unhappy history of the relationship between Christians and Jews, 'Jesus' is not, either, simply one subject among others."

53. Cf. here S. Krauss, *Das Leben Jesu nach jüdischen Quellen* (Berlin, 1902); G. Schlichting, *Ein jüdisches Leben Jesu: Die verschollene Toledot-Jeschu-Fassung Tam u-mu'ad* (Tübingen, 1982); J. Klausner, *Jesus;* S. Ben-Chorin, "Das Jesus-Bild im modernen Judentum," in *Judenhass—Schuld der Christen?* ed. W. P. Eckert and E. L. Ehrlich (Essen, 1964), 139ff.; and G. Lindeskog, *Jesusfrage*. On the rabbinic period, see J. Maier, *Jesus von Nazareth in der talmudischen Überlieferung* (Darmstadt, 1978). On Judaism today, see Trude Weiss-Rosmarin, *Jewish Expressions on Jesus: An Anthology* (New York: Ktav Pub. House, 1977); esp. on Jesus in Israeli school books, see P. Lapide, *Ist das nicht Josephs Sohn? Jesus im heutigen Judentum* (Stuttgart and Munich, 1976).

54. Klausner, *Jesus.*

55. Ibid.

56. For a correction of the view that the ninth to eleventh centuries were the Golden Age for Jews in the Middle Ages, see M. Awerbuch, *Begegnung* 13ff.

57. On the following passage, cf. Lindeskog, *Jesusfrage*, 29ff., 63ff., 94ff.

58. M. Buber, *Two Types of Faith* (New York: Harper & Row, 1961). [The present translation has been made directly from the German text.—TRANS.]

59. M. Buber, *I and Thou*, trans. R. Gregor Smith (New York: Charles Scribner's Sons; Edinburgh: T. & T. Clark, 1937); quoted from 1952 reprint, p. 66.

60. S. Ben-Chorin, *Bruder Jesus: Der Nazarener in jüdischer Sicht* (Munich, 1967). Cf. now his "Ist im Christentum etwas von Gott her geschehen? Ein Versuch jüdischer Theologie des Christentums," in his *Theologia Judaica: Gesammelte Aufsätze* (Tübingen, 1982), 72–85, esp. 80. This later contribution perhaps goes a stage further still.

61. D. Flusser, *Jesus*. Cf. his "A New Sensitivity in Judaism and the Christian Message," *Harvard Theological Review* 61 (1968): 107–27.

62. J. Bloch, "Jesus," 17–18.

63. F.-W. Marquardt, "Jesus," 67ff.; and Osten-Sacken, "Jesus," 25.

64. Flusser, *Jesus*.

65. Ibid. On the assurance of Jesus' resurrection as the essential difference between the Jewish and the Christian understanding of Jesus—and between Judaism and Christianity generally—see Eckardt, *Brothers*, 88.

CHAPTER 3

1. R. Bultmann, *Theology*, sec. 7; and idem, "Die Christologie des Neuen Testaments," in his *Glauben und Verstehen*, 3d ed. (Tübingen, 1958), 1:265–66; W. Schmithals, *Jesus Christus in der Verkündigung der Kirche* (Neukirchen, 1972), 51.

2. E. Käsemann points out here that "not even in a ghost" could "the facticity of the coming [be separated from] the modality of the appearance" ("Jesus-Frage," 50).

3. This is the title Luther gave to one of his writings in 1523.

4. Cf. Käsemann, "Jesus-Frage," 50, 52–53.

5. E. Käsemann, "Problem," 205.

6. In addition to the books on Jesus by Jewish authors already cited, see G. Vermes, *Jesus the Jew* (New York: Macmillan Co., 1974; London: William Collins Sons, 1973; 2d ed., Philadelphia: Fortress Press, 1981), 19ff. See also the essays in *Jude-Sein*, ed. Eckert and Henrix; as well as N. P. Levinson, "Jude"; Marquardt, "Jesus"; and L. Swidler, "The Jewishness of Jesus: Some Religious Implications for Christians," *JES* 18 (1981): 104–13. Opinions disputing the "Jewishness of Jesus" or minimizing its importance are gathered together in B. Klappert, "Jesus," 155–56.

7. Cf. I. Greenberg, "The New Spirit in Christian-Jewish Relations," *CJR* no. 70 (1980). Greenberg points out that if Jesus and his mother had been living in Europe in the 1940s they would have been sent to Auschwitz (p. 30).

8. J. Klausner, S. Ben-Chorin, D. Flusser, P. E. Lapide, and others. This trend is given its most pointed form in Lapide's statement "Jesus was an Israeli" (*Jesus in Israel* [Gladbeck, 1970], 63).

9. L. Baeck, "Harnack's Vorlesungen über das Wesen des Christentums," *Monatsschrift für Geschichte und Wissenschaft des Judentums* 45 (1901): 119.

10. See P. Lapide, "Messias."

11. Cf., e.g., the American writers already discussed. A slight trend in this direction is also shown by the resolution of the Rhineland Synod *Zur Erneuerung des Verhältnisses von Christen und Juden*. This is admittedly retarded by the use of the title "Israel's Messiah." For a development of the Christology implicit in the resolution, see Klappert, "Jesus," 158ff.

12. This last dimension is too often ignored. Cf., e.g., Bultmann's account of Pauline theology, in which the section dealing with Christ's cross and resurrection as saving event has no "flanking" exposition to bring out the place of the "One who is to come" (*Theology*, sec. 33).

13. "Good Teacher" is an unusual form of address, but it is not without parallel in Jewish tradition. Cf. *b. Taanit* 24b and the comment on it by G. Dalman, *Die Worte Jesu*, 2d

ed. (Leipzig, 1930; Darmstadt, 1965), 277; and I. Abrahams, *Studies in Pharisaism and the Gospels* (Cambridge, 1924), 2:186.

14. On Jesus' closeness to the "Hear, O Israel," as this is shown by Mark 12:28–34, see Lenhardt, *Auftrag*, 72; and Osten-Sacken, *Anstösse*, 209–10. These contributions also discuss the trend to suppress Jesus' closeness to Israel's faithfulness to the Torah, a trend that can be observed both then and now; cf. Matt. 19:16ff.

15. Cf. H. G. Kippenberg, *Garizim und Synagoge* (Berlin and New York: Walter de Gruyter, 1971), 94ff.

16. Cf. here J. Jeremias, *Abba*, 56ff.; and idem, *Theology*.

17. Cf. for example Jeremias, *Abba*, 19ff., esp. 23–24, 26, as well as the criticism of related and even more radical positions in Mussner, *Tractate*, 126ff. See now also the helpful articles by D. Zeller, "God as Father in the Proclamation and in the Prayer of Jesus," and A. Finkel, "The Prayer of Jesus in Matthew," both in *Standing Before God: Studies on Prayer in Scripture and in Tradition with Essays in Honor of J. M. Oesterreicher*, ed. A. Finkel and L. Frizzell (New York: Ktav Pub. House, 1981), 117–29, 131–70. On the interpretation of the Lord's Prayer in general as a Jewish prayer, see also C. Taylor, *Sayings of the Jewish Fathers* (Cambridge, 1877), 1:138–45; M. Brocke, J. J. Petuchowski, and W. Strolz, eds., *Das Vaterunser: Jemeinsames im Beten von Juden und Christen* (Freiburg, 1974); Mussner, *Tractate*, 124ff.; Pnina Navè, *Du unser Vater: Jüdische Gebete für Christen* (Freiburg/Basel/Vienna, 1975). Cf. further Osten-Sacken, *Katechismus*, chap. 3.

18. Jeremias (*Abba*, 62–63) gives other examples, though he plays down their importance.

19. *Mekhilta* on Exod. 14:19, quoted from Fiebig, *Gleichnisse*, 49.

20. *Authorized Daily Prayer Book*, trans. S. Singer (Prayer Book of the Orthodox Jewish Community, the United Hebrew Congregation of the British Empire; printed by Eyre and Spottiswoode, London). Quoted in W. S. Simpson, *Jewish Prayer and Worship* (London, 1965). My italics; punctuation slightly altered.

21. Cf. here J. Jeremias, *Lord's Prayer*. Cf. also J. Heinemann's pointer to the traditional coupling of God's lordship and his holiness in ancient Jewish prayers (*Prayer*, 223 with n. 15).

22. *Authorised Daily Prayer Book*, 208–11. See 182 n. 33 above.

23. Cf. Jeremias, *Lord's Prayer*.

24. Cf. here Bloch. "Jesus," 23, following F. Maass, "Das Gleichnis vom ungerechten Haushalter, Lucas 16, 1–8," *ThViat* 8 (1961–62): 173–84.

25. H. D. Leuner, "Jüdische und christliche Zukunftserwartung," in his *Israel*, 99–100; F. Schnider, *Söhne*, esp. 51ff. Schnider's work is also important as showing the pre-Lukan character of the parables in Luke 15, esp. Luke 15:11–32. Cf. here also I. Broer, "Das Gleichnis vom verlorenen Sohn und die Theologie des Lukas," *NTS* 20 (1974): 453–62; C. E. Carlston, "Reminiscence and Redaction in Luke 15, 11–32," *Journal of Biblical Literature* 94 (1975): 368–90; and O. Hofius, "Alttestamentliche Motive im Gleichnis vom verlorenen Sohn," *NTS* 24 (1978): 240–48. Schnider's acceptance of the traditional interpretation that terms both sons lost is problematical, however. See n. 26 following.

26. Thus J. Schniewind, *Die Freude der Busse* (Göttingen, 1956), 77: "But here, in the rejecting words of the devout man, a breach takes place that now means a separation and a lostness that *goes far beyond* the lostness of the 'prodigal' son" (my italics). Such an interpretation does violence to the text. D. Flusser characterizes its trend much more aptly when he describes what the father says to the elder son as the "sting of a mild admonition"; cf. *Die rabbinischen Gleichnisse und der Gleichniserzähler Jesus* (New York: Peter Lang, 1981; Bern and Frankfurt, 1980), 306. Flusser's description has all the more force since he is not at all mealy-mouthed in what he says about Jesus' critics (cf. p. 72 and passim).

27. In this specific, limited sense it may perhaps be said that what is in question in the case of the elder son as well is the "reacquiring of fellowship" with the Father. But Schnider's conclusion (*Söhne*, 95; cf. 66) that what is ultimately at stake is the "reacquiring of fellowship with the Father . . . by every human being" can hardly be maintained. For one thing, it levels out the difference between the two sons. For another, the extension to "every human being" would seem to be dogmatically determined. The word "ultimately" suggests that Schnider himself has a certain doubt here. It is a similar, christologically motivated strain on the text when Mussner (*Tractate*), while stressing the correspondence Schnider (p. 95) rightly sees between God's acts and the acts of Jesus (for which he coins the apt phrase

"unity of action with God"), extends this idea to mean that Jesus wanted to gather the whole of Israel "round himself."

28. Cf. R. Meyer, "*Pharisaios* A," in *ThWBNT* 9 (1973): 11–36, esp. 15. For further literature, see ibid., 11–12; and Mussner, *Tractate*.

29. For the importance of the "eschatological goal of a restored 'whole Israel'" for an understanding of Jesus' ministry, see also the references in Maier, "Jesus," 96, 99, 110. The quotation is taken from p. 96.

30. Cf. Käsemann, "Problem," 207; and idem, "Jesus-Frage," 50. Käsemann, however, shares traditional tendencies that are questionable: Jesus is presented as shattering the sphere of late Jewish piety ("Problem," 206) or as shaking the foundations of late Judaism (p. 208), and his relationship to the Torah is defined as being the reason for his death ("Problem," 208; and "Jesus-Frage," 51–52). Cf. here the following passage.

31. L. Goppelt's phrase in *Theologie*, 148. Goppelt maintains in connection with the Sabbath that the command to "keep the Sabbath day holy" was "swallowed up, as it were," by Jesus' own principle as this is passed down in Mark 3:4 (*Theologie*, 145). Since what is in question is a Jewish maxim (see *Mekhilta* on Exod. 31:12), this is so excessive that no further refutation is required. His judgment on the cult also lacks a sufficient foundation in view of his own extremely tentative attempt to ascertain Jesus' attitude to the temple (pp. 147–48). The simple question why Jesus should have "cleansed" the forecourt of the temple if he had wanted to abolish the cult should be sufficient to indicate what familiar old dogmatic interests are involved here on the part of the interpreter. For criticism of the theological stylizing of Jesus' disputes into a "fundamental conflict with 'the law,'" see Maier, "Jesus," 95ff. (quotation from p. 95). K. Berger has also shown (*Die Gesetzesauslegung Jesu* [Neukirchen, 1972], 473–74) that related views can also be found in Hellenistic Judaism, so that from this point of view too there is no reason for maintaining that with Mark 7:15 we are outside Judaism (cf. p. 476). Berger therefore assumes that the saying does not go back to Jesus himself; but in favor of its genuineness is perhaps the principle of the *lectio difficilior*.

32. *Pesikta de Rav Kahana* 40b. The actual wording is as follows: "In your lives it is not the dead who pollute, or the water which purifies, but it [the water, or the purifying power of water mixed with the ashes of the red heifer] is an enactment of the King of kings. The Holy One, blessed be he, spake: I have laid down an edict, I have given an ordinance; no man is empowered to infringe my ordinance; for it is written: 'This is the statute of the Torah which the Lord has commanded' (Num. 19:2)." For a German translation and an elucidation, see P. Billerbeck, *Kommentar* 1:719. The English translation is by W. G. Braude and I. J. Kapstein, *Pesikta de-Rab Kahana* (London, 1957), 82–83. Billerbeck also cites the parallel traditions.

33. "It is time for the Lord to act, for thy law has been broken."

34. H. Danby, *The Mishnah* (Oxford: At the Clarendon Press, 1977 [1933]), 10 n. 13. See also p. 56 below, with 187 n. 42.

35. For a criticism of wholesale judgments of this kind, see Maier, "Jesus," 49.

36. C. G. Montefiore, *The Synoptic Gospels* (1927; 2d ed., New York: Ktav Pub. House, 1968), 1:152–63.

37. As Jeremias does (*Theology*). He denies the relation to enactments such as Leviticus 11 and Deut. 14:3–21 but does so only in order to prove anew that Jesus makes an end of all "casuistry." He sweeps aside the saying in Matt. 23:3 that presents difficulties in this connection ("Practice and observe whatever they tell you. . . ."), saying that it is exaggerated in its formulation and is intended ironically. He maintains that the *whole* stress lies on the second half of the saying with its sharp condemnation of the practical behavior of the scribes, *which gives the lie to their whole theology*. This *has to* be said, apparently, even if the text maintains exactly the opposite. One might, incidentally, consider the result if Jeremias had applied the same criterion to the Christian side and had drawn the corresponding conclusion.

38. Montefiore's interpretation of the Gospels must be rated particularly highly, since he is very well aware of the anti-Judaism that colors central European exegesis. More than eighty years ago in commenting on an English anti-Jewish statement, he said, "If one met this sentence in any unorthodox [*sic*] German Protestant divine, one would pay no notice. It seems to belong to their business to misrepresent Rabbinic Judaism; it lies, perhaps, in their blood" ("Notes on the Religious Value of the Fourth Gospel," *Jewish Quarterly Review* 7

[1895]: 44 n.1). As the examples I have given show, his comment is still largely applicable today.

39. See here Lenhardt (*Auftrag*, 58–59), who points out that in Jewish life there are *not only* ritual acts (his italics).

40. Cf. here Maier, "Jesus," 90ff., 97–98; and H. Merklein, *Die Gottesherrschaft als Hand-lungsprinzip: Untersuchung zur Ethik Jesu* (Würzburg, 1978). The caution with which Merklein attempts an appropriate evaluation of Mark 7:15 is an agreeable contrast to many other investigations (p. 293).

41. For a wealth of material, see J. Gratus, *The False Messiahs* (London: Victor Gollancz, 1975). See also Maier, "Jesus," 84–85, 101; and Blank, "Paulus," 169–70.

42. Chapter 9 of the tractate *Sotah* incidentally includes other examples of the annulment of individual enactments. Cf. the repeal of individual halakhot in the Babylonian Talmud on the basis of the interpretation of Ps. 119:126 already quoted (*b. Yoma* 69a; *b. Gittin* 60a; *b. Terumah* 14b). On the rabbis' authority to suspend Mosaic laws if the occasion arose, even without support from the Scriptures, see G. F. Moore, *Judaism in the First Centuries of the Christian Era* (Cambridge: Harvard Univ. Press, 1927; New York: Schocken Books, 1974), 1:259.

43. Cf., e.g., Isa. 30:8–17; Jeremiah 6—7.

44. Cf. P. Winter, *On the Trial of Jesus*, 2d ed., rev. and ed. T.A. Burkill and G. Vermes (Berlin and New York: Walter de Gruyter, 1974).

45. Maier ("Jesus," 83) rightly stresses that in spite of all the differences between the movements, the expectations of the Zealots, the Sicarii, Jesus, and the early church all had "a political aspect . . . since they hoped for a fundamental transformation of conditions and hence called in question the conditions of the present. This was so at least in the eyes of the people who exercised power and bore political responsibility. Jesus therefore does not have to have been a political rebel for him to have been accused and condemned as such—and crucifixion was the punishment for rebels."

46. This trend in the Passion story is sensitively traced in the final dialogue between pastor and verger in Ingmar Bergman's film *Light in Winter*. Cf. F. Stolz, "Psalm 22: Alttesta-mentliches Reden vom Menschen und neutestamentliches Reden von Jesus," *ZThK* 77 (1980): 147: "In the story of the Passion everything is so arranged that Jesus is alone in his suffering."

47. The question whether this is a historical reminiscence or whether the cry is to some degree given a biblical identification can probably no longer be decided. On the antiquity of this Passion tradition, see H. Gese, "Psalm 22," 14, 17.

48. See p. 40 above.

49. See pp. 119–24 below.

50. See the apposite observation of Maria Horstmann, *Studien zur markinischen Christologie*, 2d ed. (Münster, 1973), 132: With the angelic saying pointing to Galilee (16:7), Mark is demanding "a rereading of the Gospel . . . so that the risen Jesus may be encountered."

51. Gese ("Psalm 22") has rightly perceived that the *whole* psalm is important for the interpretation of the Passion. It must be said, however, that the interpretation he himself undertakes in this light is charged with tension. On the one hand, he states that the aim is to show that the One who "proclaimed the eschatological rule of God" in his lifetime "brings about [that rule] in his death" (p. 17). On the other hand, he considers (p. 17) that the point where the end-time kingdom breaks in is both Jesus' death and the "act of God that rescues Jesus from death," and finds the "break-in" a little later even more distinctly in "Jesus' death *and resurrection*" (p. 21; my italics). The interpretation of Jesus' death as being already victory, which is the interpretation toward which Gese tends, therefore seems problematical. I myself have already defined the context of the cry from Ps. 22:2 differently in what I said about the Passion (see p. 58 above), and would see the references to the whole psalm only in the framework of the assurance of the resurrection. Consequently, in what follows also, my emphasis differs from Gese's.

52. But it is probably impossible to decide when, after Easter, the "fellowship of the table" took on the form of the Lord's Supper. For its interpretation as *todah*, i.e., as a sacrificial meal of thanksgiving celebrated as a confession of faith, see Gese's noteworthy remarks ("Psalm 22," 17ff.).

53. Cf. 1 Thess. 1:9–10; Acts 17:16–34.

54. Cf. on this pp. 120–22 below.

55. In the New Testament the story of Stephen reflects this in its own way (Acts 6:8ff.).

56. Cf. *b. Berakhot* 61b; *b. Avodah Zarah* 9a and frequently elsewhere. For a judgment on Roman rule by the rabbis, see also Schechter, *Aspects*, 106 ff.

57. W. Grundmann, "Das palästinensische Judentum im Zeitraum zwischen der Erhebung der Makkabäer und dem Ende des Jüdischen Krieges," in *Umwelt des Urchristentums*, 3d ed, ed. J. Leipoldt and W. Grundmann (Berlin, 1971), 1:286.

58. Cf. M. Stern, *Greek and Latin Authors on Jews and Judaism*, vols. 1 and 2 (Jerusalem, 1976, 1980), esp. 1:429ff., 512ff., 521ff. (Seneca, Quintilian, Martial), 2:1ff., 94ff. (Tacitus, Juvenal); I. Heinemann, "Antisemitism," in *Realencyclopädie der classischen Altertumswissenschaften* (Pauly-Wissowa), ed. A. F. von Pauly and G. Wissowa, sup. 5 (Stuttgart, 1931), 3–43; J. N. Sevenster, *The Roots of Pagan Anti-Semitism in the Ancient World* (Leiden, 1975), 89ff; and H. Conzelmann, *Heiden*, 95ff.

59. Consequently, Eph. 2:11–22, esp. 2:14, has long counted as one of the central texts for the relation between Christians and Jews. Cf., e.g., M. Barth, *Israel*, 5ff.; and most recently, Immer, *Erneuerung*, 22.

60. Cf. on this 182 n.42 above and also 198 n.7 below.

61. Barth, *Israel*, 18–19.

62. For criticism, see, e.g., K. M. Fischer, *Tendenz und Absicht des Epheserbriefes* (Göttingen, 1973), 81–82.

63. Cf., e.g., the convincing reasons W. G. Kümmel gathers together (and supplements) for rejecting the possibility of Pauline authorship (*Einleitung in das Neue Testament*, 20th ed. [Heidelberg, 1980], 314ff.).

64. Cf. A. Lindemann, *Die Aufhebung der Zeit* (Gütersloh, 1975), 253; Stegemann, "Alt," 531; Osten-Sacken, *Anstösse*, 146–47.

65. Cf. E. Käsemann, "Erwägungen," 48.

66. Cf. ibid.; among the texts, cf. esp. Rom. 5:1–11 in connection with Romans 6—8, above all Romans 8, and the comments by N. A. Dahl, "Two Notes on Romans 5," *Studia theologica* 5 (1951): 37–48; see also Osten-Sacken, *Römer 8*, 57ff., 124ff.

67. On this interpretation of *apobolē* instead of the usual interpretation of it as the "rejection" of Israel, see H. Thyen, "Heil," 175 n. 51.

68. On the Pauline statements about reconciliation, see Käsemann's comment on 2 Cor. 5:19–20 ("Erwägungen," 52): "Cosmic peace does not descend on the world in some fairytale way. It only takes possession at the points where men and women in the service of reconciliation prove that they themselves have found peace with God. The message of the reconciled world proves its truth in the reconciled human being, not without him or over his head."

69. E.g., the society Amis d'Israël, which was proscribed by the Congregation of the Holy Office on March 25, 1928 (cf. Lenhardt, *Auftrag*, 100), or the associations of Amitié judéo-chrétienne de France that were initiated by Jules Isaac. Cf. the apposite comment by R. Mayer (*Judentum*, 57) that Christian hostility toward the Jews is a "self-contradiction."

70. Cf., e.g., Conzelmann, *Heiden*, 4. His reproach (p. 3) that theologians oriented toward salvation history incline to pick out what suits their book is not, incidentally, very convincing, especially in the light of his own treatment of Romans 9—11 (p. 38), in which Paul's aim in these chapters is unrecognizable.

71. See on this p. 110 below, with 193 n. 24.

72. K. Stendahl (*Paul*) has pertinently observed that from Rom. 10:17 onward Paul no longer mentions the name of Christ. It is true that a reference to Christ is implicit in Romans 11, in what he says about faith and unbelief (vv. 20, 23); nonetheless, the observation remains significant.

73. This among other things shows the untenability of Conzelmann's apodictic assertion (*Heiden*, 238) that "it is *solely* a question of faith" (my italics). F.-W. Marquardt ("Freiheit," 161) has caught the Pauline intention much more aptly when he defines the task of Christians as being "to serve Israel among the Gentiles."

74. Cf. L. Steiger's cogent conclusion ("Schutzrede," 57): "Israel's unbelief is not a subject for Christian dogmatics and preaching; it is material on which to prove Christian ethics and doxology." As what has been said above shows, it is a question of testing Christian *faith* at its very center. See here also Barth, *Israel*. The key word "doxology" is a reference to the

conclusion of Romans 11 (vv. 33–36). On its link with Rom. 9:1–5, and on the interpretation of this connection, see above, pp. 20–21. Incidentally, Steiger's essay is both exegetically and theologically one of the best comments written on Romans 9—11.

75. My previous exegetical comments on Romans 9—11 are the result of a detailed study of these chapters made in the framework of a forthcoming book of essays on Pauline theology (to be published by Chr. Kaiser, Munich). This study too corroborates my view that when Romans 10 is summed up, as it is so often, under a heading such as "Israel's guilt," this is to mistake the intention of the chapter. J. Munck tends in the same direction. His remarks may still count as exemplary in their indication of the direction to be taken; cf. his *Paulus und die Heilsgeschichte* (Copenhagen, 1954), 32ff., 295–96.

76. Cf. here K. Kupisch's superlative phrase about Israel's "obedient disobedience" ("Nach Auschwitz: Fragen an die Weltchristenheit," in his *Durch den Zaun der Geschichte* [Berlin, 1964], 404). See also Eckardt, *Brothers*, 104, 129ff., 137–38; Marquardt, "Feinde," 311ff.; Osten-Sacken, *Anstösse*, 119–20. For criticism of the simple, undialectical talk about "Jewish disobedience," see Ellen Flesseman-van Leer, "Das jüdische Volk und die kirchliche Ökumene," in *"Als Boten des gekreuzigten Herrn": Festgabe für W. Krusche*, ed. H. Falcke, M. Onnasch, and H. Schultze (Berlin, 1982), 266–67.

77. Cf. R. R. Geis in *Versuche des Verstehens: Dokumente jüdisch-christlicher Begegnung aus den Jahren 1918–1933*, ed. and intro. R. R. Geis and H.-J. Kraus (Munich, 1966), 22ff., 134.

78. Lenhardt, *Auftrag*, 103. Cf. Flusser, "Reflections," 2.

79. See p. 18 above. On the hermeneutical significance of the change of situation between Paul's time and the present day, see also now B. Klappert, "Traktat für Israel (Römer 9—11): Die paulinische Verhältnisbestimmung von Israel und Kirche als Kriterium neutestamentlicher Sachaussagen über die Juden," in *Jüdische Existenz und die Erneuerung der christlichen Theologie*, ed. M. Stöhr (Munich, 1981), 58–137.

80. For a detailed interpretation, see Osten-Sacken, *Anstösse*, 185ff.

81. On the meaning of this conception, see J. Roloff, "Die Paulus-Darstellung des Lukas: Ihre geschichtlichen Voraussetzungen und ihr theologisches Ziel," *EvTh* 39 (1979): 510–31. It must, however, be said that Roloff's viewpoint requires correction. The period of the church that is now to come is, according to Luke, *a transitional period* before the end, at which, however, Israel's hope will be fulfilled. See the following passage, and J. Koenig, *Foundations*, 97ff.

82. Cf. E. Lohse's essay with the same title: "Lukas als Theologe der Heilsgeschichte" (1954), now in his *Die Einheit des Neuen Testaments* (Göttingen, 1973), 145–64.

83. Cf. here P. von der Osten-Sacken, "Zur Christologie des lukanischen Reiseberichts," *EvTh* 33 (1973): 476–96.

84. U. Wilckens (*Die Missionsreden der Apostelgeschichte*, 3d ed. [Neukirchen, 1974], 43, 153–56, 234–36) does not think that Acts 3:19–21 fits, and believes that in 3:22–23 Luke "clearly 'bent the text,'" lending a present-day reference to the eschatological statement in 3:20f."; i.e., he interpreted the period after the ministry of Jesus "as the time when all the Old Testament prophecies were fulfilled" (p. 43). Now, it is true that in 3:22–26 Luke is talking about the earthly Jesus; but, significantly enough, in these verses he talks not about everything that has been prophesied but about "all the prophets" (3:24). And it emerges no less clearly from 3:25–26 that for him, in fact, by no means everything has been fulfilled: the recollection of the promise given to Abraham, that in him all generations would be blessed, is followed by the precise temporal definition that God *first of all* sent Jesus for Israel's sake, to bless her through repentance—but it is this same Israel that is being appealed to in the present tense by Peter in chap. 3, with the call to conversion. This shows that, according to chap. 3, the time when the Gentiles will be blessed has not even begun, let alone been fulfilled. That Luke of all people should have "bent" a statement presupposing the ascension, like 3:20, is also extremely improbable in view of Acts 1:9–11. So the obvious reading is the complementary interpretation of 3:20–21 and 3:22–26 that avoids the need to presuppose a "bending" of the text. For the interpretation of Acts 3:19–21 as a genuine Lukan text, see E. Haenchen, *Die Apostelgeschichte*, 13th ed. (Göttingen, 1961), 170ff.; Conzelmann, *Acts*; G. Voss, *Die Christologie der lukanischen Schriften in Grundzügen* (Paris and Brussels, 1965), 28ff., 151–52; G. Lohfink, "Christologie und Geschichtsbild in Apg 3,19–21," in *Biblische Zeitschrift* n.F. 13 (1969): 223–41. It must be said that the interpretation of *apokatastasis* put forward above goes beyond the view of these authors. But it is convincingly justified

by F. Mussner, "Die Idee der Apokatastasis in der Apostelgeschichte," in his *Praesentia Salutis: Gesammelte Studien zu Fragen und Themen des Neuen Testamentes* (Düsseldorf, 1967), 223–34, as well as in his *Tractate*, 36ff. Incidentally, Luke's ties with Israel are also documented by his replacing the passage about the cursing of the fig tree (Mark 11:12–14, 20–21) with the tradition about Jesus' weeping in love over Jerusalem (Luke 19:41–44). A series of other examples of ties of this kind can be found in Koenig, *Foundations*, 97ff., 119ff.

85. Cf. A. Fischer, "Ein Wunder (Matth. 21. 33–46)," in *Gottesdienst*, ed. P. von der Osten-Sacken, 63. On the whole complex, cf. Beker's clear-sighted statement (*Paul*, 338–39): "The primary task of the Christian towards Judaism is to safeguard the peace of the Jew in the world."

86. Although M. Barth's exegetical justification (*Israel*) for his theological interpretation of the relation between Israel and the church cannot be maintained (see pp. 65–66 above), one can nonetheless fundamentally assent to the interpretation itself, in the light of other presuppositions put forward. Without going into the distinction between sinners and the righteous, Barth recognizes a correspondence between the relationship of Gentiles and Jews in Ephesians 2, on the one hand, and between the prodigal son and the elder brother in Luke 15, on the other. For Jesus as the link or mediator between Israel and the Gentiles, see also Eckardt, *Brothers*, 140; Mussner, *Tractate*, 107; and Klappert, "Jesus," 160–61.

87. Cf. Lenhardt's complementary recognition, arrived at from a different perspective (*Auftrag*, 104), "that the Jewish rejection certainly denies the fulfillment by Christianity and the church (Rom. 11:28) and is insofar negative; but that the rejection has no negative effects on the value and positive orientation of Israel, since these have been secured to it by God himself, with his call and his gifts (Rom. 11:29)." For a similar point of view, see Eckardt, *Brothers*, 129.

88. Because the title Messiah when it is applied to Jesus in the sense I have suggested binds Christians much more closely to the Jews than it divides them, the variously justified pleas to abandon it seem dubious rather than helpful—quite apart from the fact that it is the title most frequently applied to Jesus in the New Testament. Cf. here Klappert, "Jesus," 158ff. The use of the title becomes destructive if it aims at a simplistic yes or no without any differentiating exposition. Cf. pp. 39–40 above; and in addition my article "Heil für die Juden—auch ohne Christus?" in *"Wenn nicht jetzt, wann dann?" Aufsätze für H.-J. Kraus zum 65. Geburtstag*, ed. H.-G. Geyer et al. (Neukirchen, 1983), 169–182.

89. The German text follows J. Beckmann, ed., *Kirchliches Jahrbuch für die evangelische Kirche in Deutschland 1945–1948* (Gütersloh, 1950), 26–27.

90. *EvKomm* 18 (1978): 676. On the other hand, the corresponding statement of the conference of Protestant church leaders in the German Democratic Republic is of pioneer and exemplary importance (ibid., 675–76).

91. "Für ein neues Verhältnis zur Glaubensgeschichte des jüdischen Volkes: Erklärung der Gemeinsamen Synode der Bistümer in der Bundesrepublik Deutschland vom 22.11.1975," *FrRu* 27 (1975): 5; my italics. It is only if the qualifications I have italicized are left out that the two clauses in which they are included agree with the final, unqualified statement. Cf. the critical questions raised by J. B. Metz in "Podiumsdiskussion: Glaube und Widerstand nach Auschwitz," in *Auschwitz*, ed. G. B. Ginzel, 196–97.

92. epd–Dokumentation no. 42 (1980): 14–17.

93. The same intention seems to underlie the noticeable misuse of language: an ideology cannot commit crimes, nor can an ideology "be committed." For further criticism of the declaration, esp. of the way it deals with the question of guilt, see B. Klappert, "Kein Dokument der Erneuerung: Antwort auf Erwägungen von einigen Bonner Theologen zum Synodalbeschluss der rheinischen Landessynode," in epd–Dokumentation no. 42 (1980): 18–43.

94. Cf. here, e.g., Gutteridge's *Mouth*, esp. 267ff., as well as W. Gerlach, *Davidstern*, 20ff.

95. Immer, *Erneuerung*, 9ff., 12ff.

96. Cf. here F.-W. Marquardt, "Christsein nach Auschwitz," in *Schweigen*, ed. Marquardt and Friedlander, 7–34.

97. C. Dietzfelbinger, *Die Antithesen der Bergpredigt* (Munich, 1975), 18.

98. Cf. p. 14 above.

99. Cf. p. 42 above.

100. R. Bultmann, "Weissagung und Erfüllung," in his *Glauben und Verstehen*, 2d ed. (Tübingen, 1958), 2:134. For criticism see H.-J. Kraus, *Die Biblische Theologie: Ihre Geschichte und Problematik* (Neukirchen, 1970), 319–20.

101. Cf. here P. von der Osten-Sacken, "Kreuzestheologie," 169–70, 173ff.

102. Bultmann, *Theology*, sec. 55.3.

103. Cf. here C. Müller, *Gottesgerechtigkeit und Gottes Volk: Eine Untersuchung zu Röm. 9—11* (Göttingen, 1964), 104ff.

104. Cf. H. Conzelmann, *The Theology of St. Luke*, trans. Geoffrey Buswell (New York: Harper & Row; London: Faber & Faber, 1960).

105. See Acts 2:38; 3:19; 11:18; and frequently elsewhere.

106. E.g., 1 Thess. 5:1–11; Mark 13:32–37; Matt. 24:42–51; 25:1–13.

107. Cf. the interpretation of the period of delay as "time for the doers of the Torah, whose hands will not tire in the service of truth," in IQpHab VII,9–12.

108. Cf. A. Descamps, "Moses im Neuen Testament," in *Moses in Schrift und Überlieferung*, ed. H. Cazelles et al. (Düsseldorf, 1963), 193 (German trans. of *Moïse, l'homme de l'alliance*).

109. Cf. here 2 Cor. 5:7.

110. Cf. pp. 90–91 above.

111. On the related concept in Rev. 21:1–7; 22:1–5, see W. Grundmann, *"chriō,"* in *ThWBNT* 9 (1973): 569–70. For a more detailed discussion of the whole complex, see Osten-Sacken, "Theologia," 477ff. Franz Rosenzweig was the first to draw attention to the great importance of 1 Cor. 15:20–28 for the relationship between Christians and Jews. Cf. H.-J. Schoeps, *Religionsgespräch*, 134; Thoma, *Theology*, 130–31.

112. H.-J. Schoeps, *Paul*, rev. trans. Harold Knight (Philadelphia: Westminster Press; London: Lutterworth Press, 1961).

113. *b. Yoma* 86b. On this whole question, and especially on the tradition history of the prayer "And there shall come for Zion" (*u-ba le-Ziyyon*), see L. J. Liebreich, "An Analysis of U-ba le-Ziyyon in the Liturgy," in *Hebrew Union College Annual* 21 (1948): 176–209. Liebreich shows (p. 204) the messianic understanding of Isa. 59:20–21 in this prayer and also points to Rom. 11:26 (p. 204 n. 90). On the rabbinic exegesis of Isa. 59:20, see also *b. Shabbat* 98a (Billerbeck, *Kommentar* 4/2:981). The section of *u-ba-le-Ziyyon* that is quoted in the following passage here is taken from the Authorised Daily Prayer Book, 202–5. See 182 n. 33 above.

114. Cf. 2 Cor. 5:10 and frequently elsewhere. See also L. Mattern, *Das Verständnis des Gerichts bei Paulus* (Zurich, 1966), and E. Synofzik, *Die Gerichts- und Vergeltungsaussagen bei Paulus* (Göttingen, 1977).

115. Cf., e.g., *Lektionar für Evangelisch-Lutherische, Kirchen und Gemeinden: Neue Ausgabe (Probetext)* (Hamburg, 1978), 353–54.

116. See p. 10 above.

117. Cf. Matt. 18:20; 28:20.

118. See on this the more detailed exposition in Osten-Sacken, *Anstösse*, 98ff.

119. See p. 9 above.

120. D. Bonhoeffer, *Letters and Papers*. On Bonhoeffer's development, see E. Bethge's biography, *Bonhoeffer*.

121. Bonhoeffer, *Letters and Papers*.

122. Bethge, *Bonhoeffer*.

123. D. Bonhoeffer, *Sanctorum Communio: A Dogmatic Enquiry into the Sociology of the Church*, rev. trans. R. Gregor Smith (London: William Collins Sons, 1963).

124. Cf. J. Beckmann, "'Christus als Gemeinde existierend': Der Begriff der Kirche in Dietrich Bonhoeffers 'Sanctorum Communio' im Blick auf die Ökumene," *EvTh* 21 (1961): 327–38, esp. 337–38. Regin Prenter has pointed out, however, that Bonhoeffer never reversed the formula (Bethge, *Bonhoeffer*).

125. See the hints in this direction in Bonhoeffer, *Letters and Papers*. For this question and its bearing on the relation between God and human beings in the light of Auschwitz, see F.-W. Marquardt, "Immanuel ohne Zauberformeln: Die Frage nach der Menschheit Gottes fällt auf uns," *LM* 19 (1980): 701–2.

126. Bonhoeffer, *Letters and Papers*.

127. Cf. W. Gerlach, "Zwiespältig in der 'Judenfrage': Bonhoeffers Mut und die Furcht der Kirchenkämpfer," *LM* 18 (1979): 463–66; and idem, *Davidstern*, 492ff. See also P. E.

Lapide, "Bonhoeffer und das Judentum," in *Verspieltes Erbe? Dietrich Bonhoeffer und der deutsche Nachkriegsprotestantismus*, ed. E. Feil (Munich, 1979), 116–30; and E. Bethge, "Dietrich Bonhoeffer und die Juden," in *Konsequenzen: Dietrich Bonhoeffers Kirchenverständnis heute*, ed. E. Feil and I. Tödt (Munich, 1980), 171–214.

128. Cf. Rom. 5:6ff.; 2 Cor. 5:14ff.

129. For a legitimation of this variant, see also the close connection in terminology and subject matter between the end of Romans 8 and the beginning of Romans 9—11: the theme of separation *apo tēs agapēs tou Christou* or *tou theou tēs en Christō Iēsou* (Rom. 8:35, 38–39) is taken up in Rom. 9:3 by the apostle's unrealizable wish to be *anathēma . . . apo tou Christou*. But the wish has to remain unrealizable because nothing can separate either the apostle or Israel from the love of God; hence, Paul can only witness to, and live, the love of Christ or the love of God in Jesus Christ; he cannot take its place.

CHAPTER 4

1. Cf. P. Lapide, *Hebräisch*, 162; L. G. Terray, "Gemeinden," 63–64.

2. J. Beckmann, ed., *Kirchliches Jahrbuch für die Evangelische Kirche in Deutschland 1933.1944*, 2d ed. (Gütersloh, 1976), 460 (text of the statement of December 17, 1941).

3. Cf. p. 42 above.

4. An important recent testimony from the Diaspora is, e.g., the acknowledgment of the new archbishop of Paris, Jean-Marie Lustiger: "I am a Jew, and consciously so. My parents passed on to me faith in God and respect for my neighbor. For me, the two religions form a single whole, and I have never betrayed the faith of my forefathers. For me, there is no breach between the two" (*Allgemeine Jüdische Wochenzeitung*, February 20, 1981, p. 6). After regional beginnings in the nineteenth century in England (1865), the most important association of Jewish Christians today, irrespective of the different church affiliations of its members, is the International Hebrew Christian Alliance. Founded in London in 1925, this has since 1954 included a branch in Israel. Cf. J. Jasper, "Judenchrist," 145ff.; W. Schweikhart, *Mission*, 198ff. On earlier associations, see F. Majer-Leonhard, "Judenchristentum," 973.

5. On the Evangelical Lutheran congregations see Terray, "Gemeinden"; for other groups, see Jasper, "Judenchrist," 159ff.; Lapide, *Hebräisch*, 160ff., 202–3; K. Kjaer-Hansen and O. C. Kvarme, *Messianische Juden: Judenchristen in Israel*, trans. N. P. Moritzen and A. H. Baumann (Erlangen, 1983), 35ff.; and S. Schoon, *Christelijke presentie in de Joodse Staat* (Kampen, 1982).

6. The phrase is taken from Lenhardt, *Auftrag*, 126.

7. See Majer-Leonhard, "Judenchristentum," 975. However, she produces equally good reasons for supporting the foundation of a "native" church in Israel, in which the great majority of members would be Jewish Christians. But this has not as yet been implemented (see Schweikhart, *Mission*, 203).

8. W. G. Kümmel's phraseology; see his "Judenchristentum I" in *RGG*, 3d ed. (1959), 3:971.

9. On the "benediction" or "malediction" for the *minim* (heretics or sectarians), see P. Schäfer, "Die sogenannte Synode von Jabne: Zur Trennung von Juden und Christen im ersten/zweiten Jh. nChr." (1974) in his *Studien zur Geschichte und Theologie des rabbinischen Judentums* (Leiden, 1978), 45–64; G. Alon, *The Jews in Their Land in the Talmudic Age (70–640 C.E.)* (Jerusalem, 1980), 1:288ff., 305ff. Schäfer puts forward convincing reasons for maintaining that the *birkhat ha-minim* was directed against the Jewish Christians *among others*—i.e., that the separation from them was not the decisive or sole motive for its formulation. Cf. here also Heinemann, *Prayer*, 225; and even earlier, K. Kohler, "The Origin and Composition of the Eighteen Benedictions with a Translation of the Corresponding Essene Prayers in the Apostolic Constitutions," in *Hebrew Union College Annual* 1 (1924; reprint, New York: Ktav Pub. House): 401–2. Alon gives plausible reasons for his view that the essential reason for the synagogue's separation from the Jewish Christians was their aloof behavior in the first and second Jewish Wars against Rome. See here a much earlier book, I. Elbogen, *Der jüdische Gottesdienst in seiner geschichtlichen Entwicklung*, 3d ed. (1931; reprint, Hildesheim, 1967), 37.

10. Cf. here the examples Lapide gives (*Hebräisch*, 201) indicating that "local complaints

about a kind of ecclesiastical colonization [are increasing] on both the Arab Christian and the Jewish Christian side."

11. Israel's reserve here is much more comprehensible historically if one considers the part Jewish Christians played in the medieval religious disputations, or remembers the total renunciation of Judaism required of the Jewish Christians in various regional churches in the early Middle Ages. Cf. Parkes, *Conflict*, 394ff. For further reasons, see Jasper, "Judenchrist," 155ff.; Schweikhart, *Mission*, 189ff.

12. Cf. Terray, "Gemeinden," 71–72; A. Krolenbaum, "Judenchrist," 8.

13. I am drawing here on a conversation with Paul van Buren.

14. Cf. here Conzelmann, *Acts*; M. Hengel, "Zwischen Jesus und Paulus: Die 'Hellenisten,' die 'Sieben' und Stephanus (Apg. 6,1–15; 7,54—8,3)," *ZThK* 72 (1975): 151–206.

15. See the Hebrew Christian Alliance's own description of its function: ". . . in corporate witness toward their Jewish brethren, with whom they know themselves to be united not merely in their ethnological origin but above all in Israel's divine calling, and in witness towards the church, to which they try to mediate the spirit of Judaism and for which they wish to be guarantors of the unity of the body of Christ of Jews and Gentiles" (quoted in Jasper, "Judenchrist," 146).

16. Cf. H. Lietzmann, *History of the Early Church*, trans. B. Lee Woolf, 2d ed. (New York: Charles Scribner's Sons; London: Lutterworth Press, 1949); H.-J. Schoeps, *Theologie und Geschichte des Judenchristentums* (Tübingen, 1949), 320–21; G. Strecker's foreword in W. Bauer, *Orthodoxy and Heresy in Earliest Christianity*, trans. a team from the Philadelphia Seminar on Christian Origins (Philadelphia: Fortress Press, 1971). We have to thank Strecker for the differentiation that the judgment leveled by Lietzmann and Schoeps at both east and west applies only to the west: in the eastern church, right down to the third and fourth centuries, the situation was more open, and the analogous evaluation of Jewish Christians as a heretical group therefore only began to win general acceptance in the fourth century. The protest of Jewish Christian groups against the path taken by the mainstream church, esp. its liaison with political power, is worthy of very serious consideration; see here S. Pines, *Christians*, 28, 65, and passim.

17. Cf. on this p. 146 below.

18. M. L. Bass, "Christ," 169–70.

19. Cf. H. D. Leuner, "Ist die Bezeichnung 'Judenchrist' theologisch richtig?" in his *Israel*, 69; Jasper, "Judenchrist," 177.

20. Bass, "Christ," 171–72.

21. Cf. Krolenbaum, "Judenchrist," 11–12; and the influence of Leuner, which is reflected, e.g., in his volume of essays *Israel*. An unusually unprejudiced account of the various Jewish Christian groups is given from the Jewish side by Lapide in his *Hebräisch*, irrespective of his own clear position with regard to the question about the Messiah (see his "Messias").

22. See the excursus on pp. 110–14 below.

23. F. Hesse, "Anmerkungen," 283–84; the quotation is taken from p. 283.

24. For recent discussion, see Eckardt, *Brothers*, 55ff., 93; Mayer, *Judentum*, 162; P.G. Aring, *Judenmission*, esp. 1ff., 255ff.; idem, "Absage an die Judenmission," in *Umkehr*, ed. Klappert and Starck, 207–14; Lenhardt, *Auftrag*; R. Rendtorff, "Judenmission nach Auschwitz," in *Auschwitz*, ed. Ginzel, 539–75; Schweikhart, *Mission*, 119ff.; H. Kremers, *Judenmission heute?* (Neukirchen, 1979); and Klappert, "Jesus," 152ff. Schweikhart gives a critical and well-weighed summing up of the arguments on both sides (pp. 34ff., 59ff., 119ff.). It is a pity that Aring did not include the Jewish Christians in the final critical chapter of his important investigation (see pp. 255ff.). The problems connected with "mission" could then probably have been described in a more differentiated way. The Bonn "Considerations," on the other hand, in their final point (no. 10. p. 17) stress that "the proclamation of the gospel of Christ for Jews" can "neither address them as heathen nor expect conversion to the Christian faith to result in separation from the community of the Jewish people and its tradition." This is a bright spot in the declaration, but it has already been watered down in advance through the description of the Jews as "*descendants* of God's chosen people" (no. 9; my italics). So point 10 has as a whole no apparent substantial relevance.

25. See, from the German-speaking area, the study *Christen und Juden*, issued by the Council of the Protestant Church in Germany (EKD) (Gütersloh, 1975), 9ff., 31–32; the resolu-

tion of the Synod of the Protestant Church in the Rhineland *Zur Erneuerung des Verhältnisses von Christen und Juden*; and the theses included in Immer, *Erneuerung*, 9ff., 12ff. On the Catholic side, and beyond the official Vatican statements, special mention must be made of the declaration of the French episcopal commission on relations with Judaism. The German trans. of this is in *FrRu* 25 (1973): 15–18. For the ET, see H. Croner, ed., *Stepping Stones to Further Jewish-Christian Relations: An Unabridged Collection of Christian Documents* (New York and London: Stimulus Books, 1977). For an evaluation of the most important church declarations, see C. Thoma, *Die theologischen Beziehungen zwischen Christentum und Judentum* (Darmstadt, 1982), 11ff.

26. For the dialogue side, see the resolution and theses of the Synod of the Protestant Church in the Rhineland; on the mission to the Jews, apart from A. H. Baumann's contribution (*Zeugnis*), see the pamphlet "Jüdisches Zeugnis" issued by the study group on "The Church and Judaism" of the United Lutheran Church of Germany and the Deutsches Nationa-komitee des Lutherischen Weltbundes and published in *Fül* 64 (1981): 73–75. This pamphlet is no. 21 in the series "Was jeder vom Judentum wissen muss."

27. Baumann, *Zeugnis*.

28. Ibid., 29–30.

29. Ibid., 30.

30. For references, see C. G. Montefiore and H. Loewe, eds., *A Rabbinic Anthology* (1938; reprint, Cleveland: World Pub. Co.; Philadelphia: Jewish Pub. Soc. of America, 1963), 556ff.; G. Levi, *Das Buch der jüdischen Weisheit* (n.d.), 3d reprint (Wiesbaden, 1980), 199–200; and A. Cohen, *Talmud*, 65–66. As examples from a more recent period, cf. Buber's contributions in his dialogue with K. L. Schmidt (*Kirche*, esp. 560ff., 570); Lapide's work; Levinson, "Jude," esp. 204; Talmon, "Community," 610, 615; and Aschkenasy, "Mensch." Schmidt's contributions (printed together with Buber's in K. L. Schmidt, *Neues Testament—Judentum—Kirche*, ed. G. Sauter [Munich, 1981], 149ff., 163–64) bring out the borderline that is usually drawn for Christians. Guttmann gives a sensitive description of the continuity and discontinuity between the Jewish and the Christian view in *Umwelt*, 314–15: "In the church of the patristic period, the idea of election was exaggerated into the conception of the church outside which there is no salvation. In the election of *Israel* one will seek in vain for this latter theory" (Guttmann's italics). In spite of this, rabbinic literature shows that Israel's relationship to the Gentiles was ambivalent: see Urbach, *Sages*, 541ff.; L. J. Eron, "You Who Revere the Lord, Bless the Lord," *JES* 18 (1981): 63–73; and also pp. 120–22 below.

31. Baumann, *Zeugnis*, 29.

32. G. Rost, "Tempel."

33. Ibid., 57.

34. Ibid.

35. Ibid., 58; my italics. The quotation from Goppelt is taken from his *Theologie* 1:148. On the whole subject, see also pp. 54–56 above.

36. Goppelt, *Theologie* 1:148.

37. Rost, "Tempel," 59.

38. Ibid., 61; my italics.

39. J. S. Sponge (bishop of the Episcopal Church in the U.S.A.) shows that there are other more consoling ways for a bishop to talk; see his "The Continuing Christian Need for Judaism," in *CJR* no. 73 (1980): 3–10. Cf. also K. Immer, "Einführung in das Synodalthema 'Christen und Juden,'" in *Erneuerung*, ed. Immer, 5ff.; E. Lohse, "Frieden für Israel (Hebr. 1,1–6)," in *Gottesdienst*, ed. Osten-Sacken, 138–42; and M. Kruse, "Folgerungen," in *Gottesdienst*, 147–51.

40. Steiger, "Schutzrede," 57. For criticism of the "absolutist" standpoint, see Mayer, *Judentum*, 163; Talmon, "Community," 616–17; Marquardt, "Feinde," 334ff.; G. Baum, intro. to R. Ruether, *Nächstenliebe und Brudermord: Die theologischen Wurzeln des Antisemitismus* (German trans. of *Faith*; Munich, 1978); P. von der Osten-Sacken, "Von der Notwendigkeit theologischen Besitzverzichts," epilogue to Ruether, *Nächstenliebe*, 244–51, 269. H. Thyen, "Holocaust," 142ff. On ways of dealing with the similarly located so-called question of truth, see Metz, "Ökumene," 128. Ideas about a salutary restriction in the use of the absolutist concept may be found in Schoeps, *Religionsgespräch*, 153–54; U. Mann, "Christentum und Toleranz," in *Mut zur Verständigung: Fünfundzwanzig Jahre Evangelische Akademie Loccum*, ed. H. Storck (Göttingen, 1977), 109–32; and Gollwitzer, "Judentum," 173.

41. Cf., e.g., the groups mentioned in Jasper, "Judenchrist," 163–64; and Lapide, *Hebräisch*, 160ff., 200–201.

42. On this cf., e.g., Leuner, "Die Messiasfrage im jüdisch-christlichen Gespräch," in his *Israel*, 44ff., esp. 52ff.

43. Cf. J. Downey, "Der Christus der jüdischen Christen: Ein pluralistisches Modell für afrikanische Theologie," *Zeitschrift für Mission* 1 (1975): 197–214; and S. Talmon, "Anfrage," 141, 150ff.

44. On the significance of this for the interpretation of the Sermon on the Mount, see C. Burchard, "Versuch, das Thema der Bergpredigt zu finden," in *Jesus Christus in Historie und Theologie: Festschrift für H. Conzelmann*, ed. G. Strecker (Tübingen, 1975), 409–32.

45. Quoted in M. Krupp, *Vergesse ich dein, Jerusalem: Kleine Geschichte des Zionismus* (Konstanz, 1965), 195. See also Lapide, *Hebräisch*, 161; Lapide describes the group in more detail.

46. See p. 34 above, with 183 n. 48. Of course the resolution does not apply to the Jewish Christians in the sense of what has been said above. As Baumann rightly stresses (*Zeugnis*, 26), the Jewish Christians are not mentioned at all in the resolution—a weakness in what is nonetheless a pioneer document.

47. *Erwägungen* no. 4, pp. 14–15.

48. But Käsemann offers a convincing criticism of the interpretation of Paul that takes its bearings from the isolated individual; see "The Theological Problem Presented by the Motif of the Body of Christ," in his *Perspectives*, 102–21.

49. Cf. Krolenbaum, "Judenchrist," 8–9; W. Grillenberger, "Begegnung mit jüdischen Christen in Israel," *FüI* 51 (1968): 130. The Christian settlement Nes Ammim is a further important way of registering the presence of the church in the state of Israel in the form of a gentile Christian community. On its history and function, see S. Schoon and H. Kremers, *Nes Ammim: Ein christliches Experiment in Israel*, trans. W. Bunte (Neukirchen, 1978). On the theological problems involved in the self-understanding of the Nes Ammim group, see, in addition to the work already mentioned, Aring, *Judenmission*, 255ff. The christological and ecclesiological perspectives developed in the present investigation, which also include the Jewish Christians, can perhaps be of some slight help in overcoming the difficulties. On the relationship between Nes Ammim and the Jewish Christians in Israel, see Kremers's remarks in the volume just cited, pp. 192–93. On the problematical situation of the Jewish Christians in Israel and on other aspects of the "possibilities of a Christian life as church in the midst of a largely Jewish society," see also Lenhardt, *Auftrag*, 122ff.

50. Some of the points that have to be considered here have already been discussed in the framework of what has been said about Christology. See pp. 72–76 above.

CHAPTER 5

1. In Augustine, the witness is still bound up with the guarantee of the genuineness of Holy Scripture. But it was then pressed into service for other things as well. Cf. B. Blumenkranz, "Die Juden als Zeugen der Kirche," *ThZ* 5 (1949): 396–98; and idem, "Die Entwicklung im Westen zwischen 200 und 1200," in *Kirche und Synagoge: Handbuch zur Geschichte von Christen und Juden*, ed. K. H. Rengstorf and S. v. Kortzfleisch (Stuttgart, 1968), 1:93ff. See also Isaac, "Antisemitismus," 345.

2. Attention should also be drawn here especially to two essays by B. Klappert, "Erinnerung" and "Biblelarbeit über Hebräer 11,1.32–40; 12,1f," both in *Erneuerung*, ed. Immer, 79–100. Cf. pp. 123–24 below.

3. Marquardt, "Feinde," 311.

4. Ibid., 335; my italics.

5. Cf. R. R. Geis, "Auftrag"; E. Simon, "Das Zeugnis des Judentums," in Deutscher Evangelischer Kirchentag Köln 1965 Dokumente (Stuttgart and Berlin, 1965), 654–67; Mayer, *Judentum*, 188–89; J. Moltmann, *The Church in the Power of the Spirit*, trans. Margaret Kohl (New York: Harper & Row; London: SCM Press; 1977), 136ff.; and Heschel, *God*, 423–24.

6. It would be worthwhile pursuing this aspect in more detail than is possible here. Hints may be found in Guttmann, *Umwelt*, 127.

7. A. Alt, "Die Heimat des Deuteronomiums," in his *Kleine Schriften zur Geschichte des Volkes Israel*, 3d ed. (Munich, 1965), 2:250–75, esp. 253–54, 273–74. Alt's volume has been published in English as *Essays on Old Testament History and Religion*, trans. R. A. Wilson

(Garden City, N.Y.: Doubleday & Co., 1967; Oxford: Basil Blackwell, 1966). On the theme of unity in Deuteronomy, which is stressed in the following passage, see as well G. von Rad, *Old Testament Theology*, vol. 1, trans. D. M. G. Stalker (New York: Harper & Row; Edinburgh: Oliver & Boyd, 1962).

8. See pp. 62–63 above.

9. E. Bickermann, *Der Gott der Makkabäer* (Berlin, 1937), 138.

10. Contrary to Hesse's denial of this in "Anmerkungen," 285. Hesse's repudiation is all the more astonishing because it comes from an Old Testament scholar.

11. B. Klappert, "Erinnerung," 196; italics omitted. See esp. Marquardt, "Feinde," 318–19: Jewish life with the "Hear, O Israel" is a daily commitment to the God of Abraham, Isaac, and Jacob as the foundation of existence, and a struggle for the recognition of the First Commandment. Cf. idem, "Freiheit," esp. 154ff.; and Eckardt, *Brothers*, 150; Kraus, *Reich*, 124–25.

12. Klappert, "Erinnerung," 199; italics omitted.

13. Ibid., 204.

14. Ibid., 199.

15. M. Smith, "Das Judentum in Palästina in der hellenistischen Zeit," in *Der Hellenismus und der Aufstieg Roms*, ed. P. Grimal (Frankfurt, 1965), 265. See also Thyen, "Holocaust," 143.

16. See p. 103 above, with 192 n. 9.

17. See also the distinction already indicated above (p. 111) in connection with the phrase about the righteous Gentiles.

18. This is also the point theologically at which Islam can be included in reflections on the subject, but here my remarks must remain restricted to Israel and the church, that being the particular orientation of our present subject. For an important recent study of the relationship between the Christian faith and Islam, cf. J. Bouman, *Das Wort vom Kreuz und das Bekenntnis zu Allah: Die Grundlehren des Korans als nachbiblische Religion* (Frankfurt, 1980).

19. It is therefore correct enough when A. Schindler writes (in the volume of which he is editor, *Monotheismus als politisches Problem? Erik Peterson und die Kritik der politischen Theologie* [Gütersloh, 1978], 67) that monotheism "is not *in itself* a political problem" (my italics). But when does it ever exist "in itself"? Peterson's conception ("Der Monotheismus als politisches Problem" [1932], in his *Theologische Traktate* [Munich, 1950], 45–147), and the convincingly pursued critical discussion in the volume mentioned, otherwise belong within a different context and can therefore be left on one side here.

20. In 1QMXVII, 7f. the expectation is interpreted as "Israel's lordship among all flesh." For rabbinic references to the subjection of the Gentiles in the messianic era, cf. Billerbeck, *Kommentar* 4:899. Isaac Troki also draws on Dan. 7:27 as argument in his work refuting the Christian faith; see his *Faith Strengthened [= chizzuk emunah]: Twelve Hundred Biblical Refutations to Christian Missionaries*, intro. Trude Weiss-Rosmarin (New York: Ktav Pub. House, 1970), 34, 196ff. See also what Schechter has to say about the national dimension of the kingdom of God (*Aspects*, 97ff.).

21. As I have already said, the expectation is relativized by the statement in 1 Cor. 15:28 that at the end "God will be all in all." The same applies to the rabbinic tradition, in which Israel's victory is related to the era of the Messiah (cf. Billerbeck, *Kommentar* 4:881). Nonetheless, the expectation of the kingdom is in both places of the kind I have suggested here.

22. See, e.g., 1 Thess. 2:14–16; Matthew 23; John 8:40–44.

23. See Cohen, *Talmud*, 66; and R. Meyer, "Volk und Völker in der rabbinischen Literatur," in *ThWBNT* 4 (1942): 39–49, esp. 48.

24. For the Jewish tradition, see pp. 111–12 above; on its Christian equivalent, see the same pages, as well as, e.g., Mark 12:28–34, and the comment in Osten-Sacken, *Anstösse*, 209–10.

25. A depressing wealth of evidence is to be found in, e.g., Isaac, *Jesus*.

26. See, e.g., E. Grässer, "Die antijüdische Polemik im Johannesevangelium," *NTS* 11 (1964–65): 74–90; and the comment by Osten-Sacken, "Kreuzestheologie," 168ff. On these points, cf. Stegemann, "Paulus," 117ff.; Stendahl, *Paul*, as well as pp. 13–14 above and 136–37 and 143–50 below. A much more differentiated discussion of the question of Johannine anti-Judaism than Grässer's, and one that shows a much greater awareness of the problem, is to be found in J. T. Townsend, "The Gospel of John and the Jews: The Story of a

Religious Divorce," in *Antisemitism and the Foundations of Christianity*, ed. A. Davies (New York and Toronto: Paulist Press, 1979), 72–97; and esp. in Koenig, *Foundations*, 122ff. The two writers, though differing in some respects, take as background to the anti-Jewish statements the inclusion of the Jewish Christians in the "Malediction of the Heretics" in the Eighteen Benedictions. But Townsend does not bring out sufficiently the connection between the structure of Johannine theology and the anti-Jewish statements, which emerges, e.g., in John 8:44 (a passage on which Townsend does not comment). Koenig, on the other hand, quite rightly perceives the connection, commenting, e.g. (p. 135), "the fourth Evangelist's all-encompassing Christology, helpful as it must have been for his congregation, nevertheless produced a potentially hostile side-effect: total exclusivism." Cf. Koenig's further reflections (pp. 135–36) and my own remarks below, as well as my already mentioned contribution "Kreuzestheologie."

27. Among the Old Testament testimonies cited in the excursus, the closest is Deuteronomy, with its demand for "oneness" and its stricter definition of the relationship between Israel and the Gentiles (see p. 121 above). On the convential structure of the Johannine group and its dualistic attitude to the world, see also E. Käsemann, *The Testament of Jesus*, trans. Gerhard Krodel (Philadelphia: Fortress Press; London: SCM Press, 1968), and L. Schottroff, *Welt*. On the connection between the two, see Osten-Sacken, "Kreuzestheologie," 156–57.

28. On the question of realized eschatology in Qumran, see H.-W. Kuhn, *Enderwartung und gegenwärtiges Heil: Untersuchungen zu den Gemeindeliedern von Qumran* (Göttingen, 1966); on the relevance of the "knowledge" terminology for the Dead Sea community, see, e.g., F. Nötscher, *Zur theologischen Terminologie der Qumran-Texte* (Bonn, 1956), 15–79; on the Gospel of John, see R. Bultmann, *ginōskō*, in *ThWBNT* 1 (1933): 711ff.; and C. H. Dodd, *The Interpretation of the Fourth Gospel*, 6th ed. (New York and Cambridge: Cambridge Univ. Press, 1963), 151–69.

29. Cf. Osten-Sacken, "Kreuzestheologie," 169–70, 173ff.

30. Thus it probably requires a particular frame of mind to comprehend the highly eccentric conclusion that in the Christian-Jewish dialogue one could only discuss the "pious folklore of two thousand years ago"—M. Hengel's view. See his "Kein Steinbruch für Ideologien: Zentrale Aufgaben neutestamentlicher Exegese," *LM* 18 (1979): 26.

31. Cf. Ruether, *Faith*; and Osten-Sacken, "Verständnis."

32. Geis, "Auftrag," 203.

33. Ibid.

34. See pp. 44–59, 89–90 above.

35. H. Conzelmann, *An Outline of the Theology of the New Testament*, trans. J. Bowden (New York: Harper & Row; London: SCM Press, 1969).

36. Philo *Leg. Alleg.* II.86.

37. Cf. H. Hegermann, *Die Vorstellung vom Schöpfungsmittler im hellenistischen Judentum und Urchristentum* (Berlin, 1961), 70ff.

38. An attempt in this direction has been made in the present volume in chap. 3, the chapter on christology.

39. Tanchuma B *wayyera* § 7ff. (1b). Cf. Billerbeck, *Kommentar* 2:462–63.

40. Cf. here also van Buren's remarks in *Way*, 68ff., though these are not applied to the Exodus text and narrowed down by that.

41. On this point, see also pp. 31–32 above.

42. Cf. p. 26 above.

43. Cf. pp. 58–59 above.

44. Cf. Leuner, "Juden werden Christen, Christen werden Juden," in his *Israel*, 57ff. According to Leuner (p. 67), about three thousand proselytes a year are received into the Jewish community in the United States. Lapide (*Hebräisch*, 205) shows that 2,288 people were received into the Jewish people in Israel between 1948 and 1968, eighty-five percent of them Christians. Conversely, the number of Jews who became Christians or Moslems in Israel between 1948 and 1964 amounted to 201 (*Hebräisch*, 205).

45. G. Fohrer, *Glaube und Leben im Judentum* (Heidelberg, 1979), 5.

46. Cf. his review of the book in *Deutsches Pfarrerblatt* 81 (1981): 190.

47. I have added this clause to avoid being quoted and interpreted as having called for conversion to Judaism. Unfortunately there is good reason for this apprehension, in view of

the regrettable method that E. Grässer has adopted in the framework of disputes about questions bearing on the Christian-Jewish relationship—quoting passages in curtailed form and out of context, and giving them a distorted interpretation. Cf. his polemics in the Mussner Festschrift ("Zwei Heilswege: Zum theologischen Verhältnis von Israel und Kirche," in *Kontinuität und Einheit: Festschrift für F. Mussner*, ed. P.-G. Müller and W. Stenger [Freiburg, 1981] 428 n. 56) with the actual essay he attacks.

48. Bodo, court chaplain to the emperor Louis the Pious was converted to Judaism and followed up his conversion with violent attacks on the church. Cf. B. Blumenkranz, "Jüdische und christliche Konvertiten im jüdisch-christlichen Religionsgespräch des Mittelalters," *Miscellanea Mediaevalia* 4 (1966): 266ff. The Christian convert Pfefferkorn, as is well known, played an exceedingly unsavory role during the Reformation period. Cf. "Pfefferkorn, Johann Joseph" in *Jüdisches Lexikon* 4/1 (Berlin, 1930): 890–93.

CHAPTER 6

1. See Isa. 43:11; Matt. 5:14; Acts 13:46.

2. Cf. here Geis, "Juden und Christen: Ihr biblischer Friedensauftrag," in his *Minorität*, 200–219; B. Klappert, "Perspektiven einer von Juden und Christen anzustrebenden gerechten Weltgesellschaft," *FrRu* 30 (1978): 67–82.

3. Cf. A. von Harnack, *Marcion: Das Evangelium vom fremden Gott*, 2d ed. (Leipzig, 1924), esp. 30–31, 93ff.

4. Ibid., 106 n. 2; cf. 289*f.

5. Conzelmann, *Heiden*, 3.

6. Ibid.

7. For criticism of the rendering of *telos nomou* in Rom. 10:4 as the "end of the law," see pp. 31–32 above. When Conzelmann (p. 238, with n. 116) quotes my book on Romans 8 as evidence that Paul interpreted the law christologically, this is quite correct. But by simultaneously using it as evidence for the interpretation of Christ as the "end of the law" he is turning the actual facts upside down.

8. See here Osten-Sacken, *Römer 8*, 321–22; and idem, "Das Evangelium als Einheit von Verheissung und Gesetz: Grundzüge paulinischer Theologie," *ThViat* 14 (1977–78): 87–108, esp. 87ff.

9. Conzelmann, *Heiden*, 1.

10. Ibid., 234ff.

11. Ibid., 4. For an evaluation and appreciation of Conzelmann's investigation, see W. Wiefel's review in *Theologische Literaturzeitung* 108 (1983): 425–28. This combines high esteem for Conzelmann's historical work with considerable reserve toward his theological viewpoint.

12. Ibid.

13. Ibid. For the polemic, cf., e.g., ibid., 3 ("hopeless confusion," "pervert"), 4 ("wrong track," "tangle," "philo-Semitism," "philo-Zionism").

14. Ibid., 238, with n. 118.

15. Ibid., 120.

16. Ibid., 10.

17. Ibid., 241 n. 132.

18. Cf. Schottroff, *Welt*, 228ff.

19. R. Bultmann, *The Gospel of John*, trans. G. R. Beasley-Murray (Philadelphia: Westminster Press; Oxford: Basil Blackwell, 1971). On this whole subject, and hence on the question of anti-Judaism in the Gospel of John, see the more extensive account in Osten-Sacken, "Kreuzestheologie," 165ff. Thyen ("Heil" 163ff.) gives a convincing exposition of the Johannine "love-hate" for "the Jews," but he then narrows down his viewpoint in a kind of special pleading (p. 168, with n. 26). His appeal to passages such as John 3:16 and 15:13 does not provide evidence for what he would like to see in them, since here—in contrast to Paul—the love of God, or Jesus Christ, is limited to believers, his friends, those who are his. He does not unfortunately prove his assertion that the Johannine theology of the cross (esp. in its effects on the relationship to Israel) can be a "critical potential" compared with Paul's. On the necessity of a critical attitude towards the Fourth Gospel, see also Koenig, *Foundations*, 122ff.; and W. Trilling, "Gegner Jesu—Widersacher der Gemeinde—Reprä-

sentanten der 'Welt': Das Johannesevangelium und die Juden," *ThJb* 22 (1980): 222–38, esp. 237–38.

20. On the difference between Paul and John, see also Schottroff, *Welt*, 296.

21. G. Altner, *Schöpfung am Abgrund*, 2d ed. (Neukirchen, 1977), 32.

22. On the whole subject, see the general observation by H. Miskotte, which fits precisely into this context, that in hating the Jew the anti-Semite is hating humanity (*Das Judentum als Frage and die Kirche*, trans. Brigitte Toet-Kahlert [Wuppertal, 1971], 20 ff.). On the extent to which Jewish citizens were robbed of their rights as early as 1933, see the comprehensive documentation in Comité des Délégations Juives, eds., *Die Lage der Juden in Deutschland 1933: Das Schwarzbuch—Tatsachen und Dokumente* (Paris, 1934; Berlin, 1983).

23. E. Wiesel, "Die Massenvernichtung als literarische Inspiration," in E. Kogon et al., *Gott*, p. 45.

24. See above all Littell, *Crucifixion*, 8ff.; and idem, "The Credibility of the Modern University," in *The Holocaust: Ideology, Bureaucracy, and Genocide*, ed. H. Friedlander and Sybil Milton (New York: Kraus International, 1980), 271–83. See also M. Stöhr, "Erinnern, nicht vergessen," in *Erinnern, nicht vergessen*, ed. M. Stöhr (Munich, 1979), 156–74; idem, "Holocaust; oder, Konsequenzen nach Auschwitz," *Jud* 35 (1979): 103–12; and H. Schmid, "Holocaust, Theologie und Religionsunterricht," *Jud* 35 (1979): 5–11.

25. Cf. C. Gestrich, "Der 'Absolutheitsanspruch' des Christentums im Zeitalter des Dialogs: Erwägungen zur theologischen Begründung der Mission in der Gegenwart," *ZThK* (1980): 106–28.

CHAPTER 7

1. H. Gollwitzer, *Israel—und wir* (Berlin, 1958), 23. See also Eckardt, *Brothers*, 134.

2. On Kraus, see his 1951 essay "Freude" (see 200 n. 30 below), which represents a pioneer approach, and his recent essay "Verständnis." For Zimmerli, see esp. his own contributions to the Christian-Jewish discussion in his *Israel und die Christen: Hören und Fragen*, 2d ed. (Neukirchen, 1980). For Rendtorff, see pp. 153–54 below. It is impossible to give an exhaustive list, but mention should also be made once more of J. C. Rylaarsdam (see p. 6 above) and H. Miskotte (see p. 12 above). Especially deserving of note, finally, are M. A. Beek, *A Short History of Israel from Abraham to Bar Cochba*, trans. A. J. Pomerans (London: Hodder & Stoughton, 1963), esp. the brief but important concluding passage; and the contributions of H. Schmid (see 199 n. 14 and 201 n. 36 below).

3. A. H. J. Gunneweg, *Verstehen*, 21; my italics. [The passages quoted have been translated directly from the German text, not from the published English translation, for details of which see the bibliography.—TRANS.]

4. On this whole subject, see pp. 54–56 above.

5. Gunneweg, *Verstehen*, 22–23; his italics.

6. "Peace and mercy be upon all who walk by this rule, upon the Israel of God."

7. See, e.g., the weighty reasons given by F. Mussner in *Der Galaterbrief* (Freiburg/Basel/Vienna, 1974), 417; and H. Kuhli, "Israel," in *EWNT* 2 (1980): 500–501. Even if the phrase is interpreted as referring to the church, it is in any case only the Jewish Christian members who come into question, these being, at the time when the Epistle to the Galatians was written, "part of the Israelite nation" (P. Richardson, *Israel*, 74ff; the quotation appears on p. 83).

8. Richardson, *Israel*, 122, with n. 5.

9. Cf. pp. 20–40 above.

10. Gunneweg's terminology is unfortunately common coin among New Testament scholars. To take the most recent example, Conzelmann (*Heiden*, 236) tersely remarks, when talking about the New Testament, that the church sees itself as the "true Israel." In actual fact the corresponding term "new Israel" only crops up for the first time in the middle of the 2d cent., in Justin Martyr. Cf. Richardson, *Israel*, 9ff.; van Buren, *Way*, 133.

11. Gunneweg, *Verstehen*, 144.

12. Cf. here R. Rendtorff, "Bibel," esp. 104ff.

13. Gunneweg, *Verstehen*, 198.

14. For a judgment on this, see M. Honecker's vigorous comment (unfortunately addressed

to the wrong quarter, as the example above shows): "The very idea that the gospel, as the message of Christ, could be something over which the church and Christians can dispose as if it were their own possession is monstrous" ("Ein gemeinsames Glaubensbekenntnis für Christen und Juden?" *Kerygma und Dogma* 27 [1981]: 207). For what is true for one canonical part of the Word of God is surely true for the other too. When Honecker asks why, in giving up the claim to exclusiveness, "the conclusion should not also be drawn that Christianity and the church ought to be liquidated" (p. 207), one can only answer, first, that the notion of liquidation does not present itself as immediately to everyone as it apparently does to him; and second, that the question shows that he is evidently only able to think in terms of the alternative either-or. So both Honecker and Gunneweg merely offer a reason for stressing yet again the necessity of this renunciation—or, to be more exact, the necessity of giving back this "possession," which is illegitimate, because it is not theologically shared. On the "Christian robbery of Judaism," see also Mayer, *Judentum*, 57–58; and H. Schmid's important essay "Erwägungen zur christlichen Hermeneutik des Alten Testaments unter Beachtung der 'bleibenden Erwählung Israels,'" part 1, *Jud* 37 (1981): 16–30, esp. 24–25. Schmid's intention is to arrive at an appropriate hermeneutical method of treating the Old Testament.

15. Gunneweg, *Verstehen*, 38.
16. Ibid., 188; Gunneweg's italics.
17. Ibid.
18. Ibid., 189.
19. My italics.
20. Gunneweg, *Verstehen*, 143; his italics. With sentences like these Gunneweg involuntarily answers the question with which W. Zimmerli quite rightly challenged his remarks: "whether the full preformation of the language in which the Christ event is expressed, which also includes the facts of monotheism and a creator God, can be so simply understood by ignoring the validity of what the Old Testament has to say in substance about Yahweh and his acts on behalf of Israel" ("Von der Gültigkeit der 'Schrift' Alten Testamentes in der christlichen Predigt," in *Textgemäss—Aufsätze und Beiträge zur Hermeneutik des Alten Testaments: Festschrift für E. Würthwein*, ed. A. H. J. Gunneweg and O. Kaiser [Göttingen, 1979], 197).
21. Gunneweg, *Verstehen*, 198.
22. See pp. 77–79 above.
23. For more detail, see here Osten-Sacken, *Anstösse*, 11ff.; A. H. Friedlander, "Die Exodus-Tradition: Geschichte und Heilsgeschichte aus jüdischer Sicht," in *Exodus*, ed. Henrix and Stöhr, 41–42.
24. Cf. the emphatic confirmation of the connection here in the New Testament through Acts 7:17.
25. See pp. 69, 106–7 above.
26. Cf. M. Weber, *Gesammelte Aufsätze zur Religionssoziologie*, vol. 3: *Das Judentum* (Tübingen, 1921), 6–7.
27. This heading follows Kraus's essay "Freude." On the subject itself, see esp. Schechter, *Aspects*, 148ff.
28. Rendtorff, "Bibel," 113–14. Cf. also N. Fuchs-Kreimer, "Christian Old Testament Theology: A Time for New Beginnings," *JES* 18 (1981): 76–92. A remarkable point is her demand, made from the Jewish perspective, that analogous questions be put to the Jewish tradition and that here too no exclusive claim to Scripture be made, esp. in respect of the postexilic period (Ezra); see pp. 91–92.
29. Rendtorff, "Bibel," 111ff.
30. Kraus, "Freude." He shows on the basis of Psalms 1, 19B, and 119 that postexilic Judaism had by no means a rigid understanding of the law. To the contrary, in this period too it was the idea of covenant "that was the supporting force without which the Torah cannot be understood" (p. 341). For a development of this line of thought, see also F. Crüsemann, "Tora und christliche Ethik," in *Auschwitz*, ed. Rendtorff and Stegemann, 159–77.
31. Cf. pp. 53–56 above.
32. Cf. here G. Theissen, "Wanderradikalismus: Literatursoziologische Aspekte der Überlieferung von Worten Jesu im Urchristentum," *ZThK* 70 (1973): 245–71; and idem, *Soziologie der Jesusbewegung: Ein Beitrag zur Entstehungsgeschichte des Urchristentums* (Munich, 1977). See

also Talmon's recognition that Christianity, with its "impatient eschatology," is "a religion of the shortcut with a radical ethic" whereas Judaism is "a religion of the long way round, with a moderate ethic, which is more suited to life" ("Anfrage," 144).

33. Cf. Osten-Sacken, "Befreiung," 355–56.

34. Cf. on this, pp. 55–56 above.

35. See Schoeps, *Religionsgespräch*, 59ff.; Geis, "Geschichte des christlich-jüdischen Religionsgespräch," in his *Minorität*, 165–95; and among newer books, D. J. Lasker, *Polemics*; Awerbuch, *Begegnung*; and I. Willi-Plein and T. Willi, *Glaubensdolch*.

36. The interpretation of Gen. 1:26 is not in dispute, but since the revised Luther translation of 1975 still uses the word *Jungfrau*, "virgin," in Isa. 7:14, it is worth drawing attention to H. Wildberger's judicious discussion (*Jesaja I. Teilband Jesaja 1–12* [Neukirchen, 1972], 289–90). Wildberger comes to the clear conclusion, which is shared by most scholars, that "the aspect of virginity is not inherent in the term." See also the splendid example in Kraus ("Verständnis," 2–3) that shows that what was thought to be a brand-new recognition in Old Testament scholarship has long had rabbinic parallels. Kraus also points to the importance of rabbinic scriptural interpretation for Old Testament scholarship today, and to some degree for Christian biblical interpretation already at the close of the Middle Ages and in the Reformation period. This supports Schmid's earlier judgment (*Auseinandersetzung*, 27): "Contemporary research appears to be 'new' to some extent because—if I see the matter rightly—the rabbinic exegesis of the Middle Ages did not find an unbroken continuation in modern times and the work of the rabbis of this earlier period is in general too little taken into account by Christian scholars, or even not at all." On the Christian reception of Jewish interpretation of Scripture in the Middle Ages, see for more detail the works by Awerbuch and by Willi-Plein and Willi cited in n. 35. See also H. Hailperin, *Rashi and the Christian Scholars* (Pittsburgh: Univ. of Pittsburgh Press, 1963), and Beryl Smalley, *The Study of the Bible in the Middle Ages*, 3d rev. ed. (Oxford: Basil Blackwell, 1983), esp. 149ff., 329ff. Further literature is cited in Awerbuch, *Begegnung*, 237ff.

37. B. Blumenkranz, "Die jüdischen Beweisgründe im Religionsgespräch mit den Christen in den christlich-lateinischen Sonderschriften des 5. bis 11. Jahrhunderts" (1948), in his *Juifs et Chrétiens: Patristique et Moyen Age* (London: Variorum, 1977), 147.

38. According to Lasker (*Polemics*, 164–65), representatives of the Jewish side in fact took over arguments from heretical circles, rather than vice versa. This has been definitely shown for a polemical 16th-cent. work, Isaac Troki's *chizzuk emunah* (Schoeps, *Religionsgespräch*, 73). On the closeness of Jewish Christian groups to heretical circles in the church of the patristic period, see Pines, *Christians*, 13.

39. As should be clear from what has been said in the present study, this is not merely a question of benefit in philological matters. It is theological insights that can also be a particular gain here. A fine and easily accessible approach to rabbinic traditions is offered by the books of J. J. Petuchowski: *"Es lehrten unsere Meister . . .": Rabbinische Geschichten* (Freiburg/Basel/Vienna, 1979); *"Ferner lehrten unsere Meister . . .": Neue rabbinische Geschichten* (Freiburg/Basel/Vienna, 1980); *Die Stimme vom Sinai: Ein rabbinisches Lesebuch zu den Zehn Geboten* (Freiburg/Basel/Vienna, 1981). See also Osten-Sacken, *Katechismus*. It does not always have to be Billerbeck—for a number of different reasons. As examples of the attempt at a constructive interpretation of these traditions in the framework of New Testament interpretation, see Osten-Sacken, *Anstösse*, 43ff., 53ff., 169ff., 201ff., 209–10; and idem, "Geist im Buchstaben: Vom Glanz des Mose und des Paulus," *EvTh* 41 (1981): 230–35.

CHAPTER 8

1. I should like here to draw attention to the following contributions that have been published since the appearance of the German version of the present book, and in which I have discussed further aspects of the Christian-Jewish relationship: "Heil für die Juden—auch ohne Christus?" in *Wenn nicht jetzt, wann dann? Aufsätze für Hans-Joachim Kraus zum 65. Geburtstag*, ed. H.-G. Geyer et al. (Neukirchen, 1983), 169–82; "Christen und Juden—Zukunftsperspektiven ihres Verhältnisses," *Friede über Israel* 67 (1984): 98–110; *Katechismus und Siddur: Aufbrüche mit Martin Luther und den Lehrern Israels* (Munich and Berlin, 1984); "Vom Nutzen jüdischer Schriftauslegung für Christen," in *Wie aktuell ist das Alte Testament? Beiträge aus Israel und Berlin*, 3d exp. ed., ed. P. von der Osten-Sacken (Berlin, 1985), 86–106; "Staat

Israel und christliche Existenz: Möglichkeit, Grenze und Bewährung theologischer Aussagen," *Berliner Theologische Zeitschrift* 2 (1985): 74–91; "Jesus, die Gemeinde und das jüdische Volk," *Lutherische Monatshefte* 24 (1985): 72–75; "Die Entwicklung des christlich-jüdischen Dialogs auf dem Felde der kirchlichen Theologie: Die Aufgaben der nächsten Generation," in *Im Blick auf morgen: Juden und Christen in der Verantwortung*, ed. Deutscher Koordinierungsrat der Gesellschaften für christlich-jüdische Zusammenarbeit e.V. (Frankfurt, 1985), 16–27; and "Auf dem Weg zum jüdischen Volk: Eine Einführung in Günther Harders Sicht des christlich-jüdischen Verhältnisses," in G. Harder, *Kirche und Israel: Arbeiten zum christlich-jüdischen Verhältnis* (Berlin, 1986), 8ff. In this final chapter I have occasionally taken over brief passages from the above-named contributions.

2. Y. Amir, *Deraschot: Jüdische Predigten* (Berlin, 1983), 60.

3. *Glauben und Verstehen* is the title given by R. Bultmann to the four volumes of his collected essays. A selection of these essays was published in English under the title *Faith and Understanding*.

4. M. Kähler, *Der sogenannte historische Jesus und der geschichtliche, biblische Christus*, 2d enl. ed., ed. E. Wolf (Munich, 1956), 103.

5. M. Luther, "Vorrede auf die Epistel S. Pauli an die Römer," in *Martin Luthers Vorreden zur Bibel*, ed. H. Bornkamm (Hamburg, 1967), 143–59.

6. E.P. Sanders, "On the Question of Fulfilling the Law in Paul and Rabbinic Judaism," in *Donum Gentilicium: New Testament Studies in Honour of David Daube*, ed. C. K. Barrett, E. Bammel, and W. D. Davies (New York and London: Oxford Univ. Press, 1978), 124.

7. Thus, e.g., H. Hübner, "Der 'Messias Israels' und der Christus des Neuen Testaments," *Kerygma und Dogma* 27 (1981): 217–39. For criticism, see my essay mentioned in n. 1 above, "Heil für die Juden—auch ohne Christus?" 174ff.; and B. Klappert, "Welches Judentum begegnet welches Christentum?" in *Welches Judentum steht welchem Christentum gegenüber?* ed. H. H. Henrix and W. Licharz (Frankfurt, 1985), 101ff.

8. P. Melanchthon, *Loci communes* (1521), ed. T. Kolde (Leipzig, Erlangen, 1925), 63.

9. *Freiburger Rundbrief* 35/36 (1983–84): 172.

10. See my study *Katechismus und Siddur*, mentioned in n. 1 above.

11. D. Wiederkehr, "Christusglaube und Glaube an den einen Gott: Zum Spannungsverhältnis zwischen Monotheismus und Trinitätslehre," in *Das Reden vom einen Gott bei Juden und Christen*, ed. C. Thoma and M. Wyschogrod (New York/Bern/Frankfurt, 1984), 131–35.

12. Ibid., 134.

13. Ibid., 138.

14. Ibid., 153.

15. See my contribution "Vom Nutzen jüdischer Schriftauslegung für Christen," mentioned in n. 1 above.

Bibliography

Not included are books and articles that appear in only one note, or in a consecutive series of notes; these works are already cited with full bibliographical details in the notes themselves. Books and articles listed below, on the other hand, are cited in the notes with only a short title.

Amir, Y. "Jüdisch-theologische Positionen nach Auschwitz." In *Auschwitz*, ed. Ginzel, 439–55.

Aring, P. G. *Christliche Judenmission: Ihre Geschichte und Problematik dargestellt und untersucht am Beispiel des evangelischen Rheinlandes.* Neukirchen, 1980.

Aschkenasy, Y. "Geliebt ist der Mensch." In *Umkehr*, ed. Klappert and Starck, 191–206.

Awerbuch, Marianne. *Christlich-jüdische Begegnung im Zeitalter der Frühscholastik.* Munich, 1980.

Barth, M. *Israel and the Church.* Richmond: John Knox Press, 1969.

Barth, M., et al. *Paulus—Apostat oder Apostel? Jüdische und christliche Antworten.* Regensburg, 1977.

Bass, M. L. "Der jüdische Christ in der Gemeinde Christi." *FüI* 52 (1969): 165–78.

Baudis, A., et al., eds. *Richte unsere Füsse auf den Weg des Friedens: H. Gollwitzer zum 70. Geburtstag.* Munich, 1979.

Baumann, A. H. *Christliches Zeugnis und die Juden heute: Zur Frage der Judenmission.* Hanover, 1981.

Beker, J. C. *Paul the Apostle: The Triumph of God in Life and Thought,* 2d ed. Philadelphia: Fortress Press, 1982.

Berkovits, E. *Faith After the Holocaust.* New York: Ktav Pub. House, 1973.

Bethge, E. *Dietrich Bonhoeffer,* trans. E. Mosbacher et al. New York: Harper & Row; London: William Collins Sons, 1970.

Billerbeck, P. *Kommentar zum Neuen Testament aus Talmud und Midrasch,* vols. 1, 2, 4. Munich, 1922–28.

Blank, J. "Paulus—Jude und Völkerapostel: Als Frage an Juden und Christen." In *Paulus*, ed. Barth et al., 147–72.

Bloch, J. "Der historische Jesus und Paulus." In *Paulus*, ed. Barth et al., 9–30.

Bonhoeffer, D. *Letters and Papers from Prison,* trans. R. H. Fuller, 3d enl. ed. New York: Macmillan Co.; London: SCM Press, 1971.

Buber, M. "Kirche, Staat, Volk, Judentum: Aus dem Zwiegespräch mit Karl Ludwig Schmidt im jüdischen Lehrhaus zu Stuttgart (14. Januar 1933)." In his *Der Jude und sein Judentum: Gesammelte Aufsätze und Reden,* 558–70. Cologne, 1963.

Bultmann, R. *Theology of the New Testament,* trans. Kendrick Grobel. New York: Charles Scribner's Sons; London: SCM Press, 1952–55.

Buren, P. van. *Discerning the Way: A Theology of the Jewish-Christian Reality.* New York: Seabury Press, 1980.

Cohen, A. *Everyman's Talmud.* [1st ed. London, 1932]; New York: E. P. Dutton & Co., 1949, Schocken Books, 1978.

Conzelmann, H. *Acts of the Apostles.* Hermeneia. Philadelphia: Fortress Press, pub. pending.
———. *Heiden—Juden—Christen: Auseinandersetzungen in der Literatur der hellenistisch-römischen Zeit.* Tübingen, 1981.
Eckardt, A. R. *Elder and Younger Brothers: The Encounter of Jews and Christians.* New York: Charles Scribner's Sons, 1967; Schocken Books, 1973.
Eckert, W. P., and H. H. Henrix, eds. *Jesus Jude-Sein als Zugang zum Judentum: Eine Handreichung für Religionsunterricht und Erwachsenenbildung.* Aachen, 1976.
Fackenheim, E. L. *God's Presence in History: Jewish Affirmations and Philosophical Reflection.* New York: New York Univ. Press, 1970; Harper Torchbooks, 1972.
Fiebig, P. *Altjüdische Gleichnisse und die Gleichnisse Jesu.* Tübingen, 1904.
Flusser, D. *Jesus,* trans. Ronald Walls. New York: Herder & Herder, 1969.
———. "Reflections of a Jew on a Christian Theology of Judaism." In Thoma, *Theology,* 1–19.
Geis, R. R. "Der Auftrag Israels an die Völker." In his *Minorität,* 199–205.
———. *Gottes Minorität: Beiträge zur jüdischen Theologie und zur Geschichte der Juden in Deutschland.* Munich, 1971.
Gerlach, W. *Zwischen Kreuz und Davidstern: Bekennende Kirche in ihrer Stellung zum Judentum im Dritten Reich.* Prot. theol. diss., Hamburg, 1970.
Gese, H. "Psalm 22 und das Neue Testament." *ZThK* 65 (1968): 1–22.
Ginzel, G. B., ed. *Auschwitz als Herausforderung für Juden und Christen.* Heidelberg, 1980.
Goldberg, A. M. *Untersuchungen über die Vorstellung von der Schekhinah in der frührabbinischen Literatur.* Berlin, 1969.
Gollwitzer, H. "Das Judentum als Problem christlicher Theologie." In *Treue,* ed. Osten-Sacken, 162–73.
Goppelt, L. *Theologie des Neuen Testaments,* vol. 1. Göttingen, 1975.
Greenberg, J. "Cloud of Smoke, Pillar of Fire: Judaism, Christianity, and Modernity after the Holocaust." In *Auschwitz: Beginning of a New Era? Reflections on the Holocaust,* ed. Eva Fleischner, 7–55. New York: Ktav Pub. House, 1977.
Gunneweg, A. H. J. *Understanding the Old Testament,* trans. John Bowden. Philadelphia: Westminster Press; London: SCM Press, 1978.
Gutteridge, R. *Open Thy Mouth for the Dumb.* Oxford, 1976.
Guttmann, M. *Das Judentum und seine Umwelt,* vol. 1. Berlin, 1927.
Hegermann, H. "diathēkē, Bund, Testament." In *EWNT* 1 (1980): 718–25.
Heinemann, J. *Prayer in the Talmud.* New York and Berlin: Walter de Gruyter, 1977.
Henrix, H. H., and M. Stöhr, eds. *Exodus und Kreuz im ökumenischen Dialog zwischen Juden und Christen.* Aachen, 1978.
Heschel, A. J. *God in Search of Man: A Philosophy of Judaism.* New York: Farrar, Straus & Giroux, 1955.
Hesse, F. "Einige Anmerkungen zum Wort der rheinischen Landessynode über das Verhältnis von Christen und Juden." In *Umkehr,* ed. Klappert and Starck, 283–86.
Immer, K., ed. *Zur Erneuerung des Verhältnisses von Christen und Juden: Handreichung für Mitglieder der Landessynode der Kreissynoden und der Presbyterien in der Evangelischen Kirche im Rheinland.* No. 39. Düsseldorf, 1980.
Isaac, J. "Hat der Antisemitismus christliche Wurzeln?" *EvTh* 21 (1961): 339–54.
———. *Jesus and Israel,* trans. Sally Gran. New York: Holt, Rinehart & Winston, 1971.
Jasper, J. "Der Judenchrist als das Zeichen Gottes für Israel und Kirche: Eine Besinnung zur Frage nach der Judenchristenheit." *Jud* 11 (1955): 134–78.
Jepsen, A. "Berith: Ein Beitrag zur Theologie der Exilzeit." In his *Der Herr ist Gott: Aufsätze zur Wissenschaft vom Alten Testament,* 196–210. Berlin, 1978.
Jeremias, J. *The Lord's Prayer,* trans. John Reumann. Philadelphia: Fortress Press, 1964.
———. *Abba: Studien zur neutestamentlichen Theologie und Zeitgeschichte,* esp. 15, 67. Göttingen, 1966. Selections of this vol. pub. as *The Prayers of Jesus* (Naperville, Ill.: Alec R. Allenson; London: SCM Press, 1967).
———. *New Testament Theology,* vol. 1, trans. John Bowden. New York: Charles Scribner's Sons; London: SCM Press, 1971.
Käsemann, E. "Erwägungen zum Stichwort 'Versöhnungslehre im Neuen Testament.'" In *Zeit und Geschichte: Festschrift für R. Bultmann,* ed. E. Dinkler, 47–59. Tübingen, 1964.

————. "The Problem of the Historical Jesus." In his *Essays on New Testament Themes*, trans. W. J. Montague, 15–47. London: SCM Press, 1964.

————. *Perspectives on Paul*, trans. Margaret Kohl. Philadelphia: Fortress Press; London: SCM Press, 1971.

————. "Die neue Jesus-Frage." In *Jésus aux origines de la christologie*, ed. J. Dupont, 45–57. Gembloux, 1975.

Klappert, B. "Erinnerung und Hoffnung (Hebr. 11.32–40)." In *Gottesdienst*, ed. Osten-Sacken, 192–205.

————. *Israel und die Kirche: Erwägungen zur Israellehre Karl Barths*. Munich, 1980.

————. "Jesus Christus zwischen Juden und Christen (Gegen eine Christologie der Trennung vom Judentum)." In *Umkehr*, ed. Klappert and Starck, 138–66.

Klappert, B., and H. Starck, eds. *Umkehr und Erneuerung: Erläuterungen zum Synodalbeschluss der Rheinischen Landessynode 1980 "Zur Erneuerung des Verhältnisses von Christen und Juden."* Neukirchen, 1980.

Klausner, J. *Jesus of Nazareth*, trans. Herbert Danby. New York: Macmillan Co.; London: George Allen & Unwin, 1925.

Koenig, J. *Jews and Christians in Dialogue: New Testament Foundations*. Philadelphia: Westminster Press, 1979.

Kogon, E., et al. *Gott nach Auschwitz: Dimensionen des Massenmords am jüdischen Volk*. Freiburg/Basel/Vienna, 1979.

Kolitz, Z. "Jossel Rackower spricht zu Gott." *Almanach für Literatur und Theologie* 2 (1968): 19–28.

Kraus, H.-J. "Freude an Gottes Gesetz: Ein Beitrag zur Auslegung der Psalmen 1, 19B und 119." *EvTh* 10 (1950–51): 337–51.

————. *Reich Gottes, Reich der Freiheit: Grundriss Systematischer Theologie*. Neukirchen, 1975.

————. "Jüdisches und christliches Verständnis der Bibel." *Christlich-jüdisches Forum* no. 52 (1980): 1–12.

Krolenbaum, A. "Der Judenchrist und sein Volk." *FüI* 50 (1967): 8–13.

Kutsch, E. "b*rit Verpflichtung." In *Theologisches Handwörterbuch zum Alten Testament*, 339–52. Munich, 1971.

Lapide, P. *Hebräisch in den Kirchen*. Neukirchen, 1976.

————. "Der Messias Israels? Die Rheinische Synode und das Judentum." In *Umkehr*, ed. Klappert and Starck, 236–46.

Lasker, D. J. *Jewish Philosophical Polemics Against Christianity in the Middle Ages*. New York: Ktav Pub. House, 1977.

Lenhardt, P. *Auftrag und Unmöglichkeit eines legitimen christlichen Zeugnisses gegenüber den Juden: Eine Untersuchung zum theologischen Stand des Verhältnisses von Kirche und jüdischem Volk*, trans. Ursula Bohn from a French ms. Berlin, 1980.

Leuner, H. D. *Zwischen Israel und den Völkern: Vorträge eines Judenchristen*. Berlin, 1978.

Levinson, N. P. "Nichts anderes als Jude: Jesus aus der Sicht eines heutigen Juden." *ThJb* 22 (1980): 193–204.

Lindeskog, G. *Die Jesusfrage im neuzeitlichen Judentum*, 2d ed. Darmstadt, 1973.

Littell, F. H. *The Crucifixion of the Jews*. New York: Harper & Row, 1975.

Luz, U. *Das Geschichtsverständnis des Paulus*. Munich, 1968.

Maier, J. "Jesus von Nazareth und sein Verhältnis zum Judentum: Aus der Sicht eines Judaisten." In *Jude-Sein*, ed. Eckert and Henrix, 69–113.

Majer-Leonhard, F. "Judenchristentum." In *RGG*, 3d ed., 2:col. 972–76.

Marquardt, F.-W. "Die Freiheit Israels" (1960). In his *Verwegenheiten*, 152–64.

————. *Die Juden und ihr Land*. Hamburg, 1975.

————. "'Feinde um unsretwillen': Das Jüdische Nein und die christliche Theologie" (1977). In his *Verwegenheiten*, 311–36.

————. "Hermeneutik des christlich-jüdischen Verhältnisses: Über Helmut Gollwitzers Arbeit an der Judenfrage." In *Richte unsere Füsse*, ed. Baudis et al., 138–54.

————. *Verwegenheiten: Theologische Stücke aus Berlin*. Munich, 1981.

————. "Was haltet ihr von Jesus? Jesus zwischen Juden und Christen." In *epd-Dokumentation* no. 31 (1981): 67–76.

Marquardt, F.-W., and A. H. Friedlander. *Das Schweigen der Christen und die Menschlichkeit*

Gottes: Glaübige Existenz nach Auschwitz. Munich, 1980.

Mayer, R. *Judentum und Christentum: Ursprung, Geschichte und Aufgabe.* Aschaffenburg, 1973.

Metz, J. B. "Ökumene nach Auschwitz: Zum Verhältnis von Christen und Juden in Deutschland." In *Gott,* ed. Kogon et al., 121–44.

Miskotte, K. H. *When the Gods Are Silent,* trans. John W. Doberstein. New York: Harper & Row, 1967.

Mosis, R., ed. *Exil—Diaspora—Rückkehr: Zum theologischen Gespräch zwischen Juden und Christen.* Düsseldorf, 1978.

Mussner, F. *Tractate on the Jews,* trans. L. Swidler. Philadelphia: Fortress Press, 1984.

Osten-Sacken, P. von der. *Römer 8 als Beispiel paulinischer Soteriologie.* Göttingen, 1975.

———. "Leistung und Grenze der johanneischen Kreuzestheologie." *EvTh* 36 (1976): 154–76.

———. "Das paulinische Verständnis des Gesetzes im Spannungsfeld von Eschatologie und Geschichte: Erläuterungen zum Evangelium als Faktor von theologischem Antijudaismus." *EvTh* 37 (1977): 549–87.

———. "Befreiung durch das Gesetz." In *Richte unsere Füsse,* ed. Baudis et al., 349–60.

———. "Die paulinische theologia crucis als Form apokalyptischer Theologie." *EvTh* 39 (1979): 477–96.

———. *Anstösse aus der Schrift: Arbeiten für Pfarrer und Gemeinden.* Neukirchen, 1981.

———. " 'Bist du, der da kommen soll?' Jesus—Messias Israels?" In epd-Dokumentation no. 31 (1981): 17–25.

———. *Katechismus und Siddur: Aufbrüche mit Martin Luther und den Lehrern Israels.* Berlin, 1984.

———, ed. *Treue zur Thora: Beiträge zur Mitte des christlich-jüdischen Gesprächs. Festschrift für G. Harder,* 2d ed. Berlin, 1979.

———, ed. *Israel im christlichen Gottesdienst: Predigten, Ansprachen, Begegnungen.* Berlin, 1980.

Parkes, J. *The Conflict of the Church and the Synagogue: A Study in the Origins of Antisemitism.* London: Soncino Press, 1934; New York: Hermon Press, 1974.

Pines, S. *The Jewish Christians of the Early Centuries of Christianity According to a New Source.* Jerusalem, 1966.

Rendtorff, R. "Die jüdische Bibel und ihre antijüdische Auslegung." In *Auschwitz,* ed. Rendtorff and Stegemann, 99–116.

Rendtorff, R., and E. Stegemann, eds. *Auschwitz—Krise der christlichen Theologie.* Munich, 1980.

Richardson, P. *Israel in the Apostolic Church.* Cambridge, 1969.

Rost, G. "Jesus Christus—Der wahre Tempel." *Fül* 64 (1981): 57–61.

Ruether, R. R. *Faith and Fratricide.* New York: Seabury Press, 1974.

Sanders, E. P. *Paul and Palestinian Judaism.* Philadelphia: Fortress Press; London: SCM Press, 1977.

Schechter, S. *Aspects of Rabbinic Theology: Major Concepts of the Talmud,* intro. L. Finkelstein. New York: Macmillan Co., 1909; Schocken Books, 1961.

Schmid, H. *Die christlich-jüdische Auseinandersetzung um das Alte Testament in hermeneutischer Sicht.* Zurich, 1971.

Schnider, F. *Die verlorene Söhne: Strukturanalyse und historisch-kritische Untersuchungen zu Lukas 15.* Fribourg and Göttingen, 1977.

Schoeps, H.-J. *Jüdisch-christliches Religionsgespräch in neunzehn Jahrhunderten,* 2d ed. Frankfurt, 1949.

Schottroff, Luise. *Der Glaubende und die feindliche Welt.* Neukirchen, 1970.

Schweikhart, W. *Zwischen Dialog und Mission: Zur Geschichte und Theologie der christlich-jüdischen Beziehungen seit 1945.* Berlin, 1980.

Stegemann, E. "Alt und Neu bei Paulus und in den Deutero-Paulinen (Kol.Eph)." *EvTh* 37 (1977): 508–36.

———. "Der Jude Paulus und seine antijüdische Auslegung." In *Auschwitz,* ed. Rendtorff and Stegemann, 117–39.

Steiger, L. "Schutzrede für Israel: Römer 9—11." In *Fides pro mundi vita: Missionstheologie heute: Festschrift für H. Gensichen,* ed. T. Sundermeier, 44–58. Gütersloh, 1980.

Stendahl, K. *Paul Among Jews and Gentiles.* Philadelphia: Fortress Press, 1976.

Tal, U. *Christians and Jews in Germany: Religion, Politics, and Ideology in the Second Reich, 1870–1914.* Ithaca, N.Y.: Cornell Univ. Press, 1975.

Talmon, S. "Towards World Community: Resources and Responsibilities for Living Together—A Jewish View." *Ecumenical Review* 26 (1974): 605–18.

―――. "Kritische Anfrage der jüdischen Theologie an das europäische Christentum." In *Israel hat dennoch Gott zum Trost: Festschrift für S. Ben-Chorin*, ed. G. Müller, 139–57. Trier, 1978.

Terray, L. G. "Evangelisch-Lutherische Gemeinden messianischer Juden in Israel." *Fül* 64 (1981): 62–72.

Thoma, C. *A Christian Theology of Judaism*, trans. Helga Croner. New York: Paulist Press, 1980.

Thyen, H. "Exegese des Neuen Testaments nach dem Holocaust." In *Auschwitz*, ed. Rendtorff and Stegemann, 140–58.

―――. "'Das Heil kommt von den Juden.'" In *Kirche: Festschrift für G. Bornkamm*, ed. D. Lührmann and G. Strecker, 163–84. Tübingen, 1980.

Urbach, E. E. *The Sages: Their Concepts and Beliefs*, vols. 1 and 2. Jerusalem, 1975.

Werblowsky, R. J. Z. "Tora als Gnade." *Kairos* 15 (1973): 156–63.

Willi-Plein, Ina, and T. Willi. *Glaubensdolch und Messiasbeweis: Die Begegnung von Judentum, Christentum und Islam im 13. Jahrhundert in Spanien*. Neukirchen, 1980.

Abbreviations
Periodicals and Lexica

CJR	*Christian Jewish Relations*
CNI	*Christian News from Israel*
EvKomm	*Evangelische Kommentare*
EvTh	*Evangelische Theologie*
EWNT	*Exegetisches Wörterbuch zum Neuen Testament*
FrRu	*Freiburger Rundbrief*
FüI	*Friede über Israel*
JES	*Journal of Ecumenical Studies*
Jud	*Judaica*
LM	*Lutherische Monatshefte*
NTS	*New Testament Studies*
RGG	*Die Religion in Geschichte und Gegenwart*
ThJb	*Theologisches Jahrbuch* (Leipzig)
ThViat	*Theologia Viatorum*
ThWBNT	*Theologisches Wörterbuch zum Neuen Testament*
ThZ	*Theologische Zeitschrift*
ZAW	*Zeitschrift für die Alttestamentliche Wissenschaft.*
ZThK	*Zeitschrift für Theologie und Kirche*

Index of Subjects

Index of Modern Authors

Index of Passages